WORLD'S END

Donald James Wheal

WORLD'S END

Century · London

Published in the United Kingdom in 2005 by Century

1 3 5 7 9 10 8 6 4 2

Century Books
The Random House Group Limited
20 Vauxhall Bridge Road, London, SW1V 2SA

Random House Australia (Pty) Limited
20 Alfred Street, Milsons Point, Sydney,
New South Wales 2061, Australia

Random House New Zealand Limited
18 Poland Road, Glenfield
Auckland 10, New Zealand

Random House (Pty) Limited
Endulini, 5a Jubilee Road, Parktown 2193, South Africa

The Random House Group Limited Reg. No. 954009

www.randomhouse.co.uk

A CIP catalogue record for this book is available from the British Library

Papers used by Random House are natural, recyclable products made
from wood grown in sustainable forests. The manufacturing processes
conform to the environmental regulations of the country of origin

ISBN 1 8441 3682 5

Typeset by SX Composing DTP, Rayleigh, Essex
Printed and bound in Great Britain by
Mackays of Chatham Plc, Chatham, Kent

CONTENTS

WORLD'S END

This book is about what we think of, when we are very young, as a world without end. It differs from your story because it's about my family and not yours, or because it took place in the World's End and not elsewhere, or indeed because it took place during a war to the death for the civil societies involved. But essentially it contains the same elements as all our yesterdays: those crucial early relationships with the adults we call our parents or guardians, and that crucial challenge or response to *their* view of life which finally shapes our own.

We're all, of course, familiar with Philip Larkin's sour dictum. But it's only part of the story and should not be allowed to rest as the last word. This book is another part of the same story.

What follows is not fiction, nor even partly fiction. Childhood, of course, is a time of just remembered feelings. If there are errors they are errors of a small boy's memory. Less likely but possible, there are some errors of recollection on the part of my father who died young in the 1960s, or of my mother who died just months short of the new century. This book is dedicated to them. And to my brother, of course, and my grandmother, Eliza Toop.

And to all those who never survived the World's End.

ONE

World Without End

I grew up in that riverside enclave of central London known as the World's End. The area takes its name from the old World's End Tavern on the King's private road through Chelsea, a tavern which had stood in the same spot since at least the seventeenth century and was rebuilt in Victorian times as a big, roomy pub. Very roughly, World's End as an area was, and remains, the lower-reach of riverside Chelsea, the furthest point in the King's Road from Sloane Square. Its southern limit is the river. In the 1930s what locals recognised as the World's End covered the streets and houses on both sides of the King's Road for about three hundred yards in either direction from the World's End pub. Where World's End faded into propriety, and finally disappeared, was marked by a sharp S-bend in the King's Road and here the Chelsea of artists and aristocrats began, a Chelsea distinguishable by a difference in accent from ours, by freshly painted houses, by art galleries and expensive antique shops, the ownership of motor cars and the employment of hundreds of cleaning women – from, of course, World's end.

The *quartier*, if such a fancy term has ever graced World's End, was visibly and psychologically a separate entity from that other Chelsea. Although it was part of one of London's richest boroughs

World's End was in the thirties and forties an area of mouldering dwellings, some of them rat-ridden slums, others with their own Victorian elegance, unpainted, broken-windowed and tatter-demalion as they were. Its centre point was the broad, oddly shaped open space (once, I imagine, a village green or perhaps market square) outside the World's End pub. Its form was a large traffic island from which several roads radiated. Here La-di-dah ruled, no turbaned exotic from the far-flung empire, but a flat capped epileptic newspaper seller from whose toothless mouth *News, Star, Standard* burst as 'La-di-dah'. Even those who had bought papers from him for years had no better idea of his real name. Though several roads ran out from the island there was no swirling traffic and children crossed from St John's Church Hall to the Salvation Army Mission without fear. La-di's domain was the area between two underground conveniences, a Ladies' and Gentlemen's, their entrances ornate with Victorian ironwork, a hanging gas lamp yellowing the tiled steps in winter, their depths exuding warmth and the sharp smell of carbolic as you passed. Five-finger Steve (he had lost all the fingers on his left hand in the Great War) sold whelks at the end of World's End Passage of a Sunday morning.

Unlike the rest of Chelsea, the World's End had important industry: a massive flour mill on the river that formed the area's southern boundary, a louring four-stack generating station at Lots Road and a sprinkling of small factories each employing perhaps four or five men and a dozen girls. Balancing on the mud bank of Chelsea creek was Charrington's Brewery. On King's Road, opposite Guinness Trust Buildings, was a large and noisy Watney's bottling plant. The girls who worked there wore clogs against the swilling water on the brick floors and curlers in their hair on Fridays. By the time we were eleven or twelve we would pass as often as we could when the girls stood smoking in the green-tiled entrance. They thought we were dying of embarrassment as they winked and lazily rotated a breast with a free hand or honed their repartee on us as we approached. In fact, we had gone out of our way just to see and hear such things from older girls:

'What *you* looking for, Babyface? A quick jump round the bike sheds?'

'An' if I was?'

'Then you've come to the right place, love.'

And the girl would sashay forward in her clogs while the others shrieked with laugher and we'd run like madmen, though we knew we were in no danger of the offer going further. Most of the girls were no age themselves, no more than sixteen or seventeen many of them, between school and early marriage, savouring a brief period of sexual freedom only safe to exercise on small boys.

In addition to making and bottling beer, the World's End had a dozen pubs, frequented for a preferred ale, a game of crib or a street bookmaker who might, in certain circumstances, allow credit where none was due.

Each pub had its own following and reputation. The World's End Pub itself was never thought of as particularly boisterous. The Reilly and the Weatherby were recognised as the roughest pubs, the Weatherby from its position on the corner of Slaidburn Street. Now a middle class cul-de-sac of powder pink- and blue-painted houses, *Slayburn*, as it was pronounced by everybody who lived in the World's End, was known for its Saturday night fights. To my brother and me, as children who really only heard about the fights from our grandmother, my mother's mother Eliza Toop, it was known even more for its bonfire on Guy Fawkes Night. Then, the fire would be built in the middle of the narrow street and the flames would leap between the houses while the men would stumble out of the Weatherby and, against the cries of their wives, drag out furniture or hurl chairs from the upstairs windows onto the blaze.

We were nominally in my grandmother's charge but as often as not she had slipped into the pub for a 'twist of snuff' and we were free to push our way through the crowds for half an hour. The swirling smoke and leaping showers of sparks, the crack of fireworks and the whoosh of rockets all fuelled our intense excitement as we edged closer the action. At some point it always got out of hand. The bonfire would tip towards one of the houses. A flapping net curtain would singe and flame. Men and women, probably husbands and wives, would be pushing each other in big untidy fights, their children screaming. The police would be there, probably having been waiting round the corner, And, of course, there was never a Bonfire Night in the thirties without a fire engine or two in *Slayburn* Street. It was a World's End institution.

Another was undoubtedly its women. Many a 'Piccadilly girl' came from World's End. Perhaps it was in line with the area's honourable tradition (of which more later); perhaps it was the simplicity of the journey. Tuppence on the 22 bus took you, in little more than fifteen minutes, from the World's End Pub to the Eros statue in the middle of Piccadilly. Numbers are always difficult to come by but we know some things by newspaper scandals and from reports even closer to home. Two World's Enders who 'enjoyed the company of male friends' were murdered in the inter-war years. The mother of one of my later girl-friends (her father had moved on shortly after her birth) cooked us bacon and eggs in Lots Road before she left to earn enough to support her family in the dark alleyways of Soho. And my own mother's mother, Eliza, had certainly achieved part of her early struggle for independence on the fringes of the profession when she worked as a barmaid at Dirty Dick's in Spitalfields.

Any man who didn't work along the river or in the factories or breweries was almost certainly in the building trade – in or out of work. In the 1930s most World's End young men were only a generation away from field workers in Dorset or casual farm labourers in Kent or Essex. I once looked up my own family in Somerset House. No man or woman of our family name had been born outside the single village of Roxwell in Essex for a hundred years, or more probably a thousand years, before my paternal grandfather, Henry James Wheal, was abandoned in London by his widowed father and passed from orphanage to orphanage to end his childhood in a Chelsea workhouse. With no trade and only the skills of a country boy Henry James found the first job he could, inevitably as a labourer among the numberless army of men then building late-Victorian London.

The woman he married (whether or not in haste I don't know, but most certainly to repent it in leisure) was a formidable streetfighter named Minnie Woodhouse. This grandmother, my father's mother, was a rough bully of a woman, a steady drinker rather than a drunk, whose sons, my father included, snipped holes in the knees of their Sunday suits to make them valueless at the pawnshop where she would hope to raise the wherewithal to pay the street bookmaker. Minnie herself worked as a cleaning woman, in Chelsea proper, for the artist and Director of the Tate Gallery, J. B. Manson. He and his wife prized her highly as a cleaner and perhaps as an amusingly belligerent personality. Minnie was quite unfazed by the illustrious writers and artists who visited the Mansons' home. She treated them all with a breezy contempt. The Mansons were good, liberal people though I'm sad to say that they knew only Minnie's version of her home life and held a dreamland belief that they had somehow tamed her into genuine friendship. I think they saw in her one of those 'salt of the earth' figures the upper classes enjoyed believing they could cultivate.

In fact, apart from her eldest son George, and possibly her drinking companion, Mrs Bashford, Ma Bash as she was known, Minnie didn't give tuppence for anybody. My mother inherited the job with the Mansons from Minnie, and could have told them that she was less than the amiable rough diamond she pretended to be. But that would not be my mother's way – although she kept in touch with the widowed Mrs Manson for years after she no longer worked for her.

Sober, Minnie had intelligence but little discrimination. It's not an uncommon problem for working class people. If education offers anything, it's some ability to discriminate. Any amount of intelligence will not get any but the few over that barrier. An outstanding example of this was the issue that arose over my brother's bent, clearly bowed legs when he first began to walk. Minnie was recognised in the World's End as something of a medical authority and would happily pour scorn on the efforts of the occasional drunk and the few devoted (like Dr Glass on the corner of Tadema Road) doctors who practised in the area. When Keith, or Kit as he was known in the family, began walking on quite definitely bent legs Dr Glass suggested massage; Minnie insisted my mother take him to the bone breaker. His skill (he practised in Riley Street just round the corner from the King's Arms and had been known to hold surgeries in the public bar) was the breaking and resetting of rickets-damaged legs. Since my mother, even if it had meant starving herself and my father too, would have ensured Kit and I had the diet which was even then known to be necessary to avoid rickets, Minnie's was an arrogant, a preposterous suggestion flying in the face of Dr Glass's advice. But you didn't just ignore Minnie's solution to a problem. My mother went to see her, sat down with a cup of tea and calmly told her that she would break Minnie's arms sooner than Kit's legs. Nobody had ever spoken to Minnie like that. But this big, twenty-three year old girl with the friendly smile when she spoke was something different. And Min, being far from stupid, recognised it. But she was not yet prepared to accept defeat.

My mother had, in fact, already begun a six month daily course of massage for Kit's legs which would ultimately be highly successful. But the outcome was not yet known and the malicious drip drip of gossip from the King's Arms, the sagacious nods of agreement from Ma Bash, began to filter out into the World's End.

Again, my mother reacted decisively. She took Kit down to the King's Arms. Standing him on the table, (he was a particularly healthy looking, big, yellow haired, round-faced boy), she faced her fearsome mother-in-law in public.

'Look at him,' she said to Minnie, Ma Bash and the lunchtime cronies, 'does he look undernourished? Does your grandson look neglected?'

'I never said that.'

'It's what rickets means. It's what you saying he's suffering from rickets means.'

Even Minnie was silent.

'Now Min,' her daughter-in-law said, 'if I hear one more word from you about breaking his legs, it will be the last time you ever see your grandsons, either of them. Can we say we understand each other?'

Minnie worked her toothless jaws (she'd had all her teeth pulled 'for her health' at thirty). Ma Bash ruffled her shoulders to prepare a post-factum claim of having participated in the outburst she was sure would come from Min. But to everybody's astonishment Minnie nodded her head. 'He's your boy, Phyllis. It's up to you to decide. Not me. Nor old Ma Bash here.' She cackled. 'Now let's have a port and lemon, and a bag of crisps for the boy.'

It's true she wasn't always that effectively faced down. I think of Minnie as a streetfighter because she had a reputation (in some ways admirable, of course) for an eagerness to defend any battered wife against the offending husband, often driving him off to the King's Arms with a series of the left hooks for which she was rightly feared. The problem was that Minnie was not always in a condition after a quiet Sunday session in the same King's Arms, to make a nice judgement of the offence, and was too often known to haul unoffending husbands from the public bar to fight her outside on the embankment. On these occasions, her weighty sidekick, she of the dropsical legs, Ma Bash, would be required to bear witness to the justice of the 'good hiding' administered, which she did faithfully from an evenly balanced mix of fear and friendship.

Such evidence failed to impress my Temperance grandfather, Henry James. Quiet, deliberate, miserly and acid-tongued, he never took his wife's side in these disputes. Sometimes, in frustration, she attacked him to make her point, once notably, à la Roald Dahl with a leg of lamb. He was knocked sprawling across the Sunday dinner table before she was disarmed by her three sons. But sober she feared her husband's scorn.

In a curious way they admired one another for their differences. He was believed by many in World's End to have made secret savings throughout his life while Minnie openly threatened that anything that came to her she would hand to the bookmaker within six months of his death. She could imagine no more painful threat to him than to squander his money. In riposte, he claimed no saving was possible on his miserable earnings as a part time laundry porter at St Stephen's Hospital. Once he was gone, he jeered quietly, she would live and die a pauper. I remember hearing, though not clearly understanding until my father explained, several such exchanges, or barbed comments, which opposed the miser to the gambler. In this Aesopian contest, honours were evenly divided. Henry James's will revealed his savings amounted to a considerable sum for a working man of that era, £250. But Minnie kept her word. She treated Ma Bash and their cronies to many a port and lemon in the King's Arms, backed a loser several times a day – and died a pauper as her husband had predicted.

I met my father, who paid for her funeral, four or five days after her death. As usual we drank a cup of tea together and brought each other up to date with family events. I had just come down from Cambridge with a wife and twin daughters and was finding it hard to earn a salary we could live on. He gave me sparse details about his health and turned to my brother's swift advancement to a managerial post in his company, Hallmark Cards. I asked questions. He answered them. We laughed at this and that. Then, as an afterthought, he said: 'Did I tell you the old lady died on Tuesday?'

There was nothing much I could say. It wouldn't have been appropriate to say I was sorry. He knew what my brother and I felt about her, though we never really knew what *he* thought. I wonder if he knew himself.

My mother's mother was a very different woman from Minnie. Eliza-Maria Toop had been born a Webster, a family who lived in a small cottage in World's End Passage. Charles Webster, my great-grandfather, was a tall, well-built idler who preferred to earn his money bare knuckle fighting Guardsmen from Chelsea Barracks outside the Grenadier pub or in World's End's great nineteenth-century centre of entertainment, Cremorne Gardens. His wife, small and devoted to the Bible, bore him several large sons and one daughter, Eliza. The eldest son, Will, most closely resembled his father in belligerence. He spent long hours on his back gold-leafing the ceilings at the Bank of England but was ready at the end of the day to join Charlie in any contest with the Guards. Josh, a devout prude who became a cabinet maker, was successful at ingratiating himself with the folks from Cheyne Walk and the new mansion blocks which were going up around Sloane Square. The third son, Jack, was a private soldier in the Indian Army. There was in fact a fourth, much younger son, Charlie, who was seldom talked of. He had left for Canada before the Great War trailing debts and women troubles and had enlisted in the Canadian Army soon after the war began. His mother had last heard from him by letter which told her he had just docked at Liverpool – bound for France. This was in 1916, the summer of the Big Push on the Somme. The coming attack was not a well-kept secret. Families everywhere with boys in France braced themselves. Charlie Webster's mother put her trust in God and read her Bible twice a day. Twenty thousand British and Dominion infantrymen died on July 1, that first day of the battle. Charlie never made contact again.

It was natural for the time that my grandmother Eliza, as my mother's mother, would see far more of my brother and myself than would Minnie, my father's mother. Eliza's husband, Jesse James Toop, had died a month or so before I was born and was acutely missed. Eliza would have dinner (lunch, that is) with us every day, cooking it for Kit and me when my mother was working her ten-hour shifts in Hunt's, the haberdashery in King's Road. On Saturday nights she would cook our favourite supper of sausages, tomatoes and fried bread. Somehow, from her pension, she would find enough for a bottle of Tizer to wash it down. A half-gill of gin in her tea and several deep inhalations of snuff were *her* Tizer for the evening.

It's hard to say how my brother and I regarded her. With affection certainly but also with a sense of her difference, her eccentricity. First there was her unusual physical appearance. She was (presumably an inheritance from her very tall father) about five foot eight or nine inches, tall for a woman today, outstandingly so for a woman born in the early 1870s. But her clothes were what marked her out. She wore black. Her dress, coat and Victorian straw boater were all black. Indoors, she was never known to take off her coat, a light material in summer, a heavier moth eaten, fur-collared number in winter. What seemed certain to my brother and me is that she never removed her hat either. She certainly wore it in bed. Since at one period my parents, brother, myself and our grandmother lived in a one bedroom flat (my parents slept in the front room, Kit and I with my grandmother in the bedroom), my brother and I knew this was the case. It's possible, I suppose, that some Victorian delicacy dictated she should wait until we were asleep before she removed her hat. Who knows? But sitting up in bed, sipping her 'tea', a blanket round her shoulders but still wearing her black straw, Eliza Doolittle boater, is the image of her I'll never lose.

I have many other images of course. To me this grandmother, chuckling as she told her stories, wreathed in the blue smoke of fried bread, sipping gin and tea and drawing snuff up her right nostril, was one of the very stable elements in our very stable life.

We had no radio at that time and after-supper entertainment with our grandmother was usually a game of Snap in the yellow, hissing gas light, or having our fortunes told from the tea leaves. We would crouch round the kitchen range which for some reason had been built into the front room (there was a workable gas cooker in the scullery). She would create a residue of tea leaves in her cup with a flick of the wrist which sent the tea hissing into the stove. I don't imagine she ever took the predictions of good fortune for us too seriously. I think she believed we were, in any case, immune to bad luck. But I could feel her own reaction as the pattern of the leaves warned of some impending tragedy for herself. She had suffered so hard a life she could not take even the tea leaves lightly.

When Kit had dozed off and the gin had relaxed her sufficiently, she would talk to me about the past, sometimes lacing it with lurid and wildly indiscreet stories which I was somehow aware were not to be repeated before my mother. She was never maudlin in her recounting and it was only much later that I could put together the broad outline. She had grown up in World's End Passage during the 1870s and had learnt to read and write at the Ragged School open to everyone for a penny a week. Money was uncertain, dependent on her father's winnings as a street fighter. When two of the brothers, Josh and Jack, left home and took their earnings with them, money became even tighter. Her mother, struggling to feed the youngest children, Charlie and Eliza, saw domestic service for her daughter as the only way out. At the age of twelve, through whose agency I can't guess, she was put into service in a large house, perhaps Dinton Park, the Wyndham family house outside Salisbury. She seems to have stayed there nearly three years.

Living in the country, she said, was a dirty business. I'd understand when I was older. I thought at the time she was referring to the animals that, I'd heard, lived there. Today, I wonder what she was really suggesting? That some under valet or footman, some weekend guest or even family member, had pressed his attentions upon her.

That's how a sexual assault or even a rape might have been described then. I suppose, in view of her later life, this was the most likely answer. Certainly she was desperately unhappy there and developed a life-long hatred for living anywhere but London. At the age of fifteen or so she could no longer bear the drudgery, and the loneliness and the dirty business, whatever it was. She rolled up her few clothes and tied them with string, climbed out of the great house at night and started on the road back to London. Later I would learn more of her life when she arrived back in the city. But throughout my youth these stories of living and partly living in late Victorian and early Edwardian times laid down a bed for my imagination.

Effortlessly, I can see her sitting by the stove, gaslight turned down, musing over her own fortune in the tea cup. Never without the Eliza Doolittle straw hat, she adjusts the angle of it frequently, removing the long hat-pin, driving it back through the black straw into her thick grey hair. She sucks on her snuff-stained upper lip. She puts down the cup. One hand holds the hat in place, the other lifts the long hat-pin towards me. She has a floppy carmine cloth rose on the front of the hat today and she uses it to make sure the boater is well aligned. But still she doesn't drive the pin home. My brother is fast asleep on the other end of the Put-U-Up. 'This pin,' she says, with a slow shake of the head and a deep introductory intake of breath, 'could very well have saved my life, Dee.' (I was normally known as Dee in the family.)

'Saved your life?' She has me gripped. I shake myself fully awake. 'When?' I croak. 'How?'

'How?' Her voice deepens. 'Because it was the night I was very nearly murdered.'

I sit forward in my chair, praying that my mother doesn't come in. I know the story will stop abruptly if she does. 'Nearly murdered?'

'By Jack the Ripper himself. You heard of him?'

I shake my head.

'Terrible he was. That year he was more famous than the Queen.'

'Why was he called Jack the Ripper?'

An intake of breath – and a lowered voice. 'Because . . . of his knife.'

I try to stop myself gasping.

'It wasn't long after I came back to London. Sweet sixteen I was coming up . . .' She thrusts the pin back into her hat. 'I knew my mother would send me back to service if she found out I'd run away, so I'd waited all one night at the end of World's End Passage, sleeping naps ten minutes at a time, waiting for my brother Will to go to work. He was always early out the house because he was working that time gold-leafing the ceilings in the Bank of England, that's up in the City of London. He'd leave for work at about four o'clock and walk up to Sloane Square for the horse bus.

''Course, he nearly had a fit when he saw me. Told me Mum would give me the wroughting of my life – and there'd be a good hiding from Dad to go with it.

' "That's why I'm not telling 'em," I said to Will. "Least, not yet." I had no money and I hadn't eaten for two days. But I was going to get a job in London and look after myself.

'Now my brother Will was a terror and not many people wanted to get on the wrong side of him. But he wasn't like the eldest, Josh. Brother Josh I used to call him because he was always talking about the Bible. He was the smarmy type who'd tell on you and pleased of the chance. Always turned his nose up at me like I was a bad smell.'

'Did Will give you money?'

'Better than that, love. He took me with him up to the City, bought me soup and bread at a cabman's stall and told me to wait for him until dinnertime when he'd take me over to Dirty Dick's. 'Course, I wandered about the City, had a wash at a public pump, and when it got light watched the nobs arriving. Never seen so many top hats in my life! And a lot of 'em took a long look at me, I can tell you. Sweet sixteen, remember, and I was already tall and had lovely chestnut hair . . .'

I tried to imagine my grandmother the same age as the Watney's girls. It was impossible.

'At dinnertime Will came out and took me across to Dirty Dick's. Well named it was, the dirtiest pub I was ever in. But the story is it was *supposed* to be dirty. That was the fun of it. Cobwebs and dead cats hanging from the ceiling. Stuffed I'm sure. Will loved it. And the landlady loved him. So when he asked her to give me a job, any job, she said she'd teach me waiting on tables.'

'When were you nearly murdered?'

'That was later. About a year later. I'd made it all right with my Mum by then and I'd go home to World's End Passage on my night off. The other six days I bunked up in a room down by Aldgate with a couple of girls, although sometimes I was so tired out I slept in the bar. 'Course, I was lucky to have somewhere to sleep. A lot of the girls around Spitalfields had only the doss-house. A fourpenny doss it was called, all sleep together in one big room and cook your own food in the big kitchen. Some of the girls that came into Dirty Dick's never had a proper room in their lives, paying a different doss every night.

'Where did they really live?'

'They didn't live anywhere, love. If they didn't have the fourpence for a doss they wandered all these alleyways and courtyards round there asking strange men to give 'em money.'

I think I must have looked doubtful. 'To give them money?'

'Perhaps they'd give the men a kiss and a bit of a cuddle for it,' she conceded casually. 'Anyway, time I'm talking about, already a girl had been killed just round the corner from Dirty Dick's in Buck's Row. And then the next week, there was another terrible murder in Hanbury Street. 'Course, every girl in Spitalfields was scared out of their wits.'

'Were you?'

'Going back to my room in the middle of the night, what do you think? Then one night I was going home when I heard police whistles down towards the river. One of the girls was screaming in an alley nearby. And suddenly, I heard footsteps behind me in the fog.'

'Was it Jack the Ripper?'

'It was Jack all right. He called out to me. "Stop," he says. "I must talk to you, Miss." Then I saw him.'

'What did he look like?'

'A top hat and a black doctor's bag. He stopped in the entrance to an alleyway about six feet from me.'

I watched her open-mouthed. The flat of one hand holding her hat on, her other hand slowly drew the hat-pin out again, seven or eight inches of sharpened steel. She stared down at the point, then lifted her head again, eyes narrowed. ' "Come any nearer," I said, "and you'll have this hat-pin in your gut." Then I turned and ran like mad.'

'Did he chase you?'

'He did, but this hat-pin had saved me. When he saw it, for that moment he stopped just long enough for me to run. He was after me in a flash, of course, but I ran straight for the police whistles and before you knew it he'd turned off into one of the alleys and made his getaway into the fog.'

I sit staring at her.

'It was close,' she says. 'Very close.' She drove the pin deep into her hat.

For a minute I sit there. There is one thing troubling me, one thing I haven't resolved in my mind. 'Why was he called Jack the *Ripper*?'

'Because he used to rip the girls open with his knife,' she says slowly.

'Where? Where did he rip 'em?'

She takes a deep breath and shakes her head. 'No,' she says, 'no, my love. Your mother would never forgive me if I told you that.'

The origin of the detestation between my two grandmothers, Minnie and Eliza, is unknown to me. Most likely it was one of those obscure and finally pointless feuds that working-class life produced far more often than its eulogists have any interest in recording. During my mother's early life she lived with her parents in Upcerne Road in the lee of the power station. Perhaps two hundred yards separated them from my father's family in Lots Road. Later, when Jesse James died just a month before I was born, Eliza moved into a room in Hobury Street, now less than a hundred yards from Minnie in Blantyre Street. The hostility between them seems to have sprung full-grown from the moment my parents decided to marry. Yet this was no mundane objection to your son marrying my daughter, or vice versa, no working-class *Romeo and Juliet*. There were no such objections voiced on either side and, had there been any to voice, there most certainly would have been. But the implacable hostility of my two grandmothers only ended when Eliza died twelve years later.

For all those years the two women maintained this strange feud. They made a point of never using the same pubs. The Reilly and the King's Arms down by the river were ceded to Minnie and her cronies; the Weatherby (scene of a later murder) and the World's End to Eliza.

My brother and myself, out with Eliza buying fish and chips at Perry's opposite St John's church hall, would scan the ground ahead for any ill-chance sighting of Minnie approaching down Blantyre Street. We totally believed any meeting guaranteed a serious clash. Eliza was not normally belligerent, but she had a reputation for standing up for herself. One day outside St Luke's Hospital, where her ageing mother was being treated for that sickness of the very poor, scurvy, my grandmother's dislike of her devout elder brother Josh had come to a head. Although relatively prosperous as a cabinet maker, he was protesting that he couldn't possibly afford more than the half a crown a week he contributed to the upkeep of their mother. For Eliza, paying twice that and unable most weeks to pay her own rent this was too much. She attacked him with such a ferocious flurry of blows that he reeled backwards, collapsing a fruit stall under his sprawled weight. My mother, then eight years old, had high-stepped through the rolling apples and burst oranges and run all the way back to the World's End in embarrassment.

So a physical clash between the grandmothers was never out of the question. What puzzled me was why? As the years went on they each approved ever more warmly of their respective son- or daughter-in-law. Nor was there any history of friction between the two women. Indeed there had never been a cross word spoken between them – for the simple reason that for the dozen years they were forced to be aware of each other's presence on this earth, or rather in World's End which amounted to the same thing, they had never once met. Complex avoidance tactics were employed by Eliza to collect her Widow's Pension money from the same Post Office my other grand-mother necessarily used. Special care was taken in the approach to the lurking bookmaker's runner (used by them both) at the mouth of World's End Passage. Mysterious protocol ensured that the grandmothers were never together on the same family occasion – this included the original wedding of my parents, the christenings of my brother and myself at St John's, the local World's End church, or any New Year or Christmas party given by either side of the family.

Though they had never met they must have been recognisable faces to each other long before their children decided to marry. World's End had a population the size of a small town's, but crushed together in the area of a village. We all went to the same elementary schools: Ashburnham, Servites, Park Walk or St Mark's. Kit and I were taught by the same teacher who'd taught my mother. Anonymity was out of the question. We grew up believing it was natural to know, in some measure, every face you passed in the street.

In our early childhood money was never a consideration. Indeed, now that I think about it, I'm not sure I even knew it existed. Things were bought for us: a few sweets, a comic, and of course a Christmas present from our parents. But until we were about the age of seven I don't believe we handled money or realised the delights of spending it. I think, in the early years before the war, everybody was too hard up to give even the occasional penny or tuppence for a child to waste on sweets. Eliza was the one who broke the mould. She would slip us small sums, literally a farthing or two, to buy one sweet at the sweet shop opposite Ashburnham School or at the Black Man's shop where there was a whole farthing counter. By contrast I can never remember Minnie, with a husband who worked at least part-time and a son still at home, giving us anything. Never a penny when we paid her a visit, never a Christmas present could be spared from the demands of landlord (of the King's Arms) and bookmaker. More likely it just didn't occur to her.

But the consumer society finally entered our ken with the display in the shoe shop across Edith Grove on the corner of King's Road. Running the streets required proper shoes, plimsolls or slippers as we called them. They hung on long strings like drying fish and were, in ascending order of cost and merit in our eyes, dark brown, black or white. I don't think we ever possessed a white pair but even black was acceptable. One or two people, like a shop-keeper's son named Oddie from further down the King's Road, had black shorts, white plimsolls and a multi-purpose knife that hung from a tooled leather belt. Oddie and I competed for a while for leadership of our gang but although he was a good runner (which I put down solely to his white plimsolls) he didn't have the advantage of going to the same school we did. He was in and out of our gang, probably under pressure from his mother, until he disappeared at some no longer remembered point in the war – probably, we thought, to one of those schools where you slept at night and had teachers like black crows in gowns and hats called mortar boards which all our dads kept anyway in the closet for knocking up a bit of cement.

Yet I believe we grew up without any sense of deprivation. Barely even with any sense of difference.

Of course, I don't know what accent I had. Obviously I used the vocabulary of the World's End – parents would 'wrought' their children (or indeed each other) if the misdemeanour required no more than a verbal reprimand. For something more serious, it was said that he welted her (or if it were a son this could be with the thick leather belt that many men wore at a time when trousers were not constructed to stay up of their own accord); of a daughter you'd say he fetched her one across the face – or, of a wife, he gave her a good hiding. Men handed out the punishment. Women often lied or prevaricated to protect themselves or their children. Violence was not so widely condemned as now; a man's right to administer physical punishment was accepted by many, even the victims, in the World's End.

We did not swear. Men seldom allowed themselves more than a 'bloody' in front of women – so children were deprived of familiarity with today's repetitious swear words. We had nothing approaching a prep school slang either. Even the RAF slang common in comics – 'Wizard prang!', 'Piece of cake', 'Good show' – never penetrated the speech of the World's End, as I'm sure it didn't that of the East End.

Of course we dropped aitches and many favoured the glottal stop but the accent around us was cockney, characterised by a certain sharpness rather than the fashionable, modern Esturian whine. And my father's anxiety about the way we spoke at least made sure we pronounced our neighbours' names as spelt while all around us names were mispronounced. We, for instance, were never known as the Wheal family. Our World's End name was Wills. The Sapsford family were Saxford, the Corfields were Cornfields just as Slaidburn Street was always Slayburn. Popular etymology played its part but indifference was the key. Kit and I were taught to make sure our name was pronounced as was. It was part of my father's plan of escape – although he could do little about the universally dropped aitches and the plural pronoun with a singular part of the verb: 'We was . . .', 'You was. . .', 'They was . . .' which my mother dropped into comfortably until the end of her life.

We were not alone in making efforts of this kind. There were other families who tried equally hard. But most didn't find the effort worthwhile. I would guess, in retrospect, that Kit and I spoke quite well for the area, with a clear enough accent, but probably recognisably cockney. Modifying (without refining) the accent was to become a problem in later years.

What underlined a sense of difference among ourselves, however, was not accent or mispronunciation but the simple sense of smell. I think we grew up accepting that it was natural that all houses should have their unique smell and that men in particular smelt according to their trade. They smelt of sweat, of course, but also of paint, plaster, flux or oil. A few, like my father, scrupulous at the sink, smelt stingingly of soap. But there is another smell that comes back to me, surprisingly easy to conjure up after all these years, and that's the smell of real poverty, the smell of neglect. All the children at Ashburnham School were poor. Most were adequately cared for, barring a few fleas and reach-me-down clothes, but some suffered serious neglect. We knew them by their smell, a thick cloying smell that travelled with them. It hung about their houses, or more usually rooms, if you went home with them. In the World's End it could well be in a house with close to a dozen rooms. Five families might live there. The front door would be permanently open. The hall would have been painted chocolate brown perhaps fifty years earlier. By now, the handlebars of resting bicycles would have scored deep white marks in the plaster. And that smell would hit you straight away. There was nothing warm or comforting about it as was the case in other houses. Even before we were old enough to know, we told each other it was the smell of bugs, the blood-sucking, evil-smelling insects that infested many of the houses in the World's End. Later I learnt that it was.

*

My mother was twenty-one when I was born in 1931, my father just twenty-three. My brother Kit was born nineteen months later. The slump was gripping Britain as it had much of the rest of the world. Six million Germans were out of work, their discontents sweeping Adolf Hitler to power. In the headlines of La-di's *Evening News* I saw, but understood little of, the signs of war. Yet it was coming.

Jobs rather than war was my parents' preoccupation at this time. Estate building on the outskirts of Central London had virtually ceased soon after 1931. This meant the need for daily or weekly employed plumbers like my father ceased with it. The huge estates of new houses at Morden provided his last job. By 1933, he no longer had regular work. For the next four years he was on and off the dole eking out the twenty-one shillings (one pound five pence) a week dole money with any one-off building job he could find. In later years he could never pass on his way to South Kensington without admiring a high chimney he had built with a friend, posing as skilled bricklayers though lead, not bricks and mortar, was their real expertise.

He would at this time take any job so long as it did not remove him from his family. His long list of jobs, official and unofficial, some lasting no more than a day or two, others much longer, included a spell as a mortuary assistant at St Luke's Hospital. Conditions and personnel down in the underground mortuary were still Dickensian. The gaslit, flag-stoned mortuary chamber was connected to the hospital by a weeping brick passage. When he was introduced to the mortician, the hulking, staring-eyed Leslie, my father thought him barely sane. The smell down there was sickening and Leslie was keen to demonstrate his prowess at hurling the dissecting scalpels at the mortuary door which he had marked with a human outline target. When family members came down to visit the deceased, a coat was always draped discreetly over the target area.

During these visits Leslie excelled himself, a giant Uriah Heep bowing and bobbing the visitors to the table where the body was displayed. If it were a woman he would demonstrate how difficult it was to remove her rings, the hand having swollen with excess water. Then, with a menacing lift of his thyroid eyes and a sinister chopping hand movement, he would suggest that rings *could of course* be recovered – but that would involve the removal of the finger at the same time. This offer was always refused with horror by the family. The moment they left Leslie would signal my father to hand him the surgical chopper. With my father flinching at the dull thud that followed, the ring would be retrieved to find its way into Leslie's stained coat pocket, the finger tossed to my father for the waste bin.

In 1937 he was offered the chance to lay lead on the roof of a squash court somewhere near Sloane Square and took the job with alacrity. It led to his being offered the job of full-time plumber at a block of expensive flats called Whitelands House. The red brick block still stands next to the Duke of York's Barracks overlooking the King's Road, a few dozen yards from Sloane Square.

The owner of the block badly needed an intelligent and competent full-time plumber. The problem was that during construction the block of one hundred flats had been virtually finished when it was discovered the plumbing had been overlooked and would have to be installed piecemeal while the building was being completed. The result was an extraordinarily complex plumbing plan that required, for instance, entrance to flat 10 to turn off the water if a pipe burst in flat 19. On the service staircases, pipes and stopcocks were massed haphazardly to carry hot and cold water all over the building from the boiler rooms below. A Snakes and Ladders plan had been drawn up at the time. My father was offered the job of making sense of this mess. To a journeyman plumber a full-time job in 1937 was an extraordinary piece of luck. My father appreciated the opportunity and was grateful to his new employer. But survival depended not simply on doing a good job. It involved making himself indispensable.

His first act in his new job therefore was to learn by heart the complex plumbing plans, including drainage and hot and cold water, to the hundred flats in the block. His second act was to destroy these plans. Ten years later, when he had been promoted first to stoker, porter, then head porter and finally manager of Whitelands House, he still carried the plumbing blueprint in his head – and, though no longer a plumber himself, was nevertheless still indispensable to any visiting plumbing firm who came to work there.

Of my two uncles, George and Fred, my father kept his brother George at arm's length. Among his many manifestations of plain unpleasantness, he had the unpleasant habit of repaying a loan publicly, as if it were a gift to you. These things were important to a man or a woman whose pride was on the breadline. The middle brother, Fred, we only saw occasionally when he was back from sea. I don't know the details of his transgression but he had clearly stolen something. I certainly can't imagine him house-breaking, so his haul was more likely a quantity of paint from a job since he was by trade a painter. The magistrate or judge had taken the offence seriously and made him one of those offers you can't refuse: the choice between a period at sea to mend his ways or six months in Wormwood Scrubs. He became a merchant seaman. By the time I remember him he walked with a rolling seaman's walk.

Fred was clearly immensely fond of my brother and myself. For a long time I glibly assumed this was because he never had children of his own. In fact, when he left the court the day he was sentenced to the sea, he did not yet know that a girl from Blantyre Street, Janet Stevens, was already nearly two months pregnant with his child. It was a liaison he had been conducting in secret – not easy in and around the World's End. The problem, as ever, was his mother, Minnie. She and her friend Ma Bash were conducting a long-running feud with the Stevens family. It's pointless to ask what the feud was about. Pointless to ask what so many of these feuds were about. Most people had forgotten shortly after one began. It was just that, to Minnie, it was inconceivable that her son should marry a

Stevens girl. As soon as word leaked out that Janet Stevens was pregnant by Fred, she acted. In the King's Arms she began to blacken Janet's name. The girl was, she whispered (shouted is probably closer to the truth), a known tart. One who'd take any man up World's End Passage. Pregnant by Fred? A likely story! *Nobody* knew the father's name, but if it was humanly possible Minnie would make it her business to find out – and let her son know he was the victim of a Stevens trick to force him into marriage.

There was, of course, no such investigation. She simply wrote to Fred and told him flatly the whole World's End knew that when Janet Stevens' child was born it would be black. How my uncle, nineteen years old, stoking in a cargo ship between Shanghai and San Francisco, took this news I can only guess. A letter could take an age to reach the addressee if his ship were at sea. On arrival in some Pacific port he duly collected his mail. Fred was no fool. There was only one black man in the World's End, the sixty year old who ran the sweet shop next to the Cremorne Arms. My uncle wrote to Janet and asked her to marry him.

But by then events had moved on in the World's End. Fred was still not back from sea. The baby, a boy, was born. Janet could not look after him in the face of the hostility of both Minnie and her own family. It was decided, against Janet's wishes, that her aunt should legally adopt the boy and bring him up as her son – she was in any case moving to Kent where her husband had been transferred to a job in the docks.

When Fred returned a year later, he and Janet were married. They immediately asked her aunt for their son. The aunt refused. The Stevens family, who had never forgiven Janet for consorting with a Wheal, supported the aunt. Travelling back from Kent the young couple decided there was nothing they could do. They were ignorant of the law and in any case Fred was still under the interdiction of the magistrate. They were allowed to visit their boy from time to time, but only as 'uncle' and 'aunt'. I feel their sadness now through the strength of their affection then for Kit and myself. The working-class Montagues and Capulets had spoken. Fred and Janet would suffer for the rest of their lives. Where was that tolerance the myth-makers like to boast of? Where were those universal working class salt-of-the-earth values then?

My grandmother, who had orchestrated the tragedy, refused any responsibility. She was only telling as she saw. After the war Fred and Janet emigrated to Chicago, he as a school janitor, she as an elevator operator. There they enjoyed a modestly prosperous life surrounded by their classless Church friends.

I suppose my brother and I were the only beneficiaries. Fred and Janet had no more children. Instead they showered affection on us, Fred particularly. In an attempt to repay his kindness, my brother and I set out to collect a Christmas present for him. We knew he smoked Craven A cigarettes and a packet of ten, or even five, was far outside our price range. But there was something else we could do. We found from somewhere an old Craven A tin. Scouring the World's End streets, we collected dozens of cigarette butts, identifiable as Craven A by their much-advertised cork tips. Stripping down the dog-ends, we packed the whole damp, foul-smelling mess of used tobacco in the tin, wrapped it in newspaper and proudly presented it to him. He accepted it with profound thanks and not even a trace of a shudder.

The story of the lost child had one more final tragic twist. In 1940 the boy was called up for the RAF. Conscription formalities required a birth certificate. Aged twenty, he discovered his mother was his aunt, his aunt his mother. It was another twenty years before he forgave his father.

I have spent some time on the principal figures in my childhood while barely mentioning the most important. For both my brother and myself, much as we enjoyed the company of our grandmother Eliza, and respected and admired our father, our mother, born

Phyllis Beatrice Toop, was the most significant figure in our lives. Courageous enough to face down her mother-in-law Minnie in a High Noon meeting in World's End, broad-minded and sensitive enough to support and advise a neighbour who had just recognised her lesbian attraction to a nurse at St Stephen's Hospital, tall, attractive and shyly self-assured, she was looked up to, consulted for advice and respected for her calm good sense, by almost everyone who knew her. By this I really do mean almost everyone who got to know her. Her approach to any problem involved a good deal of weighing in the balance. For us, my brother and I, to be made unaware that we had fallen down on the job by my father was a deeply uncomfortable experience. To earn the disapproval of our mother for some act of meanness or unnecessarily hurtful comment was the stuff of sleepless nights.

I'm certainly not putting her up for sainthood. Thank God, she was much too ordinary for that. But she had so many of the very best human virtues. She was cheerful, friendly, interested and tolerant. In the end, even my first wife's intolerable, aristocratic mother realised she had no way to deal, as she wished to, with my mother. Arch patroniser that she was, my wife's mother was skilled in that casual, fluttering disparagement affected by some women of her class. She was intelligent and saw in herself a natural superiority. But she could not contend with my mother's unsettling straightforwardness and the realisation that, by comparison, the harder she tried, the more she humbled herself in her attempts to patronise.

I've no doubt that many of my mother's qualities were her own, distilled from her own experience – but many others clearly came from the intense feeling for children she shared with her mother. Eliza was never restrained in her defence of an ill-treated child. In those days there were many more shocking street-corner examples of beating than you would see now – and Eliza was always prepared to interfere vigorously. She was not always right, certainly not always successful, but there was great humanity there. This she undoubtedly passed on to her two daughters, my mother and her elder half-sister, May.

I have come, in fact, to realise that a sort of unspoken contract existed between our immediate family. Love and support for each other were at the core of it, but it was characterised by a clear expectation of fairness in our dealings with each other. My brother and I were expected to deal fairly with my parents and my grandmother and with each other. We could be sure in turn that they would deal fairly with us. This was not simply some unspoken rule, it was often enough articulated by my father, and his choice of punishment reinforced it when he felt we had transgressed. The source of my mother's commitment to this ideal was clearly evident in her own home life. Not so with my father. Any attachment to fairness could only have been developed in reaction to his own mother's excesses. This made him harder than my mother, more opportunistic, more ready to bend rules in the world outside. He saw life as much more of a struggle than did my mother, and he was prepared, as I will recount later, to go to greater lengths to defend our interests than I think my mother would have been able to. He was certainly a more complex character than her or Eliza, and more complex than any of his brothers and sisters.

I feel that his sometimes shifting moral values somehow harked back to his own enigmatic, mostly silent father who throughout his life conducted his own lonely struggle against poverty. Once only my father let out how much he had admired his father, and felt for him. It was a pitifully small incident. His father had asked for the loan of a shilling. It was early in the week when, traditionally, young bachelors had nothing left of their wages. My father was forced to confess he had no money. 'Disappointed in you,' his father said. 'But, knowing you, you'll learn, of course.' It had been a test, a rebuke – and a compliment my father never forgot. Expressions of love, or even affection, did not come easily in their family.

It's hard to say which aspects of my father's personality were derived from *his* father. Far easier to see how much my mother must have owed her air of reassuring calmness, her skill for putting people at ease, to her own father.

Jesse James Toop was born in the Dorset countryside in the mid-nineteenth century. His 'manner', which was remarked upon by many in the World's End, was no doubt the result of years spent in domestic service in grand houses, although he never lost a faint Dorset burr in his voice. It is not easy to establish exactly how old he was since his marriage certificates (there were two) tell different stories as he progressively shifted his birthdate back a few years on marrying younger women. What is certain is that he died in the World's End in 1931, a few months before I was born.

He was a member of another of those farm-labouring families who could no longer feed their children. In this he was not unlike my other grandfather, Henry James, whose journey from Essex to London was equally inspired by rural poverty. In Jesse James' case it was a longer walk. He was thirteen when he set off with his two brothers from the West Country. He disappears from sight at the point when (the last-remembered fact from my grandmother) their bread and cheese had run out at Salisbury and they had begged, with modest success, at the lodge of a great house. She, of course, claimed it was the house she had herself been imprisoned in years later, the house she had escaped by climbing from a kitchen before dawn and herself walking the endless miles to freedom and independence in London. But that's very much the sort of claim she liked to make. She believed in those improbable kismet coincidences.

Jesse James had undoubtedly spent a few years holding horses' heads after his arrival in London. Certainly he never mentioned resort to the workhouse. He was a proud man, reluctant to admit to that degree of failure. Perhaps it wasn't necessary. I know the three brothers stayed in touch and supported each other when they could, and at some point he secured a temporary domestic post with a titled family in Norfolk. It was initially for the shooting season, but given a line forward he advanced rapidly. By his late-twenties he had risen through the hierarchy of domestic service to become a butler. Clearly he could not be one bearing the evocative outlaw's name Jesse James, so from then on the Jesse was dropped, to be retained only by his brothers. He became the dignified butler with the perfect butler's name, no challenge to a Greville, a Crackanthorpe or Cavendish. He became simply, but imposingly enough, Toop.

When his lordship became too old to travel, the Norfolk winter weighed heavily upon his much younger wife. The lady of the house began a routine of wintering in the South of France. She kept a small staff in a house near Nice, but a French butler, all agreed, was out of the question. The young James Toop was required to accompany her and it was not long before the comforts he brought to the lady of the house were not confined to her pot of Earl Grey before retiring. In France, he shared his mistress's bed for five or six winters. But in Norfolk during the rest of the year he was, of course, obliged to live in abstinence. It was during one of these long summers that he met a fellow servant, Hannah, and applied for permission to marry. It could have come as no real surprise to him when permission was given – and with it notice of dismissal.

I know nothing about his life with Hannah except that they married from the Rose Inn, Norwich, and that she died, presumably still a relatively young woman, a year or two before the new century. In the intervening twenty years or so, Jesse James had moved slowly down the scale to become a ticket collector in Hyde Park at a wage of twenty-eight shillings for an eighty-hour, six-and-a-half-day week. In an age when people used the Park to walk and meet and talk, chairs could be hired for a penny each and the ticket collector would be at your elbow almost as soon as you sat down. It was, of course, the perfect opportunity in the last years of Victoria's reign to meet unaccompanied women. My grandmother was one of them, about thirty-five years of age at the time.

Jesse James was probably in his late-fifties then but loath to admit it. They must have got on well because she repeatedly came back to take a chair in his section of the park. Eliza may well, of course, have been in the park so regularly because she was *working* there (it was open until midnight, gaslit and notorious). At the very least she must have told him something of her chequered past because she had to tell him about her illegitimate daughter. He, in turn, told her something about his winters in the South of France, some details of which passed to my mother and then to me. Until a particularly unmanageable bill had to be paid, she told me, they kept ranged on the sideboard a collection of what sounds like Staffordshire pottery given to him among other things – a watch, cash – by the lady of the Norfolk manor.

Jesse James was a man of a calm and calming disposition. He and my paternal grandfather never met (though living cheek by jowl and the fathers of a young couple who had just married) but, had they done, they might well have exchanged views on dealing with the boisterous women they had married. Jesse James was the more successful domestically, although his task was admittedly less daunting. Though he was seldom at home, arriving there six and a half days of the week at midnight from the Park, the benign influence of the man was markedly present in the stories my mother told of her childhood. They lived in Berisford House in Upcerne Road, a small six-flat tenement overrun by mice and, on several occasions, rats. The homeless slept on the stairs, sometimes a single man, sometimes a couple to be carefully stepped over by my grandfather when he returned from work. Often enough there were sleeping children, too. By Thursday there was seldom enough money to feed either the gas meter or themselves. But on Friday his wages, twenty-eight shillings, were there to pay the Saturday rent collector. It was a precarious life and depended heavily on good health. Fortunately Jesse James remained healthy until he died. And by then my father, with his determination to break out of the World's End, had arrived on the scene.

*

When I was born we moved into a two-room flat at the top of a house in Seaton Street. In Henry VIII's time the street had been known as Hob Lane, a pathway believed to be frequented by malicious spirits, running down from King's Road to the river. By the 1930s the lane had long since gone but perhaps the spirits had simply moved over two streets to where Minnie and Ma Bash held court in Blantyre Street. A shared lavatory and sink on the landing below were the extent of the amenities offered by Seaton Street. But the rent was affordable at ten shillings (50 pence) a week and the couple who owned the house, Mr and Mrs Kitching, allowed a pram in the lower hall.

The bugs nesting under the loose wallpaper were dealt with by my father before we moved in. Windows and doors were sealed and sulphur candles lit to burn throughout the night. This was a process that had to be repeated every month or two for complete security. My mother claimed, and I believe her, that my brother and myself were never once bitten. Nevertheless, throughout the World's End these rented rooms were desperate places. Mice were taken for granted, rats were not infrequent, bugs might be anywhere. Sanitation was poor; bathrooms virtually unheard of and certainly not possessed by anybody we knew. Washing and cooking were frequently done at the landing sink with a gas ring on a small table next to it. Other lodgers might be standing in line. In the years after 1931 the expectations of working people all over the Western world were falling. This was certainly true of the World's End. All the same, in the middle of the Depression, with only the dole money to bargain with, my mother set out to improve the living conditions of her family.

Not many years before, the Guinness Trust, a charitable housing organisation with properties throughout London to this day, had rented from a generous Chelsea Council a large piece of land lying derelict on the King's Road at Edith Grove. It was, in fact, part of the

site of the Victorian era's Cremorne Gardens which extended from
the King's Road to the river. They had been closed down towards the
end of the nineteenth century as the haunt of thieves and prostitutes
and the generally licentious. The rent charged by the council for this
large piece of land was one shilling (5 pence) a year for a 999-year
lease. As a result of criticism that only the better-off poor could
afford most Peabody and Guinness Trust flats, the decision was
taken to build at the World's End a lower standard of tenement
without bathrooms or electric light, but which could be rented out at
rates genuinely possible for the poorer sort. It was the beginning of
affordable housing.

The property was built as four low-rise blocks on the King's Road
between Tadema Road and Edith Grove. Criticisms of the barrack-
block appearance of the new buildings were rightly ignored. The four
blocks with their cemented spaces or yards in between were an
infinitely better place to grow up in than most of the streets around
World's End. This was, of course, before the scourge of spray paint
brought us graffiti but the Trust's draconian rules on window
cleaning and the tenants' responsibility to wash down the white-tiled
landings on a rota were welcomed by many who had fled from the
multiple occupation of crumbling Victorian houses in the area. The
new flats on the King's Road, or tenements as they were called,
provided low-rent basic living: gas lighting (although to be fair all the
streets at the time were gas-lit) rather than electricity, and outside
lavatories on a small cast-iron-fenced balcony. Washing facilities
were a bath with a hinged pine top in the kitchen scullery, impossible
to use with any privacy in a crowded flat. We rarely did; instead the
big, square stone sink served as something between bath and shower,
my mother standing us in it to sluice us down. But the flats were
light, comfortable, and warmed by a kitchen range in the front room

Over Blantyre Street, Lupus, Seaton, Slayburn, Vicat, Bifron,
Meek or Stadium, Guinness Trust Buildings represented an enormous improvement. In the large open space between each block

young children could play safely: marbles up against the wall, a rough and tumble game of Warney Echo when in season, skipping for the girls and football with a tennis ball for the boys. Guinness Trust Buildings promised a good life. But how to get in? The Cerberus guarding the gate was a severe-looking man named Mr Caple. His title was Superintendent. On his decision a tenancy depended.

He was in every way a frightening authority figure. He wore an orange-hued tweed suit, with waistcoat and watch-chain, a bushy moustache and a bowler hat. Beyond the evident fact that he was a class above us, he had the power to evict any family for bad behaviour or non-payment of rent. To approach Mr Caple with a request for a vacancy was simply not done. Mr Caple approached you, that was simply a given. If a flat were empty he would begin to make enquiries of his most reliable tenants: was there a World's End family who would benefit from a flat – and prove suitably reliable in payment of the rent? To decide to break these rules took some courage in the London of the early-thirties. But my mother had determined this was the only way out of Seaton Street. Despite his unapproachability, she put on her best coat and went to the small office attached to the Caples' flat on the ground floor of the third block. Mr Caple at first affected surprised displeasure at her daring to importune him in this way. But he allowed her to make her case, to lay out for him the family income (the dole) and how she had managed so far to feed us all and avoid debt – and pay the Seaton Street rent with a regularity that her landlord would attest to.

The rent-book rules, a poster-sized copy of which was pinned to the wall behind Mr Caple's head, were pointed to. No wood-chopping allowed. Nothing was to be stored in the bath (I'm afraid they *were* thinking of coal). A colour wash to be applied throughout the tenement once a year, the distemper to be provided by Guinness Trust, the work to be carried out by the tenant. No clothes to be hung out of windows or in passages. Linoleum or other floor covering must not be nailed to the floor; an uncovered twelve-inch space must be left between linoleum and the skirting. Wallpaper may not be used to decorate the rooms. (These last two prohibitions were obviously to prevent the nesting of the dreaded bugs under lino or behind wallpaper.)

None of these regulations would give my parents a problem. But one, the rule against overcrowding, did. Now that Eliza was a widow, the plan had been, if we secured a flat at Guinness Trust, for her to come to live with us. But a clause on the list, in a heavy black print, proclaimed that any tenement that became overcrowded according to the definition of the Trust would result in the payment of a £5 fine by the tenant and immediate eviction. Overcrowding was defined as more than three people in a bedroom – two young children like my brother and myself to count as one person only. So with my parents we were 'three persons' and could have slept legally in the one bedroom. With my grandmother as well, however, it meant Kit and I in the bedroom with her, and my parents on a folding bed in the front room. This was against the rules. By the Guinness definition it was overcrowding. This item would cause us problems until the London blitz made all issues of overcrowding (shelters frequently slept ten times the number they were intended for) totally irrelevant.

I later heard of many in the Buildings who feared and even hated Mr Caple for the pressure he exerted for payment of rent. But I think Caple was not an unkind man behind his *amour propre* and Edwardian posturing. Perhaps, with his show of severity, he was desperately protecting his own job.

At the end of my mother's presentation of her case, Superintendent Caple paused and lit his pipe. As it happened, he said, he had been making enquiries in the area for a suitable family to take on tenement number 3, a scullery, front room and bedroom, which had just become vacant. The rent was eight shillings a week. One or two people he trusted, he said, had mentioned our name. In fact, he had already looked into the possibility of our becoming tenants, or so he claimed. My mother had a way with her, so it's difficult to be sure if he'd simply made up his mind on the spot. She wasn't naturally flirty but she was not unaware of the effect she had on men. Those few who overstepped the limits she expected to be observed received a very steely response. That afternoon, the terrifying Mr Caple gave her a rent book and the keys to number 3 on the spot. My father, who had been illegally moonlighting from the enforced idleness of the dole, came back to find we had a new home with soft gas light, a fire burning in the front-room stove and its own lavatory. No furniture, but so what? We had a flat which had no need of sulphur candles to make it habitable.

TWO

Summer 1939

Some children spent the last month of peace running through grass meadows or swimming in shaded ponds. Some rode pony trails on Dartmoor or built sandcastles on the beach at Frinton. We had read about children like this in our comics.

Some, no doubt, even played throughout that hot August unaware that war was approaching. In the World's End, we knew. There were the gas mask fittings, of course, when St John's church hall reeked of the black rubber masks forced over our faces. We spluttered and yelled that we couldn't breathe. Some were sick into their masks, some choked and coughed, until the council woman relented and took the bug-eyed clamps off our faces. It reminded me of the time I'd had my tonsils out at St Stephen's and the nurse had lied as she promised to remove the thick, cloying ether pad from my face as soon as I asked. I knew she was planning to kill me. My grandmother Eliza, on some evening of minor excess with gin and snuff, had already warned me that most people die in hospitals. But the gas masks were different. By then I understood what they were for. I understood the council woman wasn't there to kill us. She wasn't even a real council woman. My mother said she was a volunteer – that's why she wore a silk blouse and tweedy skirt and spoke the way she did.

We were to take home the rubber masks in their square cardboard boxes and thread a string through so we could sling them on to our shoulders. 'If war breaks out,' the council woman fluted through her nose, 'you must carry them with you at all times, *wherever you go*.' To forget, in a gas attack, she strongly hinted, was to die a miserable death, our small bottoms held upright only by the firm grip of the lavatory seat.

But it wasn't only the gas masks. It was being called back to school for *practice* that left us in no doubt. A sinister note from our headmaster, Roly-poly we called him (Mr Whitehead to his face), had been delivered to our homes announcing the recall. Extra school in the holidays! What, we asked ourselves in mutinous gaggles in the Guinness Trust yard, had we done to deserve this? Monday August 22, my birthday, was to be the first day of recall.

We were baffled. Practice for what? We grumbled incessantly as we played marbles up the wall or mooched down to the river to smell the mud. (It was said to have the same health-giving qualities as sea air.) Sunday was usually the day we rehearsed our projected, though never achieved, mass bunk-in into the Science Museum, but on what could easily be the last day of our freedom we were too listless even for that.

I took the problem to my father. But for once even he could not provide the answer. 'It could be some sort of drill,' he said as he towelled himself down. 'What to do in an air-raid, perhaps.' He obviously wasn't sure, but it was worth passing on.

I went down to impart my new information to the boys. Harold Hawthorn lived in the flat above. He and I were bound together by an incident of arson in our youth when we had nearly burned down the front door of his flat (we had established an Indian camp there). Fatty Chapman, who would also be linked to me by a further incident of arson in the years to come, was slightly older. Stan Hartnell lived next door. I was bound to him by our spending nearly two hours trapped together in a huge iron dustbin in which we had hoped to find some broken lead soldiers which we intended to melt down in a frying pan and recast for profit. Tony Caine sat next to me at Ashburnham School. My brother Kit, then six years old, hopped on one foot as he always did when caught up in the excitement of a new turn of events.

I told the boys what my father had told me: we could be under attack from German Spitfires at *any* moment, wherever we were. I suggested it would be prudent to carry our gas masks without waiting for war to break out. In fact we could go down to the river again and test them out by smelling the mud with the masks on. If anybody could smell mud, I suggested, we should go up to the Town Hall and make a complaint to the council woman right away.

It didn't quite work out. A clump of girls eating crisps outside the King's Arms while their parents were having a Sunday dinner time drink started screaming with terror as we swarmed over the embankment in our gas masks. People came running out of the pub, including my grandmother, the bad one Minnie, not the good one, Eliza, and started shouting for the police. After a few port and lemons, some of the women became hysterical, screaming that the Germans had landed. Unrecognised in our gas masks, we ran on and escaped under Battersea Bridge. Covered in mud by now, we tried to restore our masks by sluicing river water through them. By the time we had finished I don't know if the masks were still capable of repelling mustard gas but they were certainly ineffective against the bitter (though admittedly health-giving) stench of Thames mud.

Monday morning came. Our journey to school took a little over five minutes. We would run to the back gate of the Guinness Trust Buildings where most of us lived, cross the road past the heavyweight brickwork of St John's Church and hope to hang on the trailing chains of a horse-drawn coal cart along the length of Burnaby Street. From about here you could hear the school bell tolling. This was the bell that had dominated my mother's childhood as she raced down

Upcerne Road and squeezed into the Girls' Entrance, very often on the final stroke of nine. It was a bell that dominated my schooldays too.

As we reached Upcerne Road nausea roiled in my stomach. I never told anyone how I hated Ashburnham. I'd like to have tales to tell about the wickedness of Ashburnham, as some have of their prep schools. But in fact there was nothing wicked about our school. Our class teacher Miss Williams was strict and alarming, but essentially good-willed. Our headmaster, Mr Whitehead, cultivated a pomposity that even eight year olds had no difficulty seeing through. Ashburnham was all right – but I still hated it. As I remember it now it was partly the fault of arithmetic, partly singing and partly Greek dancing. Greek dancing was a serious problem for any self-respecting eight year old. We were told by the music and dancing teacher, Miss Savage, that by dancing we would learn to move with the grace and dignity of the Ancient Greeks.

'Imagine yourselves dressed like this,' she said, showing us a picture of men in skirts with bands tied round their heads. We cringed at the thought.

There was worse to come. The privilege of choosing partners was 'naturally' accorded the girls and, on a word from Miss Savage, Joan Bruton of Raasay Street, fleet of foot and short of sight, would speed across the room to seize me by the hand.

I came to believe that it was Mr Whitehead who had devised this exquisite punishment for World's End boys. Dragged around the lower hall by our enthusiastic partners we were competing for an evil-smelling bunch of dying flowers from his office, given out as the Dancing Prize each Friday afternoon.

To get into the Boys' Entrance, a stone arch with the words carved above it, we had to turn into Lots Road. Above us the huge bulk of the power station, with its impenetrable, dirty-encrusted forty-foot windows, rose not fifteen yards from our classroom. These great blank windows with their utterly mysterious interior had stared back at me since I was five. On a dark, winter morning you saw the faintest of lights through them, yellow or sometimes blue, and the hazy outline of enormous turbines. Men, human beings, were never visible. Machines worked in there, huge and infinitely menacing, silent as the four grey plumes of smoke and grit that rose from the great chimneys above us. Perhaps it was the silence of the place that intimidated me so profoundly. I certainly welcomed the occasional hooter signalling a break or shift change, the only real sound I ever remember emerging from this extraordinary building.

I confess I feel physically moved to this day if I go to Lots Road and stare up at the power station. A few months ago it was announced that the huge brick mass was to be demolished, its coal-fired electricity generators no longer needed to supply the London underground system. So I'll be given the opportunity to experiment. One day I'll be able to walk down Lots Road and stare across the cleared site. There'll be a river bank visible for the first time in a century. There'll be swooping gulls and swans in line astern. On the far bank, among glittering twenty-first century buildings by Norman Foster, an eighteenth-century church will be visible where Blake's premonition warned the revolutionary Tom Paine of arrest if he did not flee England. But will I feel the same dragging sense of dread as I stand beside the Boys' Entrance? Who knows or cares now, except me?

We took our places in the hall as we did every normal school morning, sitting in class order, cross-legged on the parquet floor. We began with a prayer spoken by Roly Poly and 'All Things Bright and Beautiful' with Miss Savage on the piano. 'All Things Bright and Beautiful' was Mr Whitehead's favourite hymn and definitely one of the things I hated most about Ashburnham. A little later in life I would listen more carefully to the words: '*The rich man in his castle, the poor man at the gate – God made us high and lowly and ordered our estate . . . All things bright and beautiful . . .*' At some point in my young life these words took on meaning, as a hymn, I suddenly understood, to the ordained difference between Sloane Square, Chelsea and the World's End, Chelsea. But that's a later story.

Mr. Whitehead looked grave. 'Children,' he said, 'today is an important day in all our lives. Does it feel important to you?'

'Yes, Mr Whitehead,' we chorused.

'And why is that?'

He'd stumped us there. We remained shiftily silent. Looking down, we avoided his eyes. I thought of volunteering that it was important because it was my birthday but that didn't seem the sort of thing Mr Whitehead would be telling the whole Junior School about. Miss Savage at the piano let slip her elbow on to the keys and made us all jump with fright. I looked at her and saw the blush rising from the neck of her floral dress to her blonde hair. She was always blushing when things went wrong.

'Children,' Mr Whitehead tried again, 'does anyone know what the word evacuation means?'

A deep school silence. And shuffling embarrassment. A coal cart crunched on iron wheels along Lots Road. A hooter sounded a change of shift in the power station. We all knew.

'Evacuation? Can nobody help me out? Roly Poly at his most benign. 'Come along now. Evacuation means . . . ?'

'It means going to the lav reg'lar, sir,' one of the older boys, Ronnie Tooks, volunteered from the back of the hall. 'The school nurse said even when it's so cold outside you just don't want to, you've still got to go. Fer yer 'ealf,' he added convincingly.

His voice trailed away. Roly Poly was shaking his head solemnly. 'No, Ronald,' he said. 'It does not.'

Well, I thought, that was one in the eye for the visiting nurse because as a matter of fact evacuation was one of her favourite topics and we'd all had a talking to from her. The school hall buzzed urgently. The headmaster lifted his hand for silence.

'Evacuation is something decided on by the government in case of war,' Mr Whitehead informed us. 'Evacuation means taking all the children out of London to keep them safe from the bomber.'

We were stunned. We'd heard about the idea of going down the country, but none of us for a moment believed it could happen. And here was Mr Whitehead talking about it. The headmaster.

'We will stay together as a school, of course.' He plunged his thumbs deep into his waistcoat pockets. 'Ashburnham will always stick together. You will travel to the country with your teachers and be received by kind country people. You will have fresh bread and fresh milk every day. There will be cheese and fresh eggs from the farm. If you're lucky the farmer might even let you help with milking the cows.'

We stared at one another in horror.

'So much better than running wild through the World's End,' Roly Poly said. 'But practice will be necessary to carry the school in a disciplined body to the country.' We must, he told us, always bear in mind the good name of Ashburnham – a good name, he implied, that already reverberated the length of the land.

Practice. We had come to the nub of the matter. Mr Whitehead was well prepared. He had ascertained the number of children who could travel on a London double-decker bus. 'Your teachers,' he said, 'will now divide you into units of fifty-seven.'

Teachers swooped, numbering us off into phalanxes. Of course, we ducked and pushed others forward so we might be with our friends, but the only concession allowed was that brothers and sisters were to be assigned the same bus. At least I had Kit with me.

Our school hall was supported by two lines of six slender cast-iron columns, much favoured by Miss Savage for the ritual male humiliation of her Greek dancing sessions. These columns were now to play a vital role in our practice for flight from the bomber. While we were being assembled round the edge of the hall in our respective units, the more agile teachers came forward with coloured chalks to draw on the hall floor the outline of several buses and the shape of their seating. The pole, part of the alighting platform on London double deckers, was to be represented by one of the convenient iron supports. Finally, cards had been prepared detailing our bus numbers. Each child was required to hang a card around his or her neck. In Mr Whitehead's planning, nothing was to be left to chance.

We practised. The problem Mr Whitehead had identified was that as each paired column of children reached their assigned double decker, only a disciplined approach appropriate to Ashburnham's traditions would prevent a jumble of kids pushing, shouting and dropping their gas masks, all trying to scramble on the bus at once to sit next to their friends. This problem was to be solved by each child knowing in advance his or her exact seat, whether on the upper or lower deck. On reaching the chalk outline of the bus's alighting platform the column leader on the right would call out in a clear voice, 'Right of the pole,' seize the pole and swing himself into position to proceed rapidly up the notional stairs to his seat. The second child would call 'Left of the pole,' then mount the platform and move quickly left to his seat on the lower deck. This procedure would continue until the chalk outline of the bus was full of sitting children. All three 'buses' quickly filled. We had never seen Mr Whitehead happier.

But nothing was to be taken for granted. Practice was relentless. Day after day the school hall of Ashburnham rang to cries of 'Right of the pole' – 'Left of the pole'. Teachers and Mr Whitehead himself intervened when muddles occurred and children screamed as they were pushed off the top deck (of the chalk bus) in the belief they had stolen the aggressor's seat. This, said Mr Whitehead, only under-lined the need for daily practice.

We had no idea how long we had left in London. Feelings were very mixed about leaving, even if we were only going for a week or two. We liked the World's End. We liked playing among the rotting barges along the river. I knew where there was a whole car engine concealed in the mud. Our plan was to haul it out and clean it up and get it going. Perhaps even piece by piece build a car. This would be quite a project because not one of the families we came from, or anyone we were distantly related to or even knew, owned a car. Against really exciting projects like this we weighed the idea of living in the country. We didn't like animals much. Nobody in Guinness Trust was allowed to own a dog or a cat which we thought was a pretty good thing. But in the country apparently there were plenty. In the comics, kids in the country always had a dog running along beside them trying to tear the backside out of their trousers. But then they probably had cupboardsful of others.

Then we'd be leaving our mums and dads. We never talked much about that. Some said tentatively they thought the country might be fun for a day or two, a few trees to climb and things. But what else was there? Fresh eggs? Milking cows? Old Roly Poly must be off his rocker. If we'd taken an open vote on evacuation the answer would have been a shrugged, *Perhaps*. In a secret ballot, it would have been a terrified scream of, *No, never!*

So the prospect of leaving London began to preoccupy us. It depended, of course, on who Hitler was planning to invade next. But when I put this question to my father who knew most things – or would tell you straight when he didn't – he shook his head. In this case he didn't know even though he was always reading newspapers with things about Hitler on the front page. There was another villain who had appeared in the headlines the day after my birthday. He had apparently double-crossed everybody and was now putting it out that he was a friend of Hitler's. His name was Stalin and he came from Russia. A slight confusion arose when I heard one of the teachers say he wasn't so bad after all and even though he was ganging up with Hitler it was in a good cause. I asked my father about this. He was in the scullery putting Vaseline on his hair hoping to darken it down from the blond colour it returned to after he'd washed it. He was always trying to look older. About Stalin, he said that if he was doing anything in a good cause, it wasn't *our* good cause. This was obviously something to think about.

I had already spent a good deal of time thinking about these things and had been my brother's source of largely inaccurate information for some months. What inspired my interest? The romance of war, as I saw it? Of course, in part. My imagination had first been tickled about two Christmasses ago, when a friend of my Uncle Fred's had told me a story about being in the trenches opposite the Germans last time. He had been at a place called the Somme and told me at length how the British had crept out at night while the Germans were asleep in their trenches and slipped rubber bayonets on to the Germans' rifles in place of the real, sharp ones. After that, he said, going over the top at dawn was easy. He didn't tell me how many British soldiers had died struggling through the chalk mud against the magpie chatter of machine guns that day, so I probably did retain a distinctly romantic view of trench warfare.

But when I think about it now I believe there was something more to my anxiety to understand what was happening in the world. I believe now that it was some dim awareness that knowledge is power. Of course I didn't and could not have put it to myself in that manner. But I already saw that the simple recitation of the facts supplied by my father gave me something approaching leadership in decisions made on totally different subjects in our small gang.

There was another form of power too, universally recognised among us. It amounted to who could fight whom. Or, probably more important, who was willing to fight. Perhaps it was like a modern prison. There were some boys who challenged no one. But, growing up in the World's End, if you wanted your own life, a willingness to fight for it was the route to a reasonable level of happiness, or at least freedom from the shocking degree of bullying a boy might suffer if he showed he wasn't prepared to fight. On reflection I realise I am echoing my father's views. By that last pre-war summer he had already impressed upon Kit and myself the value he put on being willing and able to stand up for ourselves.

We had, in fact, been taught by him to defend ourselves from a very early age. Very rarely did he ignore my mother's protests, but in this matter he was adamant. When we were barely four or five years of age, he would be on his knees in front of us. We, my brother and I, would take turns, ducking, wobbling and weaving into position to throw a puny punch. He would make sure that we would not get away without one or two prods in the ribs. I find it astonishing when I look back to remember that these contests continued until I was at least seventeen with my brother, myself and my father fighting bare knuckle (but with strict rules never to punch above the chest). Big teenagers by then, we would crash and thunder against the kitchen door to my mother's distress when she returned home to see the bruises proudly displayed.

Throughout my school years, in elementary school in particular, bullying was rife. Children then, as now, could be seriously reduced by it, their ability to concentrate totally disrupted, breaks in the play-ground a half hour of misery. This abuse of one child by the group was not recognised as a problem by the teachers in any of the elementary schools I went to. Thanks to my father, neither my brother nor I suffered bullying for anything more than a matter of days. At a new school, and we went to many schools during the early years of the war, it took a little time to do something about it. The solution would always be a set fight, not a scramble in the playground, but a proper fight with a challenge issued and a time set. It had the effect of making the bully fight alone in the middle of a ring of eager spectators. Even quite young children recognised that in such formal circumstances pride prevented them calling on their friends for help. I'm not claiming it worked out pat each time but Kit and I usually won our school playground battles – or else acquitted ourselves well enough to make nobody keen for a rematch – and our lives were very much happier for it.

My father's own rough World's End beginnings had been much

harder than ours because the bully was in his own family – his elder brother George. At thirteen, my father's first job was at Thomas Crapper, King's Road sanitary-ware suppliers to the royal family, later famous or notorious from the Dirk Bogarde film *The Servant*. In his year and a half there my father had proved himself the sort of boy that good management should not allow to go unnoticed. The Managing Director, or possibly even the owner of the company, I no longer remember, a Mr Warham, knew something about people. He made real efforts to keep my father when Minnie decreed he should join the building trade, which would give her a few more shillings a week to pass on to the bookmaker. In later years, though they had parted company before my father was fifteen, Mr Warham, by now Mayor of Chelsea, would always stop to talk to him in the street, discussing problems to do with the level of requisitioning or the fall in total borough income caused by the accountant-engineered vacancies of many Chelsea properties.

But this was long afterwards. When Minnie decreed my father should join the building trade, it was decided he was to become a plumber's mate to his brother George. Twelve years older, George was mean, vindictive and singularly lacking in what is fondly regarded as that universal working-class virtue of willingness to help a neighbour. Or even a member of his own family. Accounts continue to describe working-class life in the warmly glowing terms mythologised by sentimental memoir writers. Not surprisingly, the *collective* element of such lives is emphasised. But individualism was what really kept your head above water. Working-class life was hard and brutally competitive. Good neighbours came round with a bit of cheese or a shilling if they could afford it, but too many others denounced the moonlighting unemployed family man to the Labour Exchange. If my father got a casual job offered when he was officially out of work he would leave the house with his bag of plumber's tools in the middle of the night, doze outside South Kensington station for a few hours and turn up for work at eight o'clock. '*We was all one,*' is the way the early socialist romantics like to tell it. They were often enough the teachers or council workers of the time, badly paid but at least paid every week. They were believers in the Marxist way and the light which, it can be argued, has traduced more people than Christianity ever failed.

Back to George. His bullying ended dramatically on the May morning of 1922 when he decided his new fifteen-year-old plumber's mate had to be taught the traditional lesson: who was boss.

My father was not tall, but he was developing fast. Until the day he died it was impossible to miss the quickness of his movements and, in marked contrast to my mother, the general sense of hustle that he generated. In the cramped conditions of the family flat in Blantyre Street, my father slept under the sink in the kitchen. At 5.30 on his first morning as George's mate he was awakened by a bowl of cold water in the face. As he stumbled to his feet to face his grinning brother, he was hit deep in the solar plexus and sent crashing down across the sink.

But George had somehow missed what eighteen months carrying the heavy sanitary-ware of Thomas Crapper had done for his younger brother's physique. My father's dilemma was acute. Minnie insisted he work with George. Yet George could make his life hell. My father decided to hit him once, and once only. His boxing at the Three Feathers Boys' Club had sharpened his punch. He hit George once on the line of the jaw. His brother went down with a shout of pain. He was rising slowly to his feet when Minnie and Henry James came in to see what the noise was about.

'I slipped, that's all,' George tried to explain it away. 'And listen, you.' He turned threateningly to my father. 'If you slosh water all over the floor when you wash, mop it up. Or you'll be in trouble.'

'From me too,' Minnie said.

Henry James smiled into his collarless shirt and left for his morning walk to look for dropped half pennies outside the King's

Arms. My father never knew what Henry James thought about his sons fighting as he walked slowly down Blantyre Street, eyes on the gutter where a small coin might have rolled. He was a pacifist who, in the Great War, had volunteered for dangerous battlefield ambulance work in France to avoid conscription. This much Minnie had divulged. My father said he had never heard Henry James say a single word about the two years he'd spent in Flanders.

Digression is what it's about. There's no other way to tell it really, is there? I was talking about knowledge, information. Not education because that really wasn't available to any of us beyond the reading, writing and arithmetic taught by Miss Collins. No, I was talking about information about the world we lived in, something more than the impossible dream of a pair of white plimsolls or the prices at the Sunlight Bagwash at World's End. The sort of knowledge my father tried so painstakingly hard to acquire. The sort of knowledge he felt he needed as war became more likely. There had in truth been wars going on throughout my childhood. There was Japan's assault on China, Italy's attack on Abyssinia, and the Spanish Civil War. Of these and others the only one I was aware of, though somewhat after the event, was the Italian-Abyssianian campaign. I don't remember the war, but I do remember receiving from my Uncle Fred, home from sea for a week, a set of Woolworth's lead soldiers, a dozen maybe, six of General Badoglio's Italian Infantrymen and six ebony Abyssinian tribesmen, handsome and lithe in flowing white robes. It was obvious that whoever sculpted them considered the tribesmen the heroes of Mussolini's war. It was a shame their lead spears, poised to hurl at the enemy, broke so easily.

The truth is, there was violence all around us in the last years of the thirties. Domestic violence, certainly. Pub fights, of course. And every week or so, Blackshirts and Communists clashed across La-di-dah's island outside the World's End pub. These were not battles of Cable Street proportions, mostly little more than street scuffles, but several times my grandmother, the good one, Eliza, led us through jostling crowds as we watched, wide-eyed, men wasting good marbles by rolling buckets of them under the police horses' hooves. I suppose I saw Moseley speaking, although I can't honestly say I remember him. He first came to the World's End in 1933 (alternating with ill-attended pacifist meetings held by Bertrand Russell, among others) and spoke at a good many meetings on La-di's island in the following years. His headquarters, the Black House (named, presumably, as a salutation to Hitler's Brown House in Munich), was only a bus ride away up King's Road at Sloane Square. We had heard my father, who in his pursuit of information attended Fascist and Communist meetings alike, tell of the potatoes bristling with double-sided razor blades, pinned in by matchsticks, that were hurled by Fascists into Communist meetings, and vice versa. At this time we knew nothing of the great issues of the day and took our cue from our grandmother who was equally scornful of both ideologies clashing before us. But crossing our own island at World's End, ducking the imagined razor missiles, with the chanted slogans all around us, the banners waving above our heads, among blasting police whistles and dangerously slithering horses, at least hazily we knew this to be about a bigger island, about things for which men were prepared to be beaten, or run down by police horses, or cut by flying razor bombs.

On what later came to be called the Home Front there was also violence from the Irish Republican Army. In 1939 the IRA had left a bicycle outside a Woolworth's in Coventry and killed several people when the dynamite in its front basket was detonated. This very real tragedy communicated itself to us kids in a wariness of any bicycle seen resting outside any shopfront. But the next revelation was even more alarming. Not long after the Coventry outrage, rumour became a well-known fact in the way it does: the IRA had stuffed street post boxes with explosives. After that passing a red pillar box was not something the children of the World's End undertook lightly. Respectful caution was called for when approaching any box. Warily we would ease our way, backs to the furthest wall, palms stretched along the bricking, until we were far enough away to be safe from the expected explosion. Alternatively we would hurl ourselves past in a lung-bursting dash, clearing the danger as soon as possible and whooping contempt for this latest attempt by the IRA to blow us up. Whichever strategy we adopted, it always worked. 'Republican Army – all gone barmy!' we sang.

But the thunderclouds of real war felt different, and infinitely more menacing to us as children. I suppose we all, children and adults alike, had our own image of the enemy. My first sight of a German was to be when my uncle Fred, back from sea where the judge had sent him as an alternative to prison, took me to Croydon Airport to see the planes. An aeroplane was not really a novelty to me at that time. I had seen plenty of small aircraft, mostly bi-planes trailing advertising banners for washing powders or cigarettes over London, or writing *Persil* or *Craven A* in the sky with pale drifting smoke.

My grandmother Eliza had told us about the huge menacing Zeppelins with enormous black crosses on their sides that had appeared over London at the end of the first war and about a German Gotha bomber she had seen once. But for me an aeroplane was something small, probably brightly coloured, looping the loop in the sky above World's End. So Croydon was something of a shock.

A tram across Battersea Bridge and on through the low undulating terraces of South London finally brought us to distant Croydon. There we sat with other visitors in a grandstand and watched the planes busily taking off and landing. That was fun. But they weren't the planes I'd hoped to see, bombers and Spitfires. The fighter aeroplane had already seized a place in my imagination. Throughout the war to come it steadily extended its grip. Within a year or so I would be able to identify all the planes we saw buzzing around us, and of course the menacing instruments of war that Japan, America and the main European countries were constructing. But not yet.

My uncle leaned across, pointing out the airport building. 'You've heard of Mr Chamberlain, Dee?'

I said I had. I didn't want to disappoint him.

'He was here last year waving a piece of paper signed by Adolf Hitler. "Peace in our time," he said. No war, the old fool promised.'

The old fool? 'Adolf Hitler?'

'Chamberlain. Hitler twisted him round his little finger.'

'Does Dad think there's going to be a war?'

My father was the younger brother, but my uncle readily deferred to his opinions. He nodded. 'He thinks it's a certainty.'

'We'll win, won't we?' I said anxiously.

He was watching a Tiger Moth taking off. 'It'll be a struggle.'

'What does Dad think?'

Fred's eyes were still on the Tiger Moth: 'Your dad thinks it'll last two years. And this time it's the Germans who'll win.'

Then, as if to reinforce my father's frightening prediction (which he wouldn't have told me himself), a loud engine roar was heard in the sky. We both looked up and saw an aeroplane quite different from any I had seen before. It was silver, made of what I now know to be corrugated aluminium. It had *three* engines, two on the wings and one fixed to the nose. But not only did it look gleamingly modern, its sides and wings carried an enormous black cross. It struck a special kind of fear into me. You couldn't miss how it struck the watching crowd, and even the airport officials and mechanics, from the moment it appeared. As it lost height and touched down I had the feeling that everybody was holding their breath. Certainly I was.

Somebody in the crowd said it was a Junkers 52, a German mail plane. I watched it taxi up to the airport building and saw the engines trail smoke as they were switched off. For a second or two it stood immobile, huge and threateningly beautiful. Modern, I kept thinking. That's really modern.

Then the door swung open. A short ladder appeared and the pilot descended. He wore a white flying helmet, a spotless white flying suit, and laced brown leather knee-length boots. But most riveting of all was the wide blood-red band on his upper arm with its black swastika centred in a white circle. The pilot stamped his feet to restore circulation, looked around him causally, aware that he was the centre of attention, then took a dozen brisk steps forward to the shabby Post Office official who was there to meet him and flung up his arm in salute.

I saw that pilot through the lens of my father's prediction. Stamped on my imagination was that trail of smoke as the motors cut, the gleam of polished aluminium, the pilot's immaculate flying suit. Most of all I could not get the deep redness of the swastika armband out of my mind. Although I was well aware that this was a mail plane, that the pilot was civilian and on a routine delivery, I felt I knew this to be about the coming of real war. I was old enough now to know that there would be no rubber bayonets in the clash that everybody believed was to come.

THREE

Kicking Leaves

For children, tension quickly turns to boredom. Each day we attended school for an hour or so to practise our line up and approach march to the buses laid out in scuffed chalk on the hall floor. We canted obediently, 'Left of the pole . . . right of the pole,' and peeled off to enter the body of the bus or climb imaginary stairs to the top deck. The excercises were normally supervised by Mr Whitehead or, from time to time, by Miss Savage. Some of the classes had good fun cheeking her. But our class teacher, Miss Williams, had put us on our honour to behave when Miss Savage was in charge, and occasionally she stood at the back of the hall to make sure we were not playing up. There's no doubt about it, Miss Williams was very keen on honour. Personally, I couldn't stand the stuff. The thing was, she told us, the Romans were very keen on honour too – and everything that was good about the British Empire had come from the Romans. They were so keen on honour, in fact, that they'd fall on their swords and split themselves open the moment they did anything wrong. When we thought some more about it, two things occurred to us. First that these Romans, obviously unlike the Greeks, clearly preferred falling on their swords to dancing in skirts; and secondly, it was clear that none of this left us much leeway to muck about when Miss Savage was supervising, although in lieu of the broad sword Miss Williams was more than willing to whack our bottoms with a rolled-up exercise book. Mr Whitehead beamed. Miss Williams scowled. Miss Savage dimpled prettily and her mother, who was to help with the evacuation, smiled encouragingly on the scene. Then we sang 'All Things Bright and Beautiful' and went home.

There, some pretty strange things were happening too. One day my father, strongly built as he was, literally staggered in carrying four, two-foot-long tins of Spam in his arms. We'd never seen Spam before. He told us it was a sort of American meat that cowboys like Tom Dix ate round the campfire in their films. That was good enough for us. The next day he came home carrying a sack of rice on his shoulder. A couple of days later he had two heavy sacks of sugar. We had no refrigerator, of course, and were unable to store anything but canned or dry goods. But he had talked to a few people – Mr Warham, the former director of Thomas Crapper was one of them – about food shortages in the first war and had decided to invest his wages in a small stock of food to supplement the rationing he foresaw as certain if war broke out.

If war broke out . . . If war did break out, of course, Mr Whitehead would get his way and we would all be evacuated. The boredom of practising had drained the prospect of any worries for us. My friends stopped talking about it. It was a school thing. At home, my father and mother didn't really mention it. So it couldn't be important. And yet war meant leaving home. And my father was buying food in case there was a war.

There was something else too, something that I vaguely knew had to do with the evacuation. For me, it was a deeply disturbing development: I began to sense that my mother was not happy about something her mother had done or failed to do. In our family the adults never had rows or arguments. The screaming and shouting of domestic discord was for other families. Even my brother and I, who inevitably sometimes fell out over trivial, childish matters, had a pact that we always made it up before we went to sleep. We grew up believing that to lose your temper (as opposed to being genuinely angry about something) was to fail. It was like a fight in the school yard. We soon learnt the truth of my father's dictum: *The one who loses his temper loses the fight.* So, bad as it was to lose your temper as a child, losing your temper as an adult was beyond the pale.

We were in fact unaccustomed to any sort of real friction in our family lives. It's true my father was naturally impatient, always wanting to see things done then and there, but my mother seemed to handle this without difficulty, effortlessly pouring oil on troubled waters. Most important of all, they seemed to agree on the quality or seriousness of any offence Kit or I might have committed. On the very rare occasions my father thought we deserved a significant punishment he called us into the front room and told us he'd decided we were to receive one smack on each hand. He always gave us the alternative of foregoing our ha'penny or penny pocket money. My brother and I knew perfectly well that this was considered to be the coward's way out. We would be sent away to confer and always decided on the whacks. My father would sit in a chair. In turn we would hold out a hand. When the smack came it was hard and stinging. Less hard probably for Kit because he was younger. My father would then tell us he was pleased we hadn't taken the coward's way out. And would add that the smacks had hurt him more than they had us.

Surprisingly enough, we believed him. I still do.

So when I began to sense some unease between my mother and my grandmother, I began to be seriously disturbed. It was too serious a matter to ask them about, and I don't in any case think that as a child I could have put my concerns into words to either of them. Probably I spoke to Kit about it, I don't remember. Perhaps I didn't.

Instead I turned to the concerns of the yard, to the outdoor life we lived. I noticed that when we finally got out among country people they were always urging us to go outside. Their image of us was of wan creatures who seldom saw the light of day, only confirmed when we told them our school was overlooked by the power station and that grit and smoke poured from its four chimneys. In fact, we spent just as much time outdoors as any of the country children I later knew well. Perhaps the air wasn't quite as fresh at home – all right, I'll admit the Thames stank and the presence of both power station and gasworks lingered in the nostrils on bad days. But they were supposed to be good smells. Cow dung and bluebells may have been equally good for you, but we were to find that the sanitation of parts of rural England was enough to make even our World's End noses twitch.

I put behind me the nagging thought that all was not well at home and concentrated on the last few days of the summer holiday. There were running and jumping games to impress the girls or tents to be constructed, stringing blankets and old curtains from the railings to make Bedouin encampments. Before I knew it the marble season was upon us. Its opening was dictated by the Oil Shop in Bifron Street which sold paraffin for lamps, linseed oil for mixing with paint, bundles of split wood for firelighting, basic tools like hammers and axes, and could charge electric accumulators for those few who owned wireless sets. When the wooden barrels of marbles came out on display all the children in the area were immediately infected with a passionate desire to own as many of the brightly coloured glass balls as possible.

There were numerous ways they could be acquired. Some were not above trailing a hand in the barrel and slipping a marble or two into a trouser pocket, but that needed a secure pocket without holes and I'd often seen the bright new marbles bouncing across the shop floor and the guilty look of the boy who'd obviously just tried to palm them. You could buy them, of course, and sometimes we invested in half a dozen to get started in the marble market just inside the Edith Grove back gate of the Buildings. Here we traded marbles for tattered comics or broken lead soldiers. When any boy, or sometimes girl, had enough to set up shop with, they placed a marble against the wall alongside five or six other merchants and tried to outbid the others for custom. If they were offering four-if-you-hit-me (four marbles if you bowl your marble straight enough to hit mine – the loss of your marble if you missed) someone else might come in with a loud cry of five- or six-if-you-hit-me. Sharp-eyed punters would select the best deal. The line where the client knelt to bowl was clearly marked in chalk and strictly observed. By the end of the first day there was a whole variety of competitions available. There might be a skittle with a wooden ball on a string. Ten if you knock me down. Impossible. Someone might have produced a short length of iron piping. You held it pointing down at the target marble. Putting your own marble in the pipe, you tried to steer it towards the marble set against the wall. Two- or three-if-you-hit-me, depending on the length of the pipe. The novelty attracted customers.

The marbles bazaar normally continued for about a week. If you did particularly well as a dealer, 'stall' holder or punter, you began to sell your marbles at just under the Oil Shop price. The real art was to guess when the passion for marbles was about to expire (which it would mysteriously over a single night) and to get rid of your stock at a decent price before the crash.

At home the tension between my mother and grandmother continued, a subdued state of affairs where they were polite but just didn't laugh together any more. My grandmother, I noticed, was now making more effort than ever to avoid my father. Normally she avoided him because she believed that in the small flat we occupied she should not intrude on my parents' lives as a couple. 'I don't want to get under your father's feet,' she'd say. She would make sure it was time to go for a quick one at the Weatherby just before he came home, or insist she had to drop in to visit her other daughter, my Aunt May, and our cousins the Easts who lived in the same Guinness block. If he came home fifteen minutes early it would be no problem to her. They would stand in the scullery talking for a while and then she would go on her way. But now, I realised, she was desperately anxious to avoid seeing him at all. None of this I liked.

The *Evening Standard* that my father brought in carried pictures most nights of German soldiers doing the goose-step in front of Hitler or, the other name we had learnt by now, Hermann Goering. Goering looked too fat to travel in an aeroplane but he had been, my father said, a German air ace when he was thinner. That was in the Great War. In the pictures I saw he wore a white uniform, different from the one worn by the man at Croydon Airport but white all the same. I concluded that all German pilots wore white uniforms. This was information I quickly passed round to the boys.

One weekend my father brought home a wireless set. It was tall with a rounded top and had a polished wooden front with a sunray shape fretworked into it against a green canvas backing. He fixed it up, with its two accumulators to power it, on a shelf out of our reach in the corner of the front room. He explained the accumulators contained acid, and acid burnt. But we just wanted to hear it. He switched it on. A band started playing 'Red Sails in the Sunset'. I think we must have heard the wireless before but it was amazing to have it in our own front room.

Before we changed out of his work clothes he made us sit down on the Put-U-Up bed he and my mother slept on. We knew this was going to be serious when he sat down opposite us and my mother came and stood quietly just inside the doorway to the scullery.

He was still wearing his overalls. He had just received his first promotion to stoker at Whitelands House and the heavy dark blue material smelt sharply of smoke and coke dust. 'You know everybody's talking about a war,' he said.

'We won the last one,' I interjected quickly, terrified he was going to tell us we were going to lose.

He nodded. 'True, but now there could be another one. We can't be sure yet, but a lot of important people think so.'

'If a lot of important people think so, aren't they getting us ready, making guns and things?'

'Yes,' he said. 'There are plans. The government's getting ready at last.'

And suddenly it came home to me. Plans. Preparations for a war. Not just making guns and planes. My mouth went dry. I looked at my father and he looked steadily back. He knew I'd understood what the talk was to be about.

I had begun to make the connections. The real connections. Between war and leaving London. War wasn't just something exciting, it could take us to the country.

'If there is a war, will we *have* to go to the country?'

'That's what I want to talk to you about. The country's not very far away. I don't know where you'll be going but it won't be far. Just far enough to make sure you're safe from any bombing.'

Kit was silent. He half-turned and looked at our mother.

We'd practised 'Right of the pole – Left of the pole' for over a week but I'd never really thought about what would happen to us. Not in any detail. 'Where will we live? Where will we sleep?'

'You'll be going with the school. The government's made all the arrangements. You'll be together with your friends. We'll come down to the country to see you. You can show us round. Show us the pigs and things.'

'Ugh.'

'I want Mum to come with us,' Kit said.

'She's got to look after the flat,' my father said neutrally. 'She's got to look after your grandmother too.'

I heard a sound behind me. When I looked round I could see my mother was holding a handkerchief to her mouth. She was crying.

Panic seized me. 'When will we be going? Not this week?'

My father paused. 'We've just had an announcement from the government,' he said at last. 'Its tomorrow.' His voice suddenly became stern. 'Now you boys have to look after each other. You understand me? Friends are friends but they come second. You two come first.'

Kit nodded vigorously.

'And it won't be for long.'

'How long?' I wanted to know.

'Yes, how long?' Kit echoed.

'You could be back home by . . . by Christmas.' He paused, glancing behind us towards my mother.

I heard her gasp. She turned quickly back into the scullery.

Kit and I didn't know what to say. My father's face was tight, not cross. He was looking towards the empty doorway with an expression we hadn't seen before. He seemed to want to go and talk to my mother. But he stayed in the room with us.

It was troubling because he was always so sure about things. It was the first time I'd seen him like this.

He got up and rubbed our heads. 'I'm relying on you to use your intelligence,' he said. It was one of his favourite phrases. But then he came out with something completely new. 'I'm relying on you to be brave boys.'

With the pressure of his hand, he kept our heads down. He didn't want us to look up at his face. He didn't want to see that Kit and I were both crying.

I heard the details long afterwards. My grandmother had absolutely refused to leave London. She'd had more than enough of the country when she was a girl in service, she said. She wasn't going to die there. This was not as melodramatic as it sounds. She was already suffering, although I had no idea of it, from severe angina attacks. She had been warned of the seriousness of her condition but had put her trust in one of the doctors at St George's Hospital who had admitted her for treatment (not an automatic procedure in those days) for what I now know were two mild heart attacks. The truth was that she was terrified of moving off the 22 bus route which could deliver her to St George's in ten minutes.

My mother couldn't bear the idea of not being with us. Equally, she could not bear the idea of leaving her mother to face her illness alone. My father was expecting to be called up at any moment. There was no other family help available. My Aunt May was to be evacuated from London with her six children (with so many she had the right to accompany them). She, too, was begging her mother to come with her but meeting an equally adamant refusal. None of our scattering of aunts or uncles was in any position to help. Everyone tacitly accepted that for my grandmother to be looked after by her arch-enemy Minnie was out of the question.

For my mother it was an intensely painful time. The two-way pull was not helped by the fact that, unknown to us, she had gone to see our headmaster as soon as evacuation plans were announced. She had offered her services as a voluntary worker on condition she was attached to the group containing my brother and myself. She had obviously given him the Superintendent Caple treatment because Mr Whitehead, normally very fierce with mothers (as befitted his position in that strictly hierarchical world), had accepted her condition and taken her on to the roll of LCC helpers that same afternoon. But in a sense this success did not make things easier. It simply meant that, in official terms, there was nothing to stop my mother being with us.

There had been a dozen discussions while we were asleep. My grandmother had been in tears night after night. She reminded my mother that she had seen the Zeppelins in the last war. She wasn't afraid. My mother should leave her and be with the boys. My father tried to explain to Eliza that the bombing would be totally different from the raids in the last war. And that it was even possible that German soldiers would reach London this time.

Not a chance, my grandmother insisted. All mouth and no trousers, that old Hitler. 'Anyway we always start slow. We took a beating from the Boers until the Relief of Ladysmith, remember. 'She had danced all night – and a good deal more, she hinted – when that news came through. And later we'd had a bad time from the Kaiser until we finally gave him a good hiding – and we would again, against what she always called 'this lot'.

As August 1939 drew to an end and, unknown to us, the Wehrmacht moved into position for its attack on Poland, this tiny domestic dispute, so trivial against the background of the gathering storm but of extraordinary importance to the five people concerned, was still unresolved.

We heard it on the wireless as we got ready for school weighed down by the knowledge that this was evacuation day. In the early hours before dawn, German troops had crossed the Polish border. The Germans had invaded Poland.

My father had said goodbye to us the night before and had already left for work, so I asked my mother what it all meant. She shook her head and got up as my grandmother came in. The two tall women stood opposite each other for a moment. 'It's starting,' my mother said in a quiet voice.

'I know,' my grandmother said, adjusting her Eliza Doolittle hat, a floppy yellow cloth flower on it today. 'Last time it was Belgium. Now it's Poland.' She shook her head at the unregenerate elements in the German people. 'I thought they'd got over it. But they're bad as the Kaiser's lot.'

I was desperate to know what all this meant. The wireless said that German planes were attacking the Polish Army. I wondered if one of the pilots was the German I had seen at Croydon. And where was Poland? Was it close? Was it in our country, like Scotland, or abroad like other countries? Did it mean we were at war with Germany? All these questions my mother waved aside with a firm movement of her hand. She poured a cup of tea for my grandmother and they sat down opposite each other at the scullery table. How to explain how they

were these days? Warm but distant. To me, it was difficult to understand. They didn't row, or fight, and I knew what they thought of
each other but they just weren't close any more.

My grandmother spoke first. 'I've just been up to May's,' she said.
There was a pause, a silence. 'She says she's thought about it,
evacuation and all that, but she can't see how she's going to manage
the money without my pension.'

I saw my mother look up.

'So . . . I told her I'd go.' My grandmother was nodding to herself.
'In any case, she'll need help with the younger ones.'

'She will,' my mother said slowly.

'I'd better put a few things together,' my grandmother said. We
watched them both stand up. As they put their arms round each
other, I heard my mother say quietly, 'Thanks, Mum.'

We weren't due at school until eleven and it seemed creepy and sad,
even in the bright sunlight, to hear the school bell ringing at that time
of morning. Along Stadium Street and Meek Street there was a
straggle of kids carrying cardboard gas-mask boxes strung round
their shoulders, some of them lugging battered suitcases, all with
their mothers who'd been allowed by Mr Whitehead to come and say
goodbye.

We made no attempt to walk with our friends, as we would
normally have done. Nobody was laughing or joking. Kit was looking
anxious, his brown knitted sweater trailing lengths of wool he'd
drawn from it, his socks round his ankles as always. He was holding
on tight to my mother's hand and, for once, didn't care who saw. She
was wearing a flowery dress and light brown coat and beige shoes
with straps across the instep. I thought she looked much better than
all the other mothers who seemed small and fat and quite old in
comparison. Most important of all she wore an armband, not at all
like the German one. It was white and had blue letters stencilled on
it: LCC – London County Council.

FOUR

In Deepest Woking

The children sat in lines on the floor of the school hall, in their usual places according to classes rather than to their allocated buses. The mothers were ranged around the walls, arms folded across their chests, most intimidated by the school surroundings, shifting uncomfortably as they leaned against radiators or wall bars. The teachers stood together in a group at the front. My mother was with them talking to my class teacher, Miss Williams, who had been *her* teacher during the first war. Mr Whitehead's desk, which had been moved in for the occasion, stood in a prominent position facing us. He was not a man to forego any opportunity to demonstrate his authority. Meanwhile we sat cross-legged, whispering together like a hundred bumblebees. For once, the buzz of talk was allowed by the teachers. After a few minutes, Miss Williams came over and brought me to my feet with a crooked finger.

'I've been talking to your mother,' she said.

'She's coming with us, miss. She's got an armband and everything.'

'I know. What a nice girl she's turned out to be,' the teacher said. 'Young woman rather. You're a very lucky boy.' She asked me to fetch the class register she had left on her desk. As I walked along the line of the mothers, I saw that some of them were crying. Others were just chatting among themselves as if they might have met in the Oil Shop. I looked over at my own mother standing easily with the teachers and caught her eye. She smiled.

In the classroom I was picking up the register from the desk when I heard the rumble of heavy vehicles outside. I went to the window. Three red buses were pulling slowly forward along Lots Road. They had no numbers on the front. They stopped and reversed a few feet. Then they came forward again, almost the same distance. Then backed a yard or two. Leaning over the window sill, I saw the puppet-master of this operation. Little Mr Whitehead was trying to get the buses to pull up at exactly the numbered chalk marks he had shown us all the day before. A bus was waved forward, another further back. There was much pointing to the big chalk marks on the road: 1, 2 and 3. When he was satisfied he brought out three small posters and, with the help of the school caretaker, stuck one on each bus. They proclaimed: Ashburnham Elementary School, World's End, Chelsea. Bus Number 1, Bus Number 2 and Bus Number 3.

Beyond the buses the blind-windowed wall of the power station rose sixty feet high. Four chimneys topped it off at nearly a hundred and fifty feet above the ground. When war broke out, the real war we expected any day now, the power station, which supplied all electricity to London Underground, was said by some to be a prime target of the bomber. Second only to Buckingham Palace according to some of my friends' parents. But there was a fundamental division in the school of World's End strategists. Others, the majority as the war went on, thought the power station would never be a target at all and to live next to it was to be in the safest place in London. Lying as it did on the river bank, with its four black chimneys it looked, from the cockpit of a German bomber, like nothing so much as a giant overturned scullery table, while the river, glinting in the moonlight (a lot of World's End imagination went into this theory), would resemble a broad flow of spilt milk alongside the table. This image, devised and developed by people who had never flown in their lives, would be, they asserted, a navigational aid which the Germans could ill afford to be without. The power station therefore became for many their giant talisman, their protector against the coming of the night bomber. It was a belief which gained increasing currency in the World's End until proved devastatingly wrong by events later in the war.

Back in the hall the teachers were taking their registers. I handed ours to Miss Williams. 'Day-dreamer, your boy,' she said to my mother. 'How else could it take five minutes to fetch a register?'

I regained my place with the names that were so familiar to me, Bobby Wilson, Ronnie Cartwright, Joan Bruton, Maisie Harrow, spoken in the voices of their class teachers.

As the last names rolled away, the double doors to the hall opened and Mr Whitehead walked with short steps towards his desk. There was no chair. He stood, leaning forward on the desk, and scanned our faces. 'Children!' he said. 'Mothers! Today is the day we have been practising for. Today is, in a sense, the day we have been waiting for. Today will show what we're made of.' We might have been a hundred and fifty applicant kamakaze pilots.

There was no war yet but everybody expected the announcement at any time. I already knew we'd promised Poland to pitch in, so it was no surprise that Mr Whitehead made a long speech about the traditions of Ashburnham and the coming fight for freedom. And a little bit about the British Empire and sticking together and winning in the end, all of which I would have cheered had it not been Mr Whitehead saying it.

Then after a final prayer we were told to stand and re-form in bus columns. Practice, as Mr Whitehead had reminded us, makes perfect. With a minimum of pushing and shoving we reformed. We moved like the Royal Marines band, countermarching at the Military Tattoo. Within minutes we were ready for Mr Whitehead's next order which would take us in paired columns to form up in the playground.

Once there we stood in the sun. In front of us Mr Whitehead announced that we would sing a going-away hymn. He said it would be the hymn which, from this day on, we would refer to as Our School Song. 'All Things Bright and Beautiful.'

We sang as we marched in our columns from the playground to stand at our allotted buses: '*All things bright and beautiful, all creatures great and small . . . All things wise and wonderful, the Lord God made them all . . .*'

The mothers cried. My mother had tears in her eyes. Some of the teachers cried. One of the bus drivers took out a red handkerchief and started blowing his nose. Mr Whitehead surveyed the columns, the chalk marks on the pavement and the perfectly aligned buses. Miss Savage, carrying a broomstick with a card tacked to it reading *Ashburham School – Assemble Here*, and looking like a much prettier Joyce Grenfell, handed him his bowler hat, his umbrella and a black Gladstone bag. He took a deep breath, then in a parade-ground voice he commanded: 'Ashburnham Junior Elementary School . . . mount your buses!'

The leaders of each column stepped forward, 'Right of the pole,' they sang out as they stepped on to the platform and began to climb the stairs to the top deck. 'Left of the pole,' the next child cried turning on to the lower deck. Clockwork. The teachers, shuffling on last with their big suitcases, looked unpractised and slightly lost in comparison. My brother and I were on the last bus. With a final cry of 'Left of the pole!' from Mr Whitehead himself, he swung on to the platform and, with his raised umbrella, gave the signal to the driver for us to abandon school.

I've seen the films of children being evacuated from London on September 1, the first day, as the Poles rightly remind us, of the Second World War. Most of them show boys in school blazers and caps with badges or girls in neat dresses that had obviously not been bought for their elder sister. We, I fear, gave off a more ragged-trousered appearance. But we were certainly beyond reproach so far as discipline went. At Clapham Junction Station Mr Whitehead seemed already to have details of platform, carriage numbers and seats reserved for Ashburnham. There were very tearful scenes, of course. Some of the mothers had run down to the King's Road to catch a number 19 bus to Clapham Junction and had arrived there within moments of the school. Mr Whitehead was not pleased as last hugs and kisses threatened the perfect symmetry of his columns.

An hour later our train puffed and hissed into Woking Station. In between London and our destination the view outside the window had looked to me like a big Putney Common with little groups of houses scattered in the woods. I thought the tree-climbing possibilities looked quite promising, but mostly we were wondering what sort of schools they had in the country. I couldn't believe we'd really have to wear those striped long trousers and big white collars that they wore in the comics. None of the children of our age that I could see in the village streets seemed to be wearing them.

On the train green-uniformed women of the WVS – the Women's Voluntary Service – had given each child a brown carrier bag with a packet of wrapped cheese sandwiches, an apple, two oranges, a packet of tea – and a bar of chocolate. We were told we could eat the sandwiches or fruit when we wanted but should not touch the chocolate. That was for emergencies.

My mother was further up the train organising things with Miss Savage who was our group's official teacher in charge. Miss Savage's mother walked up and down the corridor looking for a tearful child to comfort.

I think we were the only school leaving the train at Woking and we marched out of the station like a column of Grenadier Guards. Three buses, green but of the familiar double-decker shape, were parked immediately outside. Their engines were rumbling, ready to go.

'Bus number one,' Mr Whitehead directed the head of the first crocodile. 'Bus number two,' he pointed with his umbrella. 'Bus number three . . .' he directed our column.

We began the procedure. '*Right of the pole . . . Left of the pole.*'

But something was wrong. I felt panic rising as my mother came running up from the back of the column. 'This is our bus,' she said to Miss Savage, nominally in charge of bus three. 'There are people already on it,' she said urgently.

I heard my brother call 'Left of the pole,' as he stepped up on to the platform.

'Get them off the bus,' I heard my mother saying to Miss Savage as I stepped up. 'This *isn't* an evacuation bus. It's an ordinary country bus. God knows where it's going!'

Miss Savage went white. The mantra died on my lips.

Then events became totally confused. Miss Savage would not decide alone. She turned and ran towards Mr Whitehead. A crowd of thirty children milled about on the pavement as my mother stopped them getting on the bus. Roly Poly was red-faced with anger as he ordered Miss Savage back with épée-like thrusts of his umbrella.

The conductor's bell rang. Miss Savage ran for our bus on which her mother and some two dozen of her charges were already sitting. My mother helped her on to the moving platform as we pulled out behind bus number two.

Then understanding must have descended on Mr Whitehead. I looked back to see him nearly run over as he tried to stop us from pulling away. Number two bus ignored his frantic umbrella signals. By now he had dropped his Gladstone bag. He seemed barely aware of the last of the three buses rolling past him.

Three green country buses pulled away taking different roads to their unknown destinations, leaving Mr Whitehead alone on the pavement outside Woking Station. Fate had decreed that he would never see Ashburnham School together again. We would never be able to sing, as one, the School Song we had acquired only that morning.

I never sang 'All Things Bright and Beautiful' again.

The scale of the catastrophe was not immediately apparent to us. Later in the war we heard that teachers in the other buses had debussed with their own groups of charges at different stages along the route. Some had hoped to recover Mr Whitehead; others thought it wiser to go to the end of the route. They surmised the headmaster would have commandeered a car and be awaiting them, or at least be making efforts to reach them. Nobody had considered that the country was as unknown a territory to Mr Whitehead as it was to us. Three buses with their engines running was a common enough sight for most people living near a country railway station. For Mr Whitehead, they could only be *his* buses.

It was our first experience of how big a blunder even the Mr Whiteheads of this world can make. We never saw him again, or even discovered what happened to him. Perhaps he took the honourable way out and fell on his umbrella.

On our bus my mother took charge. We were out of Woking by now and approaching a straggle of houses along the main road. She strongly advised Miss Savage to take the remnant of our group off the bus here and then my mother would telephone the LCC at County Hall for advice. Miss Savage reared back at the boldness of the plan. She had probably never telephoned that distance in her life and the idea of speaking direct to County Hall was something she found hard to contemplate. But my mother was going to do it for her so Miss Savage agreed.

We stood in the main street, a line of red-brick houses with gardens and a few shops. We were about twenty-five or thirty children, all boys between the ages of six and eleven, plus Miss Savage and her mother. My mother had gone up to the village phone box. She had been on the phone for quarter of an hour now.

People were interested, there was no doubt about that. Women in flowered aprons were standing at their windows, holding back the lace curtains to look at us. One or two of the men strolled past to look Miss Savage over. Mrs Savage was breaking into sobs every few moments. We were already bored and most of us had surreptitiously eaten at least half our bar of Cadbury's Fruit and Nut. The dried milk and tea wasn't a lot of good to us, but we began swopping our apples and oranges for conkers that Freddie Digweed had brought with him.

My mother came back a few minutes later. The LCC were receiving calls from railway stations all around London. Mr Whitehead was not the only headmaster who had lost his school. The solution was to be local. We should now consider the village we were in as our destination. The local vicar and the WVS would be notified of our plight. The village school would absorb us as pupils. Miss Savage would come under the authority of the local head-teacher. My mother would assist the WVS to billet us on the local population. This was all explained first to Miss Savage and then, in shorter form, to us.

Mrs Savage sobbed, grateful that the problem had been taken out of her daughter's hands. Miss Savage, looking red-eyed and unkempt with panic, hugged and kissed my mother and kept asking what she would have done without her. I asked if we could go exploring until the people who were going to find us places to sleep arrived, and got a firm 'no' from my mother. I realise now she was fighting to keep control of the two dozen boys who knew they could handle Miss Savage but had not yet taken my mother's measure.

The WVS arrived, bustling cheerful women who immediately identified my mother as the natural leader of the group. Moving from house to house along the village street, they tried to persuade the inhabitants to take us in. I heard the man cutting the hedge behind us say to his neighbour, 'I'll take that one in, the good-looking one.' I was surprised to see that he was nodding towards my mother.

It took all the rest of the afternoon and much of the evening to billet the children. Some of them were from other classes, older or younger than me. Some of them were a bit rough-looking but gradually, as the evening wore on, women came out from their houses and offered for all of us, one by one. Standing there on the pavement, exhausted by the hours of waiting in the sun, we were picked off for billeting. My brother and I ended up with my mother at the house of the man cutting his hedge, Mr Pink.

The drama of the outbreak of war two days later is something I only know about from the history books. To my chagrin, at the time my mother never told me it had happened. Sometime later, perhaps on September 7 or 8, I heard the colourless Mrs Pink make some reference to an air raid on London. I was on to it like a terrier. 'It's only partly true,' my mother said. 'It was a false alarm. It was just that the sirens sounded and everybody thought it was the German planes coming over.'

'They thought the war had started?'

'It has. It started last Sunday.'

I was outraged. 'And you didn't tell me?'

'I was trying to stop you worrying.'

I'm not sure even now why this affected me so strongly. 'The Germans declared war on us and you didn't tell me!'

'We declared war on them,' she said. 'Because they invaded our friends in Poland. The French are on our side.'

It took me a few minutes to feel less betrayed.

'I should have told you,' my mother conceded.

'You should have.' I was adamant. 'If anything else happens . . .'

'Yes, I promise to tell you.'

That was better. 'Are the Germans very strong?'

Like me, she could not conceive of our losing the war. 'They're strong. But we'll give them a good hiding if they try to come here.'

I didn't care much about a German invasion of Woking. But having to give those Nazi salutes when you ran into your friends down the World's End didn't appeal. 'Have they bombed London yet?' I asked her.

'No. The government says they'll have a lot of trouble getting through the guns down at the coast.'

'Then we can go home.' I glanced around at Mr Pink, looking at my mother but pretending to tie back his roses. 'Kit and me don't like it here much.'

We were living a strange life. Mornings all twenty-five of the evacuees went to the village school. There Miss Savage taught us with my mother keeping discipline. Even the toughest older boys like Teddy Alexander were afraid to answer her back.

Sometimes the country headmaster came in and gave us a lesson on country matters, how to walk across a field with cows in and such. What you might see in the field. Common birds. The names of trees. It was quite interesting stuff in its way.

In the afternoons we just sat about on the village green eating our sandwiches which the WVS brought us, playing football and climbing trees. Most of the village came to look at us in the first few days. I don't think they were being unfriendly but they hadn't seen a bunch of kids like us before. Their own children, no doubt sweltering in their Eton collars, were kept well away from us.

The evenings were the worst. Whereas in London we had run about with our friends after school, Mrs Pink insisted we were indoors, all washed and ready for our tea. There was one good thing about this and that was the bathroom. Kit and I had never seen one before but we had to be very careful not to pee on the fluffy mat under the lavatory or use the Pinks' towels instead of the one she'd allocated to us.

Mrs Pink prepared tea for all of us. This was always eaten round a table with a cloth in what she called the dining room. The Pinks definitely got the best of anything going. We mostly got a big sausage sliced up, bread, some lettuce and a cup of tea. Mrs Pink was always explaining to my mother that this was as far as the billeting allowance would go. Afterwards we would go up to the one bedroom we slept in and play endless games of cards. If this was war, it was definitely boring.

Less boring for my mother. It didn't take long for her to discover Mr Pink had more than the billeting allowance in mind when he took us in. He made his move one afternoon when she was alone in the house. I would imagine it was short-lived. We came home from afternoon 'school' bursting with the story of Freddie Digweed who had fallen bare-chested off a big log and rolled across a bed of nettles. We were all fascinated by the rash that covered every exposed part of him. Miss Savage had taken him to the doctor in the village and we were anxious to know not so much whether he would live as whether he would die.

We came into the house to be met by an atmosphere that even the travails of Freddie Digweed could not dispel. My mother was rigid with anger. Mr Pink slunk about like a fox in a fairy tale. I don't know whether I had any idea of what had happened or not. Somehow I think I did.

'We're leaving,' my mother said to Mr Pink. 'You can tell Mrs Pink we don't feel welcome here. I shan't say any more than that.'

'You don't have to go,' he said feebly, and looked at us. 'Just a bit of fun. A laugh.'

My mother glared at him. 'We'll be out of here in a week. Before if possible,' she said in an icy voice. 'Any more laughs and we'll see if Mrs Pink shares your sense of humour.'

I recognised that as one of our old teacher Miss Williams' ways of talking when one of us pleaded that a whisper behind a hand was just a joke. 'Just let's see, Ronnie,' she'd say, 'if you and I share the same sense of humour.' And you knew she wouldn't.

When she heard that we were leaving, Mrs Pink became more

objectionable every day, insisting that we had tea by ourselves and forbidding us to use the garden which she could not keep under observation from the kitchen.

My mother had already told us she was looking for another billet. Within a few days the WVS had helped her to find us a place with Mrs Bullen at the other end of the village. Mrs Bullen was older than Mrs Pink, and quite fat with a slow country voice. You only had to look at her to know that she was warm-hearted and generous. We still wanted more than anything to go back to London but we were happy at the prospect of leaving the Pinks. Until my mother told us she would not be staying in the country with us.

The problem was my grandmother. She had been taken ill near Windsor where my Aunt May was evacuated and had insisted on going back to London. My mother talked to us for a long time, explaining why exactly she had to go back to look after her. She gave me a stamp and told me to write her a letter, there and then. If we were *really* unhappy, I should post the letter and she would come and fetch us right away.

Sticking it out became a point of honour. Kit and I both knew what my father would have thought of an immediate collapse the Monday after my mother left. Mrs Bullen was marvellous. Her husband was a big cheery policeman, her son in the army stationed nearby at Pirbright. We were given lots of food and comfortable beds with pillows. Mrs Bullen's house wasn't modern. The lavatory was outside, past a leaping Dalmation on a long chain. There was no proper bathroom which didn't matter to us. But the World's End felt a long, long way away – and that letter burnt a hole in my pocket.

We held out throughout the winter. Christmas came and my mother and father came down to visit us with a present on Christmas Day. Mrs Bullen gave us a present too. The year 1940 began.

The Bullen family would listen to the nine o'clock news as did the rest of the nation. Kit and I were allowed to sit and drink our hot milk on either side of Mrs Bullen on the sofa as long as we were quiet and only asked questions afterwards.

We didn't seem to be beating the Germans very much, although we'd sunk one of their battleships, the *Graf Spee*, somewhere near South America. Mr Bullen showed me on the map. There was also the troubling question of Finland. I tried to explain it to Kit in bed after Mrs Bullen had the light out. 'Russia is a big country attacking Finland, a small country.'

'So we're on Finland's side?'

'Yes, because Russia is a friend of Germany and they've just signed a pact to prove it.'

'What's a pact?'

Very awkward question. 'Don't worry. Thing is, you heard on the news that the Finnish Army ride on skis and capture millions of Russian prisoners. These prisoners are so dirty they have to be rolled in the snow and whipped with birch branches if they don't obey orders.'

That seemed to sum it all up. Until Kit asked, 'Who are the Soviets?'

Another awkward question. That's the trouble with younger brothers . . . The nine o'clock news often talked about the Soviets without telling us who they were. 'They're friends of the Russians,' I said casually. 'Old friends,' I added. I hadn't yet acquired my father's ability to admit I didn't know.

We had a bed each which we had pushed together till they touched. Alone, we worried about the war. The longer it lasted, the longer it would be before we could go home.

'Will we beat the Germans next week?' my brother wanted to know.

He made me feel guilty for our lack of success. 'Maybe not next week,' I admitted. 'But we're preparing for a Big Push.' That's what Mr Bullen said anyway. I was prepared to elaborate when I realised Kit was drifting off. I wondered what good news I could tell him. In

France, on what they called the Western Front, there was no fighting at all. Only football games for our troops against the French. I told Kit about the football in an effort to keep him awake.

'I expect we always win,' he said drowsily.

With absolutely nothing to go on I confirmed that we usually won. But beating the French at football seemed a poor substitute for giving the German Army a good hiding. I began to realise for the first time that nothing was as simple as it seemed in the adult world – especially between countries.

The winter of 1939–40 was a cold, hard time. We went to school in the mornings and Miss Savage and her mother tried to find somewhere for us to keep warm in the afternoons. As always the WVS was our main support, supplying cups of tea and biscuits in church halls, or finding us a real football we could kick around on the green. But we were all struck by how little there was to do in the country. And we were desperate to get back home.

At the centre of this desperation we missed our mother. Straightforward enough. We missed our friends, too. And we missed the World's End. At Woking we had food we liked well enough and all the boys in our group slept in good, comfortable beds, some alone for the first time in their lives. Good people that they mostly were, what the country folk didn't understand was that we were not ungrateful (as was often said), we were just not grateful. We were too young for gratitude. They spoke as if we had spent our lives just waiting to jump into the first hot bath provided. But we saw no virtue in that. We didn't want hot water baths; some of us had never even been much used to daily washing. We were terrible snobs. Our way of life was just naturally better. They talked of a good hot bath and walks to put the roses in your cheeks, but what we really missed was La-di-dah spitting his ferocious obscenities at any boy he thought was trying to nick an evening paper. We missed hanging on the tail chain of brewer's drays and dodging the flick of the whip as the driver tried to force us off. We missed going down to the river and standing knee-deep in the mud and trying to work out if you could cross Battersea Bridge from the crossed girders underneath. Then there were all the games that the country boys didn't know: Kingy, Warney Echo, Knock-down Warney... People in the country (Mrs Bullen excepted) were always trying to put those elusive roses in our cheeks, as if we'd caught something in the World's End and couldn't wait to be cured. They couldn't have been more wrong – the miracle cure for us was to get back home, to the *fons et origo* of all they saw as amiss in our young lives. To London. The World's End.

In my pocket was the letter already written that could effect the miracle for Kit and myself at least. He urged me to post it. Sometimes I would lean against a letter box and balance the crumpled envelope on the lip of the posting slot and let the wind make the decision for us. But whether because the wind was unfavourable or because I had deliberately balanced the letter against falling into the box, I never got the result that would have taken us back.

Then, sometime early in 1940, my brother had a brush with some boys from a gypsy encampment as he came back from playing football. They had stolen the ball the WVS had provided and, Kit said, thrown him in a gorse bush.

Mr Bullen was off duty that afternoon but he put on his uniform and went over and recovered the ball almost immediately. It was a darkening February afternoon and Kit insisted we went out for a walk. Mrs Bullen told us not to go too far and to be back before dark.

I knew what he wanted.

'The letter,' he said. 'Post the letter, Dee.'

I could feel the excitement bubble up in me. This was as close to a legitimate excuse as we had had. And I could blame it all on Kit. It's only fair to say that according to his memory of the afternoon's events, this minor tragedy with the gypsies had happened not to him, but to *me*. That, of course, would make me responsible for what followed. But since we were both desperately anxious for the same outcome, I suppose it doesn't make a lot of difference who was the initiator.

I drew the letter from my pocket. We had kept it for four months. Only the week before I'd had to over-write the address where it had badly faded: 3 Guinness Trust Buildings, Chelsea, World's End, London, SW10.

We walked to the end of the road and stopped at the letter box. I knew that to post the letter was a huge betrayal of the affection Mrs Bullen had shown us. The thought alone made me gasp with shame. 'Do you really want me to send it?' I said to Kit.

Silently, lips pressed together, he nodded his head.

I took it out of my back pocket. I wondered whether I ought to open it and write something about the gypsies in it, but that would have ruined the stamp.

'Put it in the box,' Kit said.

I looked at the letter, seamed and crumpled. I hadn't read it since I wrote it when my mother left, but I'd rehearsed the few words it contained every night we'd been at the Bullens:

'*Dear Mum, We want to come home. Love, D*'.

I dropped it in the box.

FIVE

In Darkest London

My mother was already at the Bullens' when we got back from morning school. She told us to say nothing about the letter at all and spent a long time with Mrs Bullen in the front room. When they came out Mrs Bullen was crying and hugged us a lot and said we must come straight back if there were to be any air raids. She was a remarkable woman, again more for the ordinariness of her goodwill, and the breadth of her sympathy, than for any intellectual qualities. As I grew older I began to discover that we talk a lot about the 'salt of the earth', but the term, as often as not, is tinged with disparagement. They're the salt of the earth despite their obvious social limitations, you're given to understand. But people worthy of the description come from all classes, all walks of life. Perhaps my brother and I did not sufficiently appreciate it the day we left, but it was a certain kind of privilege to have met Mrs Bullen.

We packed our things. By six o'clock we were back at Clapham Junction Station crowded with soldiers in dank-smelling greatcoats. By five-past we were on a number 19 bus riding towards the World's End. No street lights, no shop window lights, not a light to be seen in the rooms above the shops, almost no cars, and those we saw with headlamps dimmed down to pinpoints. Traffic lights shuttered to show no more than faint green, amber or red strips. The bus itself had very faint blue lights inside and thick canvas mesh glued on the windows to stop them shattering in bomb blast.

We got off at the World's end outside the familiar Sunlight Bagwash and crossed the King's Road, Kit and I carrying our case between us. I looked from the bottom of World's End Passage towards the island and was startled and somehow immensely cheered by the shriek from behind the Victorian lavatories. Lah-di-dah's unmissable cry: *News, Star, Standard*. As we crossed the island there he was unchanged, the flat cap, the overlong mac, the strange alarming scuttle to one or other edge of his island to shout his wares into the wind and rain. But his wooden stand was different. No longer lit by the gas streetlights that ringed the island, the open-fronted stand, with its three piles of papers protected by an oilskin against the rain, was now only very faintly illuminated by two storm lanterns, their glass thickly painted blue, placed on the low tarpaper roof. La-di was the first really familiar sight we had seen since we came back to this new, slightly forbidding London. I'd never thought of it before but now I wanted to spend some of the money Mrs Bullen had given us, to buy a paper from him, but my mother said my father was waiting for us and he would certainly already have a *Standard*. I kept my eye on La-di as we passed. He never welcomed us back although he must have seen us a thousand times and had known my mother since she was a young girl. But another scuttle to the kerb and a shriek from him as he turned could have been his form of greeting. With La-di who could ever know?

By daylight we saw many other changes. My father had told me that long ago Battersea Bridge was built of timber. Now, built alongside the present stone Battersea Bridge, was another wooden bridge, ready for use if the Victorian bridge were bombed. All around, into odd scraps of unconcreted earth, short posts had been hammered with flat squares of plywood, eighteen inches by eighteen inches, nailed into them to face the sky. These were painted with a chemical solution and expected to turn green in the event of a gas attack. Shelters were being built everywhere. Posters showed you how to apply for a Morrison Shelter which was a big black steel table you were all supposed to sleep under if there was a raid. Kit and I laughed at that one at the time. Our father's youngest sister, Aunt Nell, had one out in the country at Streatham where they lived. For people with gardens, there was also an Anderson Shelter. They dug a hole and the council men came and made an arch of corrugated iron over it and covered it with earth. It was like a First World War dug-out, and like a dug-out rapidly filled with mud. There were also public shelters being dug. As we arrived back from the country a massive machine was digging a long deep trench in the yard outside our block at Guinness Trust. It zigzagged round towards the second block and had one main entrance and three or four emergency exits. There was another shelter being dug between blocks 3 and 4, or 'round the Hundreds' as we used to call those blocks. Kit was worried about where he'd play football at first, but when the diggers had gone the trench was roofed and concreted, and apart from the entrance you wouldn't have known it was there. What you couldn't miss, however, was the fact that the railings that surrounded Guinness (before the war, one of the rules was that the main gates to the Buildings were locked at midnight) were torn out for melting down for the war effort. The walls where they'd been looked sad, lined with stumps of broken iron teeth – and there was nowhere to tie our Bedouin tents any longer.

Black-out curtains and blinds were up in every house; shops often painted part of their windows black. At night in the Guinness yard all the outside gas lamps had been turned off and people picked their way across to their blocks with the aid of a small hand torch covered with red or blue paper to dim the beam. There were a lot of jokes at this time about people (usually men and women) bumping into each other in the black-out. Grown-ups found these especially funny.

To Kit and me, this wasn't the London we knew. It had a slight edge, an air of menace even. But it was still the London we loved.

We went back to school, at first at Park Walk and then, a few weeks later, to Ashburnham where a scratch headmaster and staff had been brought back from retirement to take in the many children who were now returning from evacuation. Classes grew in size daily and lessons, I seem to remember, were a bit confused, but children arrived every day and on time. Registers were taken. The same excuses for absence were rejected or accepted. 'Please, Miss, no shoes,' was still the excuse for absence that was always nodded through without question, as it had been before the war. Things, in short, seemed relatively normal to us at least. The bomber, people said, was obviously a scare tactic. The Germans were afraid of the RAF and the anti-aircraft fire and the huge silver barrage balloons that were tethered in hundreds of parks and open spaces all over London. Confidence ran high that the Germans, who were clearly unwilling to advance against the French and British Armies on the Western Front, would soon be asking for an Armistice.

I asked my father if he agreed. He said people forgot that the Germans hadn't seemed afraid when they invaded Poland and, although the Poles had fought them fiercely, the German Army had won in six weeks. As for the German Air Force (I was beginning to hear the word Luftwaffe for the first time), Lindbergh had said before the war that they were stronger than us. And the bombing of Warsaw and Rotterdam had shown what they could do.

'Best to wait and see,' he said. 'Germany never likes to fight at its back and front doors at the same time.'

'What does that mean?'

'It means Hitler could be waiting till he's cleaned up Poland at his back door, and got it completely under control, before he takes on the mob at his front door, that's us and the French. Truth is, son, that nobody knows yet how things are going to turn out. Most people in this country want to fight until Germany is beaten.' He paused. 'But there are also quite a lot of people who want peace.'

This really was news. 'Spies?' I said hopefully.

'People who think Hitler is right about a lot of things. Listen,' he put his arm round me, 'I'll tell you a secret. At my work the other day, at Whitelands House, there was an admiral, an old man, retired now. Perhaps he'd had a bit too much to drink as he came through the hall. But he said, in his opinion, we should make peace straight away – said he thought Hitler was *a god*.'

This really shocked me. 'Does *that* make him a spy?'

My father smiled. 'Too old for spying. But there'll be plenty about like him. And remember, I just told you a secret. Secrets are to be kept. Don't say anything to your friends about the admiral.'

'I won't.'

'It could get me into trouble. Promise?'

'I promise. What do spies do?'

'They pass information to the enemy. Things like when ships are leaving Liverpool or Glasgow or the Port of London. Some people think they shine lights to signal to the bombers where there's an important factory . . .'

'Like the power station?'

He laughed. 'You just watch out for anybody shining lights in the blackout.'

'I am already,' I said. Behind Guinness Trust there was a large block of Edwardian mansion flats, more part of the Chelsea of Cheyne Walk than World's End. There was a persistent rumour, and not just among the children of Guinness, that lights had been seen signalling to German planes from one of the upper windows. 'Some people,' I told my father, 'have already seen someone in Ashburnham Mansions shining lights.

'Really?' he said seriously. 'What at?'

'German planes,' I told him.

'Not had a lot of luck then, have they?'

I hadn't really thought about that.

He picked up his paper and turned to the racing results. 'Use your head, Dee. Shining lights won't do a lot of good if there are no planes up in the sky to see them yet, will it?'

This was a convincing argument. And useful. I could use it to pour scorn on anybody giving me a shining light story about Ashburnham Mansions. But when would there be German planes up there in the sky? 'When Hitler's ready to fight at his front door, will he send his bombers first?'

My father lifted his hands in mock surrender. Unlike almost all workmen of the time, at home he always had clean fingernails. 'I'm not an expert in these things, Dee,' he said. 'And I don't want to pretend to be. All I'm saying is that it's quiet now but it's odds on this war's far from over. Which is why your mother and I didn't bring you back from Mrs Bullen's earlier.' He paused. 'And why you should remember that you might have to go back if things hot up.'

Mr father was not the stuff of heroes. Heroes are prepared to sacrifice themselves and thus the happiness of those around them. My father, on the contrary, was ruthless in his determination to provide for and protect his family, by which he meant my mother, my brother and me, and my grandmother Eliza though perhaps on some slightly different level. He was not a liberal, though his view of his immediate family was infinitely easy-going. Nevertheless his unusual levels of energy often made him impatient with us for what he saw as our lack of commitment to any job to be done. Politically, he was not riddled with the clichés of class conflict yet certainly saw no inherent superiority in the mere fact of birth. But he recognised what a central factor social self-confidence was in achieving any sort of real advancement and knew that it was less a personal trait than a class asset. The key, he believed, lay not in wealth but education.

He undoubtedly suffered difficulties until the end of his life when on unknown ground in social gatherings. He would never, for instance, take my mother to a restaurant without Kit or myself being present. Bewildering arrays of cutlery, French labels on wine bottles, *faux*-superior waiters, all took their toll on his comfort and enjoyment. In those days (and it's saddening that it's almost as true today) working-class people were confident enough within their familiar surroundings, but the balance tipped the moment they moved outside. Though they often talked among themselves of the upper classes with derision and contempt, faced with them attitudes fluctuated between servility and belligerence. My father managed to avoid this trap.

He understood, especially after he had worked for a while in Whitelands House, what a vast gulf in opportunity wealth and education offered in those days. Far greater than today because then it was bolstered by an intact class system.

He saw himself, I believe, as a practical man, whose chief ambition was to take us as a family out of the World's End. Born among the poorer sort, barefoot in the streets on all but school days until he was eleven or twelve, he saw no virtue in the way his mother lived or in the abject poverty of his elder sister's life. He deeply regretted not having had an education but never saw education as a possible route out of the World's End for himself. He knew, by the age of twenty-eight, that it was too late. Had he grown up in a Welsh mining valley he might have joined the many who gained their BAs through the Workers' Education Association when the demand for coal collapsed and alternative work was impossible to find. But this was London where, if you were out of regular work, there was always something to be found, schemed for, and sometimes fought for. My father was a broad-shouldered, hardened young man, committed to making his way in a world where the odds had been stacked against him from birth. In order to even those odds for himself, his wife and children, he was prepared to go further than most. He saw nothing wrong in buying a black market leg of lamb when Claridge's, the Savoy and the Dorchester's restaurants were open every night. Exactly how far would he have gone? During the worst period of the Depression, compulsory schemes were bruited to send the long-term unemployed to logging camps in Scotland. He said then that he would have chosen to go house-breaking and *risk* a prison sentence rather than submit to the certain imprisonment of a logging camp.

At Whitelands House the platform of advantage that the tenants' families started from particularly affected him. On an admittedly more trivial level, it was not easy to be addressed peremptorily by your surname and given instructions by a seven-year-old. But he contained his resentment. He never suffered from that knee-jerk class consciousness that has hidebound, even poisoned, so many talented, young working-class minds.

He had no ideology; was no extremist in politics. He was naturally pragmatic, leaning neither to right nor left. But if the Germans *had* come, I can't now rid myself of the thought that he may well have been, before the Occupation revealed its true colours, an early collaborator.

SIX

Lammas Land

The health of my grandmother Eliza (the other one, Minnie, had gone with Ma Bash to Hemel Hempstead to cause trouble there) had, for the moment, very much improved. When I told her what my father had said about the war (but not about the admiral) she straightened up in her long black dress, apron, and of course hat held at a rakish angle by the Jack the Ripper pin, and thought for a moment. Then she nodded and reached out to shuffle the frying pan. I knew what those gestures meant. She could never quite approve of my father's belief that any question asked by his sons should get as straight an answer as he was capable of giving. But then neither did my other grandmother, or my Uncle George, or my Aunt May. Most people didn't. My mother stayed silent, listening as he explained events, but would probably have preferred him to describe what was happening in less detail. After all, she had kept the outbreak of war a secret from me.

'You're too young for all these things,' Eliza said, giving me the familiar snuff-tainted hug, 'Stick to your comics for a while.'

But I didn't want peace. It was like being either Oxford or Cambridge. You chose one and you supported it through thick and thin. In the yard we all chose our boat race side when we were about five and ran around with a dark blue, or in my case light blue, paper streamer from the Oil Shop. Nobody knew exactly what a university was but people stayed with the dark blues or light blues for the rest of their lives. I felt that way about the war. I was English, how could I be on Hitler's side? It would be like defecting to Oxford.

I was outraged by this admiral who thought Hitler was a god. The truth is I was already caught up in the war, in the questions to be asked and answered. I had an old historical atlas I'd found in a bag of rubbish outside Ashburnham and now I studied it closely. The trouble was that on every page the shape of the countries seemed to be different from the maps shown in newspapers; sometimes countries even had new names. There were problems galore. Where did the Holy Roman Empire stand in all this? Was Athens on our side in this war? And if so, did that mean that all the good fighters from Sparta were on Hitler's side?

I suppose I first encountered history through my grandmother's eyes. I'm sure it made a difference. My father's measured answers to my questions on the state of a world at war were a valuable counter-balance to her exotic ramblings. But her stories were always so deeply imbued with an attractive sense of drama. Perhaps that's why I finally spent most of my life writing novels rather than history.

Despite my grandmother Eliza's disapproval of my father's explanations, she was quite prepared to dip into her own rich fund of stories about the past. When I look back I can see that, given the tales she was prepared to tell me, she had no grounds for complaint against my father's infinitely more sober accounts of the war's progress. But of course the war was here and now. We were living it. It might end suddenly making all the pains of evacuation for nothing – or it might become dramatically more dangerous, more directly threatening to number 3 Guinness Trust Buildings. My grand-mother's past, however, was not so much another country as somewhere where troubles were always lightened by singing and dancing, by health and youth. She certainly censored my view of her world but it was in an eclectic and haphazard fashion. Usually things came out right in the end. Of course, she never mentioned that, before my mother's birth, she'd had an illegitimate child in her twenties and had struggled alone to bring her up in the last harsh days of Victorian London. She never told me about living on the fringe during the many years she worked as a waitress in pubs and restaurants around Knightsbridge, although she hinted at it. I remember just before she died a rare mention of her husband, my grandfather. She'd had her tipple for the night and a few snorts of snuff. Perhaps it was a question of mine about him that caused her to fall to musing. 'I was a bad lot when I was young, Dee,' she said. 'Paid for it though. But I never wanted to tie myself to one man till I met your grandfather.' She put down her empty teacup and adjusted her hat. '"Jesse James Toop, you sound like an American outlaw to me," I said, first time I met him.

'"You can see what I am, Liz," he said. "A ticket collector. I've been up when I was younger, but I won't be moving up again. A ticket collector. At my age never will be anything more."

'I liked that,' my grandmother said. 'Straightforward. So I was straightforward with him. I told him straight I was a bad lot.'

I didn't know what she meant. I suppose the truth is I'm still not absolutely sure. But that was when she was a few months away from death, so maybe she meant what I now think she meant. She wasn't often in confessional mood. Preferred to tell me about the night her father, Long Charlie Webster, fought Tom Collen in the Cremorne Gardens for a five-sovereign purse and broke all the knuckles on his right hand to win. Everybody knew he was nearly six months behind on the rent on the cottage in World's End Passage. To have been defeated that night would have put the whole family out in the street.

'Of course fighting was forbidden in the Gardens, though plenty went on. But for a big fight like this with a titled lady (so they said) supplying the purse, they had to find a quiet place among the elm trees, surrounded with bushes where the bookmakers could take their stand for side bets, and the girls all spread out keeping look-out for P.C. Thompson from Chelsea police station who was on that night.'

'What girls?'

'Girls who worked the gardens. There were always a dozen or two about to help out. They'd no reason to thank the law.'

'But your father won. He knocked the other man out.'

'They fought for an hour. It was a record at the time. At the end of it Tom Collen was flat on his back. My dad's legs gave way seconds after they gave him the five golden sovereigns. The titled lady was pleased – if that's what she really was. They said she won a hundred guineas from her fancy man that night. As for Tom Collen and my dad, friends carried both of them to the Fountain of Light and threw them in. That brought them round.'

'What's the Fountain of Light?'

'You're sitting on it, love. Before they built these flats, this was a corner of the pleasure gardens. The fountain was here . . .' She pointed down with her index finger. 'It had water coming up cascading over big round gas globes. One of the sights of the gardens. And there were plenty, I can tell you.'

'What about your dad's broken knuckles?'

'He was all right. His friends carried him up to the World's End pub. They knew what they were doing, didn't they? My dad brought them round after round non-stop, whiskies too. He was a generous man. Here,' she leaned forward, warmed by the memory, 'when he arrived home he had this big silly smile on his battered face. And only sixteen shillings left! Not enough to knock off the back rent for more than a month, but just enough for the rent collector to give him another chance. Next night we bought jam tarts with the few coppers left and bottles of beer for the older boys,' my grandmother said, laughing. 'And danced outside in World's End Passage, showing off how rich we was.'

She stood up, excited by her memories of the past, again that distant past, dominated by dancing and singing, and began to dance round the table, singing to the tune of 'The Old Grey Mare':

'The Old World's End
It ain't what it used to be,
Ain't what it used to be, ain't what it used to be . . .'

It was many years before I began to find out what the Old World's End really used to be.

I found that my grandmother's stories about Cremorne Gardens germinated slowly in my mind. To my surprise, the teachers at Ashburnham had only heard of Cremorne Gardens because there was a Cremorne Road running down towards the embankment, or because there was (before it was bombed) a Cremorne pub. Yet the school they taught in stood bang in the middle of the pleasure gardens' former site. Even my mother, who'd lived in Upcerne Road, close to the centre walk of the gardens, knew them only by my grandmother's stories, mostly of the rowdiness of the young bucks and the music and dancing and the sparkling magnificence of the gas lighting among the trees. But because my grandmother's description had brought the Gardens so richly into existence for me, they began to play a part in my own dreamworld. I began to ask her more about Cremorne, and about what people did there. I asked her did we really live on top of them, and she'd tell me that my great-grandfather would leave World's End Passage in the evening, take refreshment in the World's End pub then stroll down the King's Road to the big gates of Cremorne which were at the very place which was and is now the entrance to Guinness Trust Buildings. Then he'd swagger . . . he was a great swaggerer . . . down the avenue of long-gone elms, not a penny in his pocket, to find a backer for his next fight. Usually, my grandmother said with some pride, a lady of some standing. By which I now think she meant that higher class of prostitute, a kept woman.

'What happened to the Gardens then?' I asked her, baffled that all those lights and cafés and bits of finery should have disappeared.

'A lot of people ganged up on them,' she said with a flourish of her hat-pin. 'A lot of people didn't want them to be there. Old Vysh across in Hortensia Road was one of the leaders. Very high and mighty, old Vysh. And there was the church, they was against the Cremorne to a man. Don't take a lot up here in the head to see why. They may have been thinking about saving their souls, but they weren't thinking much about saving the kids from going hungry, were they?'

'What kids?'

The kids of people who worked in the Gardens.'

Of course, I understood little of what she was really saying, but she always seemed content to talk to me in this way, knowing that I felt currents and eddies of her meaning, but content that I didn't understand in full. 'You'll understand more when you grow up a bit,' was a favourite line of hers.

'So what happened?'

'They all clubbed together. Old Vysh, the church, builders and the like – and they got rid of the Gardens.'

'Pulled down the lights?'

'It was terrible to see,' she said. 'They had a great big sale. All the bits and pieces. All the signs and the light globes and beds and furniture. People came from miles off. Then the gangs of navvies moved in. They was out there, pulling down the lights, digging up the gas mains, knocking down the stadium and the assembly room and everything in sight.' There were tears in her eyes. 'They was tearing up the bushes, fixing chains round the trees, hauling them down with teams of horses. I tell you, Dee, it shouldn'tave been allowed.' She wiped her eyes with her snuff-stained handkerchief. 'There was a lot of World's End people shed a few tears in those days. But not the churchmen. Not old Vysh. They say they gave him a medal for what *he* done.'

I asked my father about all this because Henry James and Minnie had lived in Lots Road before they moved to Blantyre Street and their eldest son George had been born there. They must have moved in barely ten years after Cremorne Gardens had been closed down. My father confirmed what my grandmother had told me but knew very little about why the Gardens were closed and had never heard of the mysterious Mr Vysh. He did send me down to the brewery on the corner of the King's Road and Lots Road to look at the cast-iron gates there. They were huge and impressive and carried a sign saying they were the original gates of Cremorne Gardens. The only piece of Cremorne known to have survived.

A half-century later I came back to the mystery of these enormous Victorian pleasure gardens in the middle of the World's End which seemed to have disappeared virtually without record or trace, or without trace except for that very fine pair of cast-iron gates. Today they stand before a sliver of grass and riverfront which Kensington and Chelsea Council have recently preserved where the steamboats once landed crowds of Londoners bound for the pleasures of Cremorne. I stumbled on the gates while walking with one of my daughters past Ashburnham and the power station, shortly to be demolished. Strangely there is no account on the park board of the original Cremorne other than a simple mention of the pleasure gardens formerly there. No details of their true size, and the excitement and variety of entertainment provided there. I don't believe Kensington and Chelsea Council has any reason now to bowdlerise the true nature of what was once the greatest pleasure garden in London. Perhaps this terse reference is just a coy hangover from Victorian times.

And even now, I would guess, this modern apology for Cremorne Gardens is unknown to the majority of Chelsea inhabitants.

As I stood there, looking downriver as far as Canary Wharf, I wondered what part the pleasure gardens had played in the making of this area, in employing its Victorian inhabitants, in creating this strange enclave at the World's End which lasted for nearly forty years in the face of the unceasing process of the enrichment of the rest of Chelsea. And I wondered why the story of Cremorne had been almost totally ignored ever since.

Why, for instance, did English painters shy away from painting it? You can see the Parisian equivalents of Cremorne Gardens painted and repainted by Manet or, for a less polite gathering, by Renoir in his *Bal au Moulin de la Galette*. Art historians will insist that, in Britain, the Pre-Raphaelites or Art for Art's Sake movement had other preoccupations, and this may be so. But Chelsea was thronged with artists of every quality, school, interest and eccentricity in the second half of the nineteenth century. Cheyne Walk, the location of so many studios, actually touches the old western boundary of the Gardens. Yet extraordinarily, and perhaps significantly, I can find few paintings of the subject. Lesser painters like Phoebus Levin painted Cremorne a few times and the Greaves brothers resorted to the Gardens once or twice among the dozens of studies they did as they recorded Chelsea and all its sights. But Cremorne was, overwhelmingly, the most popular sight in Chelsea, indeed the most popular sight in Victorian London, and several million entrance tickets were sold there in its thirty-five years or more of existence. While Cremorne flourished, its entertainments were sketched and its visitors often enough caricatured in the cheap prints like *Day To Day*. But no major artists recorded the Gardens.

And why can I find only one reference, after its demise, to Cremorne in fiction or memoirs, a description in the pornographic and anonymous *Walter* of the author's attempt to hire a wealthy prostitute whose carriage was parked under the elms on the main avenue which ran down to the river? To Walter's chagrin, the woman turns him down as being unlikely to pay the sum she is accustomed to. Walter was a gentleman, and though not rich considered himself a great deal wealthier than any member of the 'carriage trade'. Until she told him she earned £7,000 a year, over £200,000 today.

Of course, even a small fraction of that sort of money would have been rare earnings for most young women working Cremorne. And perhaps the lady in the carriage doubled or tripled her true income when rebuffing Walter, but there is no doubt that many earned well. They were not the pale-faced, half-starved wretches who certainly existed in the East End at this time. After this rebuff, Walter doesn't mention another visit to Cremorne in his memoir. I suspect the young women there were too independent for his tastes.

But that doesn't account for the way in which Victorians veered away from any real mention of the Gardens once they were closed down. Perhaps part of the answer lies in the great Whistler v. Ruskin court case of 1878 just after the Gardens were forced to close. At issue was a painting of fireworks at night over Cremorne Gardens. Ruskin, the country's foremost art critic, had written, on seeing the picture exhibited: 'I have seen and heard much of cockney impudence before but never expected to hear a coxcomb ask two hundred guineas for flinging a pot of paint in the public's face.'

The coxcomb or dandy was, of course, the American artist, James McNeil Whistler, and unsurprisingly he sued. Art historians have appropriated the significance of the *cause célèbre* that followed and are no doubt right in seeing it as a key moment in the history of modernism in Britain. But Ruskin saw himself, and was seen generally, as more than an art critic. His social criticism had elevated him to the status of a moral arbiter. And this is where the aesthetic offence of Whistler's impressionist treatment of the subject was compounded by the unseen subject itself. That the artist's subject was in fact the most notorious rendezvous of prostitute and client in the country was denied by Whistler himself. He had painted, he claimed, a Nocturne in Black and Gold and skirted the issue of its undoubted provenance in an exchange with Attorney General Holker, Ruskin's counsel.

WHISTLER:	It is a night piece and represents the fireworks at Cremorne Gardens.
HOLKER:	Not a view of Cremorne?
WHISTLER:	If it were called a view of Cremorne it would undoubtedly bring about nothing but disappointment on the part of its beholders.

But the issue at stake here was clear to most Victorians. Cremorne represented the dissolute life in their midst. The Gardens and the painting were different aspects of the conflict of cultural values of the time. The trial took place within a year of the decision to bring the pleasure gardens to an end. To many, it was a commentary on that decision.

As it happened Ruskin lost. But Whistler can hardly be said to have won. He had made his case for art but not for the life of Cremorne. He was awarded damages of a farthing, which, polished up, he hung on his watch chain.

So we know, in part, why the Cremorne was pushed gently out of sight. It was unacceptable because it showed the Victorians in their raw enjoyment of sex. When I started writing this book I thought I had to find out more. Where exactly were the gardens? What did they look like? What connection do they have with the World's End of the first half of the twentieth century?

Lammas Land is not a term anybody in my World's End knew. From Anglo-Saxon times, it was a tract of land attached to Chelsea village, divided into individually owned lots or strips, thrown open for common pasturage after the summer harvest. It appears under this name on many old maps. In other documents, like the 1544 *Perticular Booke of Chelsey Manor*, the west field at the manor boundary is described as the Lots. Today's Lots Road clearly has a long history.

Early in the nineteenth century Chelsea Farm, the house at the centre of the lands, was owned by Viscount Cremorne and his wife,

a descendant of William Penn named Philadelphia. The property
had changed hands at least once before the widely advertised sale of
23 July 1840. Considerable changes had already taken place under
the 'enterprising owner'. What was on offer in 1840 was described on
the sale posters as:

One noble mansion
Ten acres adorned by stately trees
Extensive river frontage
The Stadium Canteen Public House
A Lodge and Tower in the castellated style
Ten thousand trees
An ornamental basin and islands with chain bridge and other
bridges.

The prospectus continued: 'The march of progress advances at
railroad pace from Buckingham Palace towards the World's End!
The property may indeed be termed A GOLD MINE enabling the
purchaser to secure a princely fortune!'

The purchaser of the ten-acre property did in fact go on to make
a princely fortune. He was soon licensed for Musical Performances,
Fêtes Champêtres, Dancing, Masquerades, Balloon Ascents, Public
Breakfasts and Dinners.

A small sampling of the pleasures offered on a night at the
World's End in July 1861 (billed as the Fête for the Million!)
included: a vocal concert *al fresco* with the Great Cremorne Band,
M. Rivière, Conductor, and the new Grand Ballet Programme
entitled *Fortunatus*. On this same night, perhaps sitting somewhat
uncomfortably alongside the high-art pretensions of the vocal concert and *Fortunatus*, there was juxtaposed Mr Cooke's celebrated
Troupe of Educated Dogs & Monkeys and Signore Buono Core,
The Italian Fire Eating King. All rounded off in good Victorian
style with a Grand Display of Fireworks. Brilliant enough, as

we've seen, to attract the brush of as distinguished a painter as Whistler.

Balloon flights quickly caught the imagination of the public and could be relied upon to draw crowds. But the showmen of Cremorne were not content with sedate ascents like that painted by the Greaves brothers in 1872. Risks had to be taken – though some additional excitements were clearly not intended as when the captive balloon broke its moorings and carried terrified passengers across London through the freezing upper air to land at Tottenham. Or when a professional balloonist found himself landing in Dieppe. Other spectacular events *were* carefully planned. A monkey dropped by parachute; or Madam Poitevan, dressed as Europa and accompanied by a bull, surviving both the balloon flight and a show of bovine friskiness. Vincent de Goof, however, attempted to glide from a height of 500 feet using fabric wings with a 37-foot span. He crashed to his death into St Luke's Church just off the King's Road.

Gaslight was a major attraction. From the discreetly lit shrub-lined *allées* to the grand carriage approach between the brightly illuminated elms, light was an unforgettable feature utilised to maximum effect by the showmen who owned Cremorne. The dancing platform, the Ring of Light, offered gas globes within cast-iron arched tracery, and the reflections of coloured glass in crystal drops swooping through the darkness like the hem of a dancer's skirt.

But not long after the opening of the Gardens in 1845 it had become evident that prostitution was its main attraction. Hypocrisy spawned a dozen different terms for the profession. The most elegant (and most expensive) women were 'ladies of the night', or 'dress ladies of the town'. The girls who worked the bushy alleyways of the Gardens were 'fallen women' or even 'women of the abyss'. Within a few years the World's End had become the greatest brothel not just in London but in Europe, probably even the western world. Contemporary complainants insist that most women there at night, even on the arm of middle-class or upper-class gentlemen, were prostitutes. Cremorne did not call itself a pleasure garden for nothing.

There were countless places to seek and find sexual pleasure. There was, centrally, the Ring of Light, the dance floor which boasted that it could hold a thousand dancers. On any spring or summer weekend night it might be circled by seven or eight hundred potential customers and up to two or three hundred girls. There were private 'dining alcoves' for couples. There were the dimmed, gas-lit *allées* of bushes and shrubs where women trawled for custom. There were grottoes. There were the dozen open-air cafés where a passing women could be invited for a drink as a prelude to retiring to a dining alcove or to her rooms in one of the many brothels in the streets of the World's End.

But there were also other entertainments for a daytime family audience. William Acton, the Victorian investigator of prostitution, suggests there was a day and a night-time garden, each quite different in character. Switching with nightfall from one clientele to another, the ownership of the Gardens kept up its relentless commerce. 'The homely calico of daylight leaves by steamer eastward,' William Acton observed, 'before the silks and satins of the night arrive by Hansom cab.'

The Ordnance Survey Map of 1864 shows that Cremorne Gardens contained three large buildings. The most impressive was an assembly room called Ashburnham Hall, the site of the later Ashburnham Mansions. In addition there was New Hall, a building closer to the river, constructed for purposes unknown, and a hotel for purposes not difficult to guess at. There was also a maze, a shooting saloon, a pagoda, several large fountains, a circus, a stereorama, a stand for the gas balloon ascent, and a sports stadium.

My grandmother told me she often climbed the fence into Cremorne Gardens as a very young girl. I sometimes wonder if it was not fear of the influence of the older girls already working there that caused her devout mother to banish her to domestic service in Dorset and a hoped-for life of moral rectitude.

For thirty years the august members of Chelsea Vestry struggled with the problem of the World's End's disorderly houses: 'The Board resolves that the pleasure gardens are promotive of profligacy and vice. That in consequence of the said gardens, the surrounding district of the World's End has become the favourite residence of dress women of the town who frequent the said Gardens'

Lamont Road, just across the King's Road from what became La-di-dah's pitch, was made up of almost as many brothels as family houses. Numbers 33 and 36, 41, 43, 57 and 59, were all fingered by local objectors. For a short road not completely built up at this stage, it was an impressive number. But there were other such streets too. Luna Street, Hobury Street (where my grandmother Eliza lived), and Limerston Street, Blantyre Street (where Minnie lived), Seaton Street (where we lived fifty years later), all contained disorderly houses. Slaidburn Street was said to ring with cries of '*Murder!*' from the girls working there.

By 1877 complaints against the Gardens had reached, if not fever pitch, at least some sort of crescendo. In July seventy-eight parishioners on the fringes of the World's End complained, without the usual polite euphemisms, to the Vestry: 'The nuisance to our neighbourhood caused by the number of prostitutes is very great and we should consider it a great boon if anything can be done to lessen the evil.'

Reading the Vestry documents of the period I came upon two of the leading elements in the protest movement. The first was my own baptismal church, St John's in Tadema Road, as close to Cremorne Gardens as you could possible get. Significantly, this was built in 1876 and immediately launched into protests against the continued licensing of Cremorne Gardens. Another leading element in the struggle to get Cremorne closed down was the new owner of a famous nursery, Knight's Exotic Nursery, at what is now Hortensia Road just off the King's Road.

The new owners developed the nursery into a highly fashionable Victorian garden centre with floorwalkers wearing frock coats and top hats to receive the many distinguished visitors. We can imagine the Exotic Nursery did not sit well with Cremorne Gardens, indeed was possibly even confused with the pleasure gardens from some inebriated viewpoints. Whatever, it was the Scots family of James and then Harry Veitch, owners of the Exotic Gardens, who led the local protests. As I read the name, it rang a bell. Harry Veitch was undoubtedly 'old Vysh' whom my grandmother had talked about. His Exotic Gardens were also, I realised, the later site of Sloane School, Chelsea's only grammar school, which I was to attend from 1942–50.

The chorus of complaints had become a barrage. How and why the protesters sharpened their focus so effectively at this point is difficult to understand. After all the gardens had been in existence some thirty-five years. It's possibly true that prostitution had become the predominant part of Cremorne's activities, but there is little evidence that there had been any augmentation of the trade in the few years before Cremorne was closed down. Sex always had been at the centre of the entertainments on offer there. Nevertheless the protesters, literary, devout, and members of the many different interest groups along the King's Road, intensified the struggle. Some even complained direct to Scotland Yard, though they received, on 15 September 1877, the somewhat haughty reply:

Sir –
I have to acknowledge the receipt of your letter of the 13 inst. And to acquaint you, in reply, that the matter is one which does not pertain to the duties of the police.
I am, Sir, your obedient servant,
D. Labalmondiere,
Assistant Commissioner

The struggle continued into the autumn, but such was the scandalous nature of the Gardens in the view of some of the most influential people of Chelsea (Carlyle among them) that for the proprietors it had become a losing battle. The annual licence due for renewal in the autumn of 1877 was duly applied for, but the attempt was doomed. The Vestry had, in effect, put its foot down. More important, the new owner of the land, a Mrs Simpson, was receiving tempting alternative offers. The *Telegraph* put it concisely and not unsympathetically: 'It is not that Cremorne Gardens have intruded on respectability but that respectability has intruded upon the gardens.'

The final act for the pleasure gardens comes in an extract from the minutes of the Board in the autumn of 1877: 'Letter from solicitors Lee & Pemberton dated October 16, 1877. In re Cremorne Gardens licence, notifying that the application for (renewal of) licence for music and dancing was withdrawn that morning and that the licence was accordingly not granted.'

The effect on the World's End was devastating. It was the end of their employment for many hundreds of people. It was the end for all those who'd earned a living as gardeners, as sweepers of the leafy alleys, as entertainers and dancers, as waiters and waitresses, cooks and cleaners, grooms and stable boys . . . It was the end for almost all of the several hundred girls who lived in the World's End and made a living in the Gardens. 'They did for us,' my grandmother said. 'They got together to close the Gardens down. They never thought of what it would mean to the people,' she said naively: 'My dad was finished for any real paying work. Once they closed the Gardens the nobs stopped coming. And once that happened you'd be down to a tuppenny fight with a guardsman at the Grenadier with a side-bet on yourself if you fancied your chances. My dad was a good man, never beat us without cause even if he was, as everyone in World's End Passage said, a bit workshy. He used to claim he had asthma, then fight like a tiger. Died of the chest though,' she'd say, tapping her breastbone.

She would pause to refix her hatpin.

'Now my brother Josh did well out of the Cremorne. He was a sly bounder, you see, keeping out of trouble with the law, never getting into a fight although he was as big as Will or my dad. Not a carpenter or joiner, a cabinet maker he called himself. He'd just walk around the pleasure gardens with small steps and say to his wife, "I think the wood-working there is very pleasing, don't you, Theresa?" And the bosses would hear him and give him carving jobs for the woodwork over the cafés. Big paying jobs to carve bunches of grapes and naked women and things like that. He never minded if it was paid work. One day he came by chance to price a job in a house where I was cleaning in Cheyne Walk . . . number 28 I think it was . . . two big women in trousers who smoked pipes and spent their lives painting each other in the altogether. Anyway, one day I open the door and there's me brother Josh.

' "You don't know me," he hisses in my ear as we're waiting in the hall.

'I said, "Right!" I turns to Miss Parkinhurst or whatever her name was as she's coming down from her studio, and I said, "Mr Josh Webster," I said. "He's my brother but that don't mean anything. As he says, I don't really know him. Except he won't give more than half a crown a week to support my mother who's living with us. So I shall be off." And I took my coat from the hook in the hall and walked straight out. Down to the World's End pub, though I wouldn't normally use that one. I'd walked out on a good job. But you have your pride, don't you?'

In its nearly forty years of existence, the Gardens had generated unaccustomed wealth for what was, as late as 1835, a country district of farmland and nursery orchards. That wealth had demanded the solid middle-class housing which became evident from the 1860s around the area of the World's End Tavern. Much of this new wealth came from prostitution, of course, but these were not the poor prostitutes of the East End, frittering away their pitiful earnings on

gin and snuff and a fourpenny doss. Many had permanent lodgings
in the originally elegant stuccoed terraces which were replacing the
riverside meadows to become Blantyre, Luna and Seaton Streets,
and across the King's Road, Hobury and Limerston Streets, Edith
Grove, Fernshaw Road, Edith Terrace and Gunter Grove. These
were women who spent money locally, had their apartments cleaned,
their gardens tended, who bought materials and had dresses and hats
made. They were employers of World's End labour. Of course there
were girls who were pimped, there were underage girls, there were
country girls drawn in from Fulham or Putney, there were girls who
succumbed to alcohol or laudanum. But I can't help thinking that
what the Gardens provided, even for the less fortunate, were safe
surroundings and something closer to a reasonable living wage than
most girls otherwise gained from the life of prostitution in Victorian
England.

That autumn when the licence was withdrawn by Chelsea Vestry
a new wind blew hard across the World's End. The area would retain
its separateness from the rest of Chelsea, but a new role was being
marked out for it by a new generation of industrialists and
developers. As the *Telegraph* had again pointed out when listing the
offences of Cremorne: 'But the most heinous offence is that it is a
large, open space in the middle of a surrounding neighbourhood long
since built over or laid out in eligible building plots.' In other words,
it was ripe for 'development'.

Alfred Beaver confirmed the accuracy of this assessment in his
Memorials of Old Chelsea. Describing the changes which rapidly
followed the dissolution of Cremorne Gardens, he writes: 'The creek
[Chelsea Creek] is now a dirty ditch, lined with ugly wharves
and sheds. The once pleasant fields are now covered with huge
gasometers, shrieking railway engines dash past constantly and a
wilderness of more or less dingy streets covers the farm-lands and
gardens.'

A comparison of the Ordnance Survey Maps of 1865 and 1894

shows what the protests of local dignitaries like Mr Veitch of the Royal Exotic Nursery on Hortensia Road (there is still a Veitch Medal presented by the Royal Horticultural Society) and Thomas Carlyle, who lived less than a hundred yards from Cremorne, inadvertently achieved. The twenty years of Victorian industrialisation saw the birth of the World's End as I knew it. The whole appearance of this end of Chelsea changed dramatically. From eighty percent fields, woods and orchards in 1860 to one hundred percent industry and cramped working-class housing in 1900.

In one sense, Cremorne Gardens did not disappear completely without trace. Its presence held up the gentrification of the lower reaches of Chelsea for over a century, though the gardens themselves lasted for less than half that period. The existence of Cremorne Gardens impeded the movement of Upper Chelsea into its western corner because the upper-middle classes, even the bohemian artists, were unwilling to live in an area of universal ill-repute. When the pleasure gardens no longer occupied the Lammas Lands, the developers and speculative builders began to move in. But what replaced the gardens were not the elegant terraces of Upper Chelsea but a mixture of industrial sites and cheap, often tenement housing for the country families that began to flock to London looking for work.

We must assume that the girls of Cremorne Gardens for the most part moved on, though some certainly remained and they and their daughters continued a tradition that lasted into at least the 1930s. But most left. Soon, the grander houses in Lamont Road and Hobury Street and in those streets running south of the World's End to the river where the 'ladies of the night' had lived, were turned over to multiple occupancy. Gradually they descended into slum dwellings. The Gaslight & Coke Company bought a large tract of land along the river. Coke wharves and mills and the power station replaced the rural softness of Cremorne's riverfront. The rest of the gardens were sold off as low-class workers' housing and became

Meek Street, Tetcott, Uverdale and Upcerne Roads, and, in a casual nod to the past, Stadium Street and Lots Road. Ashburnham Elementary School was built there in 1908.

Even the smallest houses were soon occupied by at least two families. The tenements, grandly named six-flat buildings like Seymour House or Beresford House where my grandmother Eliza was to live, had shared lavatories, front doors open all night, drunks habitually sleeping on the cement stairs, and were soon overrun by mice and sometimes rats. The Dickensian quality of that world is preserved in the names of the families who shared the tenement known as Beresford House. Besides the Toops there were Cowpers, Dickweeds (pronounced Digweed) and Brawns. Toop, Cowper, Dickweed and Brawn. How do such names disappear?

The puritans and developers had struck the first blow against mid-nineteenth-century World's End where the first example of a large-scale sex industry created a degree of prosperity for the area. The industrialisation that built the early-twentieth-century World's End might have provided work for more people but it was of a kind that left them little time for living and even less money to live on.

Although long gone by the time I arrived in the World's End, Cremorne Gardens occupied a front row seat in my imagination. And unlike some who write of their childhood, (I think of Anatole France's *Livre de Mon Ami*), I can still see myself, *be* myself, as I run back home from school, from Lots Road, down Burnaby Street, past Ashburnham Mansions, through the back gate of Guinness Trust, past Blocks 3 and 4, the hundreds, into our territory, Blocks 1 and 2 populated, we were certain, by people who didn't smell at all, or as much, or at least not in the same way . . . And that run, five minutes going to school, twenty minutes back, was of course, although I never really thought about it, from one end of Cremorne Gardens to the other.

SEVEN

Blitzkrieg

As the spring of 1940 arrived, the war changed dramatically. This was a time when we began to fall back on the support of our families, the beginning of a year when we saw less of friends of our own age to play football or fivestones or Warney Echo within the yard. We were, I suppose, withdrawing behind the last ramparts. When the bombs began to fall there were no whining requests to go out to play. Everything was directed towards the coming night and how, as a family, we would get through it.

But total disaster had not yet struck. When I check the dates I see it must have been May 10 1940. I was coming home from Church Lads' Brigade, proud of a black uniform I now recognise as something Nazi youth leader Baldur von Shirach might have envied. Ahead of me there was chaos on World's End island. La-di-dah was going mad with excitement as the evening papers were coming in. He was selling at a rate I doubt he'd ever sold before, screaming his mantra, racing over to the delivery van to beg for more copies, running back to wet his thumb and peel off newspapers for the heaving crowd of customers. Loud as La-di screamed the titles, nobody cared whether they got a *News*, *Star* or *Standard* as long as they got a paper. It was the only time

I can remember when men didn't look first at the racing results.

I heard the name Churchill. I heard him called a warmonger. I heard him blamed for something the Germans had just done. I got home bursting to know what was happening. My mother was working at the haberdasher's shop. My grandmother was looking after Kit. My father's two brothers, Fred, kindly and cheerful, and George, with a permanent sneer on his wet lips when he looked at me, were in the front room. They were going to the Weatherby Arms with my father who ran a savings club there.

Two things, it seemed, had happened that day. The Prime Minister, Neville Chamberlain, whom Uncle Fred had told me about at Croydon Airport, had been thrown out of his job as leader. The new Prime Minister was Winston Churchill. On the very same day, Hitler burst through his own front door and began a charge with tanks and Stuka dive-bombers to cut off the British Army from the Channel ports. Of course I know now that the French Army was much more numerous and formidable than our own small Expeditionary contribution in 1940, but that's how the newspapers put it. The BBC news, to which we all listened, my brother and I crouching under the high-placed wireless set, described the German advance through the Low Countries. My father said he wouldn't put his money on Belgium this time.

I looked at Kit. Russia's attack on Finland seemed ages ago and infinitely far away. This was happening now, just across the Channel. It's certainly true I only had a hazy idea of where the Channel was, but I knew it wasn't far away. In my mind's eye I conjured up an amalgam of all those newspaper cartoon figures of German soldiers. Huge men in helmets with big hands and small, cruel, eyes. And I didn't like what I saw.

George liked to be thought generous without paying for it. As my father and Fred were talking he was flipping a penny, to go to whichever one of us, my brother or myself, could snatch it from the air. When we found (which he'd probably worked out from the beginning) that we couldn't reach the coin, he caught it and dropped it back in his pocket. 'In this world you don't get something for nothing,' he taunted us. He turned away. 'It's this Churchill business that set Hitler off,' he said to my father. 'Churchill's a warmonger. Always has been. Hitler knows that. Knows it's a fight to the finish now.'

'Let's get over to the Weatherby,' my father said. Very deliberately, he took two pennies from his pocket and, with George watching, flipped one to me, one to my brother.

'There. Something for nothing,' George smirked. 'What a good dad you boys've got.'

It was the beginning of days of mounting excitement. Nothing it seemed could hold back the advancing Germans. There were maps in the *News Chronicle* with thick black arrows on them showing the route of what I had learnt to call the Panzers to the Channel coast. Within days Rotterdam was bombed and Holland was occupied. In just over a week, German tanks reached the Channel. A few days later, Belgium surrendered.

I saw Dunkirk on the news at the King's Picture House on the King's Road. It never occurred to me that we had suffered a stunning defeat. The soldiers were smiling as they came off the ships, big and little, and some of them waved or blew a kiss at the camera.

But there was no doubt I was worried. A week or two ago we were just waiting for the chance to give the Germans a good hiding. Now it seemed different, with us having to evacuate troops from Dunkirk to save the Germans from giving *us* a good hiding. I looked to my father for reassurance. He explained that this evacuation had saved the soldiers but they had no guns or tanks or even lorries with them. That was important.

'What do we have to stop the Germans with if they try to come here?'

'Not much. But it'd be a big job to bring hundreds of thousands of Germans soldiers across the water. Don't forget, in between us

and the Germans we have the English Channel, twenty miles across.'
He looked thoughtful. 'We still have the navy. It's the strongest in the
world, but the RAF will have to stop the Germans bombing our
ships. Anyway, there's going to be no invasion while the French are
still fighting. The Germans were turned back at the gates of Paris in
the last war. And we won in the end, remember.'

Yes. But I would have felt better about that if I hadn't known that
what he really thought was that the war would last two years – and
we would *lose*. I didn't understand why, but I couldn't quite bring
myself to ask him about this. It was like questions about sex later.
You couldn't quite bring yourself to ask the questions because you
were afraid of the enormity of the answers. From about now onwards
I tried to comfort myself, never quite effectively, with the thought
that maybe he had changed his mind.

From the front page of the *News of the World* on a Sunday a week
or two later my memory conjures up an enormous quarter-page
cartoon, centrally placed below the no-longer-remembered headline.
Two massive wooden gates inscribed 'Paris' are bending inwards,
about to burst under a weight hurled against them. French soldiers,
in their distinctive helmets with a strip of metal from front to back
and long greatcoats, strain their shoulders against the thick planking
of the gates to hold back the near-intolerable pressure. Bayonets split
the woodwork around their heads in a dozen places. Where a plank
has snapped German faces under German helmets are visible, their
rifle butts hammering on the woodwork. Underneath in thick bold
letters the words: **'They shall not pass!'**

My grandmother told me that's what the French said last time –
and they were right. 'They pushed the Jerries back at the gates of
Paris in 1914. They'll do it again. They're good fighters, the French.
You can rely on them.'

A few days later Paris fell. German soldiers streamed through it
and on down to much of the rest of France. Six million French and
Belgian people left their homes and trudged south before the

advancing Germans. The government had moved from Paris to Tours, Tours to Bordeaux. In another ten days France had surrendered. 'So much the better,' said my grandmother with newfound satisfaction. 'We're on our own now. No bloody foreigners to look after.'

These were days when there was no good news anywhere. Norway had already been forced to surrender. Italy had declared war on us. I thought of those Abyssinians in their flowing white robes. Funny to think we were now on the same side. Did we have any other friends?

About this time Winston Churchill made a speech. We listened to it on the wireless:

What General Weygand called the Battle of France is over. I expect that the Battle of Britain is about to begin. Upon this battle depends . . . our own British life, and the long continuity of our institutions and of our empire. The whole fury and might of the enemy must very soon be turned on us. Hitler knows that he will have to break us in this island or lose the war. If we can stand up to him, all Europe may be free . . . But if we fail, then the whole world, including the United States will sink into the abyss of a new dark age . . . Let us therefore brace ourselves to our duties, and so bear ourselves that, if the British Empire and its Commonwealth last for a thousand years, men will still say, 'This was their finest hour.'

It was a speech that sent cold thrills up my back. It gave everyone in the country a new role, a new image of ourselves, no longer as a great empire, ever victorious, unchallengeable in its might, but now as a tiny determined island, opposed by a whole continent dominated by Hitler who was in turn backed by his shifty friend Stalin. If my chance came, I was determined to fight on the beaches or at least down by the river for Lots Road power station.

*

The speech seemed remarkably prescient. Six days afterwards, the French signed the most humiliating Armistice in their history. The Battle of France was indeed over. On July 10, less than a month after Churchill's speech, the Battle of Britain began. I don't think it is any exaggeration to say it was the most important air battle in the history of the twentieth century. If the RAF had lost, Britain would have been overrun. The Germans later claimed the battle was drawn, and it's true that in the skill and courage of the pilots and the technical equality of the new fighter planes involved, the two sides were evenly balanced. But the RAF and their allied Czech, Polish, Canadian and American squadrons were never forced to abandon the air to the Luftwaffe. And my father was right. Without German air superiority there could never be an invasion of Britain. For Goering and the Luftwaffe, that fact alone constituted a massive defeat.

Few in Britain and no one in the World's End was aware that the Battle of Britain had already started. BBC reports of German attacks on coastal shipping were not seen by the ordinary citizen for what they were – an attempt to provoke the RAF into battle over the Channel. Goering, we now know, had nearly 3,000 modern aircraft deployed in three Air Fleets, outnumbering the RAF by four to one. But a large part of each Air Fleet was made up of Heinkel 111 and Dornier 17 bombers, neither plane fast enough to escape the British Spitfires and Hurricanes. The Messerschmitt 109, however, was a different proposition, slightly superior to the Hurricane, roughly equal to the Spitfire. In terms of modern fighter aircraft the two sides were more or less equal. But, of course, Britain already deployed a rudimentary system of radar detection.

By August we were all fully aware that the air battle had begun. At the beginning of the month Hitler had ordered the Luftwaffe to attack RAF aerodromes and over Kent the first clashes of modern fighters in squadron strength was seen. Every day now each side published its casualty figures and its pilots' claims on the enemy force. For my brother and myself the excitement was intense. We learnt the word 'dog-fight' for aerial combat. We learnt 'Bandits at Angels One-Five' to denote Messerschmitts at altitude 15,000 feet. With zooming hand movements I lectured Kit about coming at the enemy out of the sun, about the destructive power of 20-millimetre canon, and the vulnerable snail's pace of the Heinkel and Dornier bombers. He was very patient with me. My grandmother Eliza ran a sweepstake on each day's number of German aircraft downed. She didn't feel the privations of the time because she had never known much luxury anyway. The Post Office still had a twist of snuff for her and the Off Licence still sold gills of gin. The sweepstake added a shilling to her pension once or twice a week. She was beginning to enjoy her war.

But still we hadn't seen an aircraft over London, friend or foe. We thought this was how the war would always be, and nobody was surprised that it was almost as distant at this stage as the Great War had been. After all, for us the airfields of Kent were almost as far away as France.

In fact, the battle was turning against us. But Goering had boasted so intemperately of the might of his Luftwaffe that Hitler began to doubt that victory was in sight. A few more weeks attacking RAF airfields might have done it, but Hitler lost patience. His own belief was that only daylight bombing of London would finally secure him victory. On September 7 he ordered Goering to send 300 bombers and 600 escorting fighters against London.

I was playing down by the river with some friends. A new coaler was manoeuvring towards the wharf at Lots Road power station. We were excited to see that it had double anti-aircraft Bofors guns mounted on its deck. When the sirens went we were supposed to go straight home but we stayed to watch the Bofors guns rotating towards the south-east. Then something caught our attention in the sky. High up where the blue fades to grey, groups of small silvery dots caught the sun. As they approached we could see the shape of wings and hear the throb of engines. A minute or two more and we could see that the centre of the armada was made up of hundreds of two-engine bombers, and that surrounding them, protecting them from above and on both flanks, were even more squadrons of Messerschmitt fighters. Nearly a thousand aeroplanes in the sky at once is a breathtaking sight. Nearly a thousand *enemy* aircraft in the sky above your head is nothing short of terrifying.

My brother pulled hard on my sleeve and tried to get me to run home but, scared as I was, I was desperate to see more. The riverside was the perfect position with no buildings far to the east to block our view. Now black puffs of smoke were bursting around the German planes. Perhaps some were hit, perhaps I was just praying for some to be hit, but by now there was too much smoke from exploding shells to see.

Nowhere was there any sign of the RAF. Was no one signalling 'Bandits, Angels One-Five'? I scanned the skies. Not an RAF fighter in sight. Not a single Spitfire barrel-rolling into the attack. Where was Flight Lieutenant Rockfist Rogan of the *Champion* comic with his big gloved fists on the joystick, his thumb calmly calculating the range for his four wing-mounted, 20-millimetre canon?

As the first bomber squadrons reached the Thames, I saw what appeared to be a haze rising from the ground, thickening and rising higher and turning a swirling pink and red as the sun caught it. Then the huge frightening column of smoke boiled and bowed and turned up river towards us, still several miles away but infinitely menacing. I wasn't to know the oil and timber and wheat and tar and munitions of the London Docks were on fire. Or that RAF Fighter Command had deliberately allowed the Freedom of the City to 300 bombers to persuade Hitler that the RAF was finished, that its fighter strength could never challenge the Luftwaffe again. I grabbed Kit's hand. Most of my friends had already left when together we clambered over the embankment and scampered home.

We heard it on the BBC while the raid was still on. London Docks under attack. No mention of the RAF. Even before the All Clear sounded there were lots of people out in the yard looking towards the slowly twisting plume of pink smoke, watching it make its way upriver towards us, watching it flare out at the head and darken in the setting sun. Most of the men smoked cigarettes or pipes. It was warm weather so they wore braces and a shirt without a collar. The women wore floral aprons and folded their arms across their breasts. Very few people spoke. For a while my mother and father had joined them. When they came back they looked grave. We were sent into the front room while they talked. I knew they were going to talk about evacuation.

Now the Luftwaffe attacked London by day and night. Suddenly we were in a different war. For a whole week the RAF disappeared to recoup its strength. My grandmother suffered most. Her pains had returned and with them a new fear of the raids. Like many very old people her experiences of other wars did nothing to protect her from the terrors of this one.

At the end of the week, my father called us in the front room for the talk we dreaded. It was a full year since Mr Whitehead's evacuation.

'If we have to go to the country without Mum, I'm going to run away from home,' Kit whispered to me as we went into the room.

I sat on the floor on the striped sisal mat in front of the unlit stove. My mother sat beside my father on the Put-U-Up, hugging Kit to her.

'We want you to know what we've decided,' my father said. 'Your grandmother doesn't want to stay in London. She wants to go to stay with your Aunt May and the children in a new place called Windsor. Auntie May says the people are very nice there.'

We waited for the decision.

'If the bombing gets worse, your mother will take you down there to join your grandmother.' Uniquely among the people I knew, my father always spoke like that. He never relaxed his air of slight formality. I think he would have said that 'Speech and spelling maketh man', by which he meant that they were the big give-away. Somehow he achieved an accent balanced between the World's End and Sloane Square in which there was never a dropped 'h' or a glottal stop in sight. And his favourite spelling test for us was, 'A harassed cobbler met an embarrassed pedlar studying the symmetry of a lady in a cemetery with unparalleled ecstasy.' He could spell far above the level of his thirteen year old's education. But then I have to admit his mother, Minnie, could too.

'We'll try to stay together here in London as long as possible,' he told us. 'But it depends on the bombing.'

Unknown to us Hitler had established September 17 1940, just a week away, as the date for his invasion of Britain. Beforehand he required from Goering one more mass attack on London to reassure himself that the RAF was indeed incapable of taking to the air. On the afternoon of September 15 massed squadrons of Heinkels and Dorniers, escorted by Messerschmitts again headed for the capital.

But this time the RAF, which had been rebuilding its strength, came up to meet them. I remember the relief and excitement of the *News Chronicle*'s headline the next morning: *187 German planes shot down.*

We were ecstatic, so excited that we went running round the yard shouting the news to anyone who cared to throw open a window and ask what was happening. 187 German planes! 187 Jerries down! We gave Tarzan calls to our friends and marched through the yard singing (to the tune of 'Colonel Bogey' long before *The Bridge on the River Kwai* made it internationally famous): '*Hitler, he's only got one ball. Goering, he ain't got none at all . . . Himmler, he's very sim'lar . . .*'

It wasn't true, of course. Not the leadership's testicular status, but the pilots' reports. Young pilots exaggerate, or two or three claim the same enemy plane as it spirals smoking from their guns. The post-war figure was well under 100 German planes down, but still a much higher level than the RAF losses and representing massive pilot wastage for the Luftwaffe in a single day's warfare. Hitler knew that such losses were unsustainable. It was probably the moment when he lost confidence in Goering's dreams of air victory. We now know that it was at the end of that day that he ordered the indefinite postponement of the invasion of Britain, and switched the Luftwaffe to the destruction of civilian morale by night.

The Battle of Britain had been won. The Battle of London was about to begin.

EIGHT

Blitz

It came with a terrifying roar of gunfire from Battersea Park, the sound of bombs falling and explosions in the dark. The air raid siren, which had for the most part been signalling daylight raids, at night became the most chilling sound imaginable. Its hollow warning was of 1,000lb bombs, of baskets of incendiaries, even of sinister green parachutes, dangling their river-mines, floating silently through the night. A few weeks ago I had used this image to terrify Kit into submission on some trivial issue and now felt deeply ashamed as he kept harking back to it at the howling of the sirens.

My grandmother had been taken down to Windsor (just a bit further up the Thames from the World's End, my mother said) and was staying with our Auntie May and her six children, the family we always called collectively 'the Easts'. Although it meant there was no one to look after my brother and myself when my mother was working on Saturdays, at least she no longer had to worry about Eliza who at that time had been living in a room fifty or sixty yards away in Tadema Road opposite St John's Church.

From the first week it became clear that London by night was the main Luftwaffe target, although it is of course true that many other British cities were being heavily attacked. My father, as ever, began planning for the worst. The shelter in the yard outside our flat had become a grim, damp concrete tunnel lit by low blue lights and lined by narrow wooden three-tiered bunks with less than a shoulder's width between them. The screams of babies, the noise of younger children, the constant shuffling movement of older people in the queue for the lavatory, the heat and smell of sweat – all this made a night in the shelter a new and special kind of hell.

Ever resourceful, my father converted the bedroom of number 3 into our own shelter. The bed had a substantial frame and barred-steel support for the mattress. By inverting it, he created a shelter about two feet high. Then using thick planks nailed and bound to the top of the bed, and an additional mattress from the Put-U-Up next door, he strengthened the shelter 'roof'. My mother cut thick hessian and stuck it with carpenter's glue to the bedroom window panes. With the black-out curtain pulled to we were safe inside. We hoped.

That first night we all four crawled under the bed. There was no room for a mattress under the bed frame (no mattress to spare come to think of it) so the linoleum was covered with a blanket. My mother had a bag of biscuits for us to munch and a bottle of milk if we were thirsty. There was a packet of sandwiches for the adults when the raid began later that night. In the meantime, tea could be made in the scullery.

It was a bad night. I didn't hear the sirens but the hollow AA-gun explosions from Battersea Park brought me awake with a jolt. My father's hand was pressing down on my forehead to stop me hitting the iron struts above our heads. My mother was holding Kit down. The noise was terrifying. The windows rattled with the gunfire; the shrapnel of exploding shells snapped and ricocheted across the yard outside. Above us we could hear the throb of German engines. The bomber had arrived.

We slept very little that night. But we were up early the next morning, stretching our legs and dying for a cup of tea. It was Saturday morning, so no school. Although school had become voluntary, attendance was a hundred percent most days. This was naturally felt to be a missed opportunity by most of us. The day before, Stan Hartnell who lived next door at number 4, had told me that the Oil Shop were getting their marbles in today and I was anxious to be round there early to see if I could pick up an unusual oncer, a big gaudy marble that I could swop for several times its worth of ordinary, workaday marbles. I went out with Stan and Harold Hawthorn and headed along the block for the back gate to Bifron Street. This involved us turning the end of the block to pass the wall where we had held our marble bazaar from time immemorial. A group of kids from the buildings were there already. Some of them had marble bags in their hands.

Shock and outrage silenced me. A large crater about twenty feet wide and perhaps five feet deep had replaced our marbles pitch. A bomb had landed exactly on it. It had blown out the windows of the flat more or less corresponding to ours at the other end of the block but it hadn't torn down the brickwork. 'Must have been a titch,' one of the older boys said. 'Hundred-pounder top weight.'

It was the first High-Explosive bomb crater I had ever seen. I looked at the broad concrete slabs that had been laid to make up the yard. In the middle of the hole the slabs had simply disappeared into the hundreds of small chunks of cement we were crunching through. At the rim of the hole the broken edge of the concrete had been lifted at an angle two or three feet from the ground. A titch, a little bomb. The older boy, I think he was one of the Benjamin brothers, said they had bombs ten times as big. Even twenty times.

We gave the Oil Shop a miss that morning.

At home my mother was looking worried. Edith Grove and Dartrey Road (where La-di-dah lived) had been hit. Most worrying for her, Blantyre Street was said to have 'caught it', which was always the term used. My grandmother Minnie was away in Hemel Hempstead but my grandfather Henry James was still there. She hurried away to check on him.

So far all this was quite exciting. I felt myself to be in the middle of events, full of boyish bravado. At least, I felt like this during the day. Huddled under the upturned bed during the night with bombs, it seemed, coming ever closer, I wasn't so sure.

Saturday night and Sunday night there were more heavy raids. We were beginning to feel very short of sleep. Monday morning we made our way to school without the usual whooping or chasing after coal carts to hang on their trailing chains.

The first change was that there was to be no assembly that morning. In fact the school hall had been put out of bounds to us and plain paper was being unrolled across its windows. I could see trestle tables inside. Then, in our classroom, after register we were allowed to do drawing while our teacher kept looking out of the windows and going out to talk to the teacher next door in the corridor. We were given strict orders to stay in our seats. In particular nobody was allowed to go near the windows. Didn't worry us, we could still see Lots Road power station from our school desks.

Then, when the teacher was out on one of his frequent visits to the next class, we heard the noise of lorries outside. I was reminded of the buses on evacuation day and my heart sank. Perhaps I was first to the forbidden window, I can't remember. But I can remember the two open-back lorries parked below and, when the drivers peeled back the tarpaulins, the mummy-shaped figures shrouded in blackout cloth lined up six or eight to a lorry.

Throughout that morning we crowded to the window whenever our teacher left to speak to the one next door. There wasn't a lot of work done. Looking down we saw people come to the entrance under our window. Most of the women wiped their eyes as they passed under us. We went home for dinner and announced, with that deep satisfaction you get from riveting an adult's attention, that they had been filling the school hall with dead people all morning.

*

The tiredness was beginning to tell on all of us. We still went to school. My mother went to work at the shop. My father stoked the boilers at Whitelands House. But in the month after the beginning of the night raids there was no single night without interrupted sleep, without thunderous explosions, without real rather than cinematic danger. There were crisis nights. I can see from the records that October 14 was one of them. That night the sirens opened up at about eleven. Within minutes, it seemed, the German bombers were overhead. Guns and bombs exploded together. One bomb was loud enough to make our block shake. I could hear screams outside on the stairway and my father got out to let Kitty Corfield and her son, my friend Billy, into the flat. They lived on the top floor and before they could get out of their flat, they had seen Watney's bottling plant in Fernshaw Road take a bomb somewhere at the back.

Somehow, we all huddled under the bed. There was also a big fire burning behind Guinness Trust. It might have been, Mrs Corfield thought, St John's Church where my brother and I were christened. The next night it was the same. Hudson's Furniture Depository, about fifty yards down the King's Road, went first, then during the night bombs fell on Stamford Bridge, Lots Road, Edith Grove, Fernshaw Road, Upcerne, Meek and Tetcott Roads.

The next night was the worst night of the blitz for us. World's End was hit heavily for the third night running. To us, it seemed like a hail of bombs: Lots Road, Upcerne Road, Meek Road and Tetcott Road again. At about two o'clock, as the raid intensified, my father decided our improvised shelter was not good enough. We should run for the public shelter below the concrete of the yard. We left the flat and shivered, despite the blankets wrapped round us, in the entrance to the block. The sky was alight with lightning flashes, criss-crossing searchlights and red and white flares. Anti-aircraft batteries all around us boomed their unique hollow echoing thunder. I could hear aircraft engines. I looked at my parents, at Kit. Under the kaleidoscope of light in the sky their faces seemed to change colour every second as we huddled just thirty yards from the shelter entrance. Then, at a word from my father, we ran for the steps. In the open I felt exposed as if I were running naked in a dream. Urged on by my mother we ran down the steps and hammered on the shelter door.

It was dragged open. Inside, the low blue lights cast frightening shadows. Everybody was wide awake. We crowded on to two empty bunks and lay there while the ground shook from a bomb in Edith Grove and another in Slaidburn Street, not eighty yards from the window of the bedroom where we had been sheltering.

That night Guinness Trust Buildings received its second bomb of the war, again a fairly small High-Explosive, again falling relatively harmlessly, if noisily, in the yard clear of the flats or shelters themselves. Even so the crater was six or seven feet deep. If it had struck the shelter, it might easily have proved powerful enough to have burst through the reinforced concrete of the roof.

Dirty, still sweating from the humid underground atmosphere, we came back to the flat about six in the morning with the All Clear. Sitting round the scullery table still wrapped in our blankets, we drank tea and waited for my father to come back with his damage report from the bomb on the far side of Block 4. When he joined us in the scullery he had talked with the Air Raid Wardens. If any connecting section of the shelter had received a direct hit the blast would have travelled sufficient distance in the confined space to have killed most of the people inside. We must find a safer night-shelter if we were going to stay in London. He had in mind Whitelands House, his workplace in Sloane Square.

NINE

Whitelands House

Whitelands is a name almost as old as Chelsea itself, derived from the medieval White Friars' ownership of land to the south of what became the King's Road. Whitelands College, a teachers' training school for women, occupied part of the land in the early-twentieth century but had moved to Putney in 1933, leaving the building temporarily empty. Within a year it attained notoriety when Oswald Moseley rented it for his Blackshirt headquarters. In the early-thirties two men with polished jackboots, black jodhpurs and black rollneck sweaters stood permanent guard outside. William Joyce, later to be known as Lord Haw-Haw when he broadcast from wartime Berlin, worked as Propaganda Director from there and was a familiar figure in Chelsea at that time when he aspired to be its MP. Whitelands, just west of Sloane Square, was of course very conveniently placed for a march down the King's Road and a rally at the World's End and presumably accounts for the frequency with which Moseley and his lieutenants (like Nancy Mitford's husband and William Joyce), visited our area, to a good deal of muscle-flexing but little or no political avail. When the new king, George VI, ascended to the throne in 1937 the Coronation celebrations were enthusiastically received in Guinness Trust and, indeed, the whole of the World's

End. There were innumerable children's parties and, for us, a fancy dress competition. I had a yellow blouse of my mother's and a spotted red bandanna tied round my head. I didn't imagine I was in for a prize from the judges when I had to explain to all my friends that I was 'a Hungarian gypsy, of course'. I had no chance against the boy who had covered himself in brown boot polish and had a straw skirt and a bamboo stick with a bit of shaped plasticine on the end for a spear. The Zulu warrior won.

Kit was dressed as a clown and pulled off a second prize in the younger children's division. But it was a great day with every child getting a mug and a Coronation spoon and iced cakes for tea. Union Jacks waved. *Poor but Loyal!* the hand-made banners read with a suitable touch of schmaltz for the occasion. There was no sign of a Blackshirt in the World's End that day.

Although the Blackshirts did not lack support in the upper reaches of Chelsea, they soon moved on. The Black House was to be demolished and on its site, some would think not entirely inappropriately, Whitelands House, a new block of expensive flats, was erected. Here, my father was employed first as a plumber, then stoker two years before war began.

The Whitelands House position ended a period of shortage and uncertainty for the family. The four years from 1933 were not one unbroken stretch of unemployment for my father. There were dozens of short-term jobs, like his spell in the mortuary or chimney-building in Kensington, but the erratic flow of work, the impossibility of budgeting, the total absence of any money at all some days, placed a great strain on my parents and I'm sure many other parents throughout the World's End. Christmas was the hardest time for them, and the Christmas of 1935 the hardest of all. There had been no casual work for several weeks. The twenty-one shillings dole money paid the rent, fed the gas meter and bought some, not enough, coal. My grandmother's pension might have yielded a shilling more and my mother's half-sister May would pass her a shilling on Fridays whenever she could possibly spare it. Beyond that, there was no work, nothing to sell. There was no other source of income.

Then on Christmas Eve, a couple of hours before Thwaites' the butcher's auctioned off the last of their meat at midnight, there was a knock on the door. When my mother opened it there was no one there. I know it sounds a bit like Bing Crosby playing the priest in *Going My Way* but somebody had dropped a ten-shilling note in the letterbox. To the end of his life my father was visibly moved when he talked of that Christmas. On Christmas Eve, shops were open later than the pubs. The ten shillings was enough for him to buy something for my mother, a toy for Kit and myself, snuff for my grandmother, and still make it to the auction for a piece of beef.

There was no way of knowing who had dropped the ten-shilling note in the door. Just possibly Mr Newson, the local curate, but we were not churchgoers and he was, in any case, likely to have made it clear the money was from the church. Nobody within the family was even remotely a candidate for having ten shillings to spare that Christmas. It was a mystery I believe my father long pondered out of sheer gratitude. Oddly, in the end, he came down to believing it was the ferocious Superintendent Caple. And I'm not sure that's too far off the mark.

The new permanent job dispelled the uncertainties of a difficult period. Whitelands was now a word we heard daily. Perhaps because of the way my mother and father regarded it, it had a magical, a cornucopian, ring to me. At this time my brother and I had never been to my father's workplace, although on forays up the King's Road we had seen ahead of us the big, new brick building that seemed to hang over the Sloane Square end. Anatole France in his childhood memoir speaks of the days when walks with his nurse used to take him to the Champs Elysées. From there, marvelling at the way the Arc de Triomphe filled the view beyond, he would invest it with special significance. He would imagine that if he could scale it he would find the seaside sparkling on the other side. When I was much younger, possibly even before my father worked there, Whitelands House was invested with a similar significance by me. It barred the road to the seaside we had never visited. But here our paths diverge. Anatole France called his book *Le Livre de Mon Ami* and saw the child of his childhood as a separate being. A young friend whom he knew well but whom, as an adult, he could never quite touch, however hard he reached out. If I understand him, what he is feeling as he looks back is an intense pity for the child he was and regret that he is unable to step back in time to help that child out of his isolation. The Arc de Triomphe, stripped of its historical significance, is for Anatole France a symbol of his own unhappy childhood.

I find no such distance between me now and me then, when I think back. The nine-year-old boy trying to pretend he is not shivering with fear under the upturned bed is not some young friend, it is me. (It is I, I suppose I should say, but then old habits die hard. I still can't bear to pronounce *nougat* any other way but *nugget*. Liquorice just has to be *likrish*).

This sense of a single identity, this lack of distance between myself and the past, this absence of aloneness, I observe to some degree in all the more recent members of my family. It is strong in my brother and his sons, in my two daughters and in their children. I feel sure it is the result, in some sense, of the way we were bound together by the tribal values my mother gave us and helped us pass down to the two generations that have followed. When you factor in my father's contribution, (not that many of his values would qualify under the general heading of morality) they make for a strong, although I think not aggressive, belief in ourselves and our call upon each other. There is more than one way of being born with a silver spoon in your mouth.

In Whitelands House all the tenants had known the taste of silver from birth. They were, like any group of beings in some sort of

authority, a mix of benign and insufferable. But over my father, both
the benign and the insufferable held a power unknown to them. He
was still, at this stage, the stoker, and still awaiting his call-up papers.
There is a definite mystery here. Perhaps one connived at by the
owners of Whitelands House. I know that a request had been made
for deferment on the grounds that my father was making an
important contribution to the war effort. This argument was based
first on the grounds that there were several very senior civil servants,
some government junior ministers and a sprinkling of generals living
in the block. Indeed, the Parachute General, 'Boy' Browning, who
later planned Arnhem, lived there with his wife Daphne du Maurier,
as did Lady Ritchie, the wife of one of the commanders in North
Africa, General Sir Neil Ritchie. Should the six massive coke boilers
explode through accident or act of war, it was argued, the effect on
national morale would be serious. My father, it was further stated,
was the only man to keep the boilers running safely. This, we think,
might just possibly have kept him from being called up. On the other
hand, at his army medical he had been graded 4F because of a near-
fatal peritonitis, badly resewn, in his late teens. This equally could
have been the reason. But if anybody in authority had put the two
together it seems reasonable that they might have asked how a man
with the lowest army medical grade was fit enough to rake clean and
stoke these massive furnaces? Or alternatively, if the man was fit
enough to do it, as he demonstrably was, how then had he been
passed 4F?

It was a mystery (if it was indeed entirely a mystery to him) which
my father was definitely content not to solve.

Now began a new-after school routine. At about five o'clock we had
tea. My mother had opened one of the giant tins of Spam and my
brother and I were happily obliged to eat Spam fritters and fried
potatoes for our tea every evening. We would already have savoured
Spam and potato pie for our lunchtime dinner and almost certainly

Spam for breakfast. With no refrigerator it was a race between consumption and degeneration.

My father came in at about six and had his tea of Spam fritters. By now it had been dark an hour or so and we hurried. Spam sandwiches were made by my father, blankets collected by us and packed in two suitcases by my mother. We would leave home about seven o'clock.

If there was no warning we would try to catch an 11 or 22 bus. This we succeeded in doing most nights. But if the sirens had already sounded, the buses, though still running, were few and far between. It's roughly a mile between the World's End and Sloane Square. We probably walked no more than a dozen times but they were the blackest of nights. October, November, December 1940. A car was a rarity and, with its headlights obscured, was visibly only as a pair of slitted eyes moving slowly past. The rumour was that you could be hanged for attacking anyone or looting in the blackout and I found that a comfort as we straggled along the King's Road, a little river mist rolling up from the Thames to remind me of my grandmother's Jack the Ripper stories. During these walks I developed several ingenious plans (or so they seemed to me) to catch him. The fact that he was by then certainly approaching a hundred or long dead was of no concern to me.

But if the night's raid was anywhere near Chelsea I had no time for thoughts of Jack the Ripper. Then the blackout would suddenly be punctured by multiple flashes of gunfire layering the sky with light, by the frightening hollow clatter of the heavy guns in Battersea Park, and sometimes by the rattle of red-hot shrapnel dancing along the pavement beside us. On such a night we would take cover for a few minutes, then hurry on another thirty yards before ducking into the next doorway. High in the sky there would be that unmistakable deep throb of bomber engines and the searchlights would spring out of nowhere and perhaps a German would be caught in the crossfire of light, twisting and turning as the flak exploded around him. Bombs would fall, but not for us.

We travelled swiftly through the darkness, my father carrying both bags. His energy and concern for us combined to propel him along at a pace we couldn't easily match. I suppose he was afraid, too. Sometimes, if the bombers seemed to be directly overhead, he would carry Kit, my mother would carry one case, I the other, and we would scuttle from one doorway to another towards Sloane Square. I remember one night when we were all four pressed deep into the doorway of the pawnshop, bombers somewhere overhead, the constant clatter of gunfire drowning out the sounds of separate explosions, when suddenly a stick of bombs came screaming down. It was as if all other sounds had merged into the background. Despite the common belief that you never heard the one with your name on it, we were all four convinced these were for us. I can't remember ever having heard bombs fitted with screamers before but I was rigid with terror as they seemed to come straight down on us. Then in a great rush of sound they passed over our heads, the screaming died away and they exploded one after the other somewhere in Battersea. Despite the noise of the guns it seemed, for a few seconds, as if silence had descended on the King's Road. Dazed, we gathered ourselves together and began again to run towards Whitelands House.

Perhaps these details seem barely relevant now. They're not the stuff of recorded history, and as moments in a life recalled they'll soon enough disappear. But in that black street, with the huge hollow crash of gunfire and the throbbing aircraft and the crossing searchlights, we seemed to be running towards Sloane Square played along by some crazed orchestra in the skies. How could the swinging sixties or the punk eighties even imagine *their* glittering King's Road on such a night as this?

Why did we not go earlier? Leave our home shortly after it grew dark, before the sirens opened up as they did fifty-seven nights running in that winter of 1940/1? Because it was my father's workplace and officially we weren't allowed to shelter there. Every occupant of a building at that time had to be identified and reported to the local Air Raid Wardens, for rescue purposes. Besides, some of the tenants of Whitelands House, although most certainly not all, would have objected to the stoker sheltering his family in the boiler room. Only by sneaking us in, unseen by anyone but the friendly night porter, through the darkened hallway and across to the door leading down to the boiler room, could my father be sure not to offend any of the tenants. Even at that stage, he believed his job depended on it.

That boiler room is not easy to describe. To begin with it was really several rooms, beginning with one under a huge coal-hole through which untold tons of coke had been poured, forming grey dusty slopes that looked more geological than utilitarian. There were several smaller rooms off this coke store full of floating dust and grime and each lit by shadeless electric bulbs. My father had a small changing room with a single-tap sink in one of them. His boiler suits and tattered undervests hung on hooks there. An old pair of shapeless ammunition boots sat below them, and a copy of the *Sporting Life* with yesterday's racing results marked up.

My father gambled very little but he was deeply interested in racing: in odds, in probability, in form. He had an unusually quick mind for figures. Perhaps today he would have been one of those young cockney men recruited to deal from dollars to pounds to euros to pesos at the nod of a head in the City of London. Not then.

The main boiler room, or more properly furnace room, was perhaps forty-five feet long and at least as deep. It was approached down a short Art Deco open stairway. Two eighteen-foot-long, drum-shaped water tanks stood on short brick supports. They were covered in black-painted asbestos and held an array of dials like something from a ship's engine room. The centrepiece, of course, was the furnaces themselves. They were called, inaccurately, the boilers, six iron monsters about six feet across and some twelve deep.

There were four blazing at any one time, two to be lit on any shift and two to be raked out of their white-hot solid coke.

The pokers with which this lava clinker was broken up, and the rakes to drag the hot coals out into a spluttering, face-burning heap in front of the furnace door, were of solid iron, three-quarters of an inch thick and fourteen feet long. Later in my life I worked as a boilerman down there myself in long vacations, so these dimensions aren't just the product of a child's exaggerated memory.

Ushered across the thick-carpeted hall with my father anxiously watching the lifts for any tenant to appear, we would pass through the equivalent of the green baize door and descend into this hell-hole of heat and glowing furnaces and swirling coke dust. It wasn't, by any twenty-first century perception, a healthy environment, but it was safe. And although my mother, Kit and I hated the dirt and dust, I think my father was deeply satisfied to have found us a bomb-proof shelter.

We slept on a concrete landing, thick with coke dust, about the size of two double beds. Each night my mother would cover the landing with copies of the *Sporting Life* and *News Chronicle*. There was little point in trying to sweep the coke dust from the landing first. In that bone-dry atmosphere it hung in the air. We'd be choked before we settled down to sleep. A blanket underneath us and one on top made the bed, rolled up coats our pillows. Kit and I would eat sandwiches and read comics and my parents would sit up in bed drinking tea and talking. Every so often my father would disappear for fire-fighting duties on a rota I didn't understand.

Mornings were waking with eyes full of coke grit, faces comically blackened, the dust itching in your shirt like a thousand fleas. Usually, we would leave with my mother. Sometimes if we had overslept my father would be about to start the early-morning rake-out and refill of the furnaces. This was the equal of any scene from the ship's boiler room in *The Cruel Sea*. He would be wearing his overalls, belted at the waist so that the top flapped down, a dirty and

sweat-stained singlet and the heavy ammunition boots. All movement for him was an impressive display of quickness and decision,
but work lay in a different category. He attacked the task before him
with ferocious energy, his face reddening alarmingly, sweat flying off
him in great droplets.

The first morning task was to light the two reserve boilers. This
involved opening a burning furnace and confronting the blaze of
heat perhaps four feet away while you wielded first the huge poker to
break up the clinker, then the heavy rake to pull it out, glowing and
spitting and jumping at your feet. The second stage, shovelling this
white-hot mass into an empty boiler and hurling hundredweights of
fresh coke on top of it, had to be achieved at speed. When the new
coke caught, a pale blue flame would flicker like marsh gas across the
surface of the black mass and the iron door of the boiler would be
flung to. Thereafter glowing clinker would be shovelled away and
watered down in a ferocious hissing of steam and the remaining
boilers filled with coke.

My father never rested between boilers. When he had lit the
second, he moved on immediately to raking and reloading the
remaining boilers with coke. Whenever, in our late-teenage years, my
brother or I helped him, working in that heat and at that manic speed
left us stepping back from the completed job with legs shaking, arm
muscles aching beyond the possibility of lifting another shovel load
of coke, and feeling certain that we had sweated off a significant part
of our body weight.

The heat, the sudden belching flame from an open boiler and the
clouds of coke dust swirling round the bare electric lights are the
things I best remember from those nights spent in the boiler room.
They made me ask myself again why we slept in this extraordinary
place and then answer myself with recollections of the times we spent
cowering under the bed or sweating in the concrete corridor of the
shelter at Guinness. Later in the war when the flying bombs and V2
rockets were sent to plague us, my mother, Kit and myself spent

nights sleeping on the platform of the Underground at Lancaster Gate. This was safe and relatively comfortable, if noisy from the passing trains, and happily crowded with generous young GIs who, while eyeing the half-dressed girls, handed out their chocolate and Hollywood chewing gum to every child supplicant.

Each morning that winter we would sneak out of Whitelands House, my mother having made an effort to clean up her face for the bus ride back to the World's End, my brother and I less scrupulous about our appearance. The King's Road would already be busy with women queuing at the local shops. Sainsbury's, opposite Whitelands, would have a mixed queue of maids, from households where they still existed, and mistresses where they existed no longer. Unless there were still a fire burning and a drift of smoke across the Duke of York's parade ground, there might well be no sign of last night's raid. Once, I remember, after a bad night of thunderous explosions, our number 11 bus was diverted from the King's Road where a water main had been hit, into the backstreets towards the river. It had snowed heavily overnight and the side streets were still carpeted. Somewhere near Chelsea Old Church we stopped for a few minutes while a lorry negotiated a narrow turning. Kit and I sprawled sleepily in the front top seats which were always our favourite places, but I could see my mother was anxious to get back to the World's End to see if there had been any bombing there.

In front of us was a bombed house, the roof half-collapsed, the still-furnished bedrooms visible. Perhaps it had been bombed that night. Under a covering of snow it was impossible to say. But blast had carried off a bright red bedspread and draped it round a cupboard. The time of year, the covering of snow, the red robe, all dispelled the experiences of the night and comforted me with thoughts of Father Christmas.

That memory of a few moments staring from the front of a bus stays with me. But then I was a child, and interpreted what I saw as a child. Now what I find striking about that scene is the way in which snow absorbs violence as easily as it absorbs sound.

I was about to write that up to the time of these visits to Whitelands House I had no sense of class difference, but I'm not sure that's so. Every child at Ashburnham knew there was a difference between the teachers and our own parents. This would partly be evident in the way they dressed, or more particularly in the way the men dressed. Mr Whitehead, for instance, always wore a suit with waistcoat and watch chain. The other teachers at the elementary school wore suits which were quite shabby, but suits nevertheless. Our fathers wore work clothes, and most of them (my father was the exception) kept them on throughout the evening. Differences between the women could be equally noticeable. The young teachers were clearly better turned out than many of the older mothers whose bandannas tied round the head disguised their unattended hair and whose lisle stockings were either rolled down to the ankles or allowed to droop towards the plimsolls which were the favoured footwear.

All children knew that teachers were posher than we or our parents were, just as we knew that the doctor was posh. In fact, doctors were especially posh. When giving us our annual examination for symptoms of the widely prevalent TB, the school doctor would always address the child's mother, not by her name, but haughtily as 'Mother'. As in, 'You need to make sure this lad drinks more milk, Mother.'

And, of course, a doctor's word was law. It was a law particularly respected when death from diphtheria or TB was, if not common, most certainly not unknown among us. Our small friend Arthur Fox, blond, round-faced and healthy, had died in what seemed no time from TB. Kit himself had contracted diphtheria and survived after six weeks fighting for his life in an isolation hospital at Tooting Bec. He came home white-faced and shy but within a week was chasing me round the kitchen table with a sprat.

At Whitelands House I rarely saw a tenant, though sometimes there would be a glimpse of a couple walking through the hall and I might hear a few words as we pressed back into the shadows waiting for my father to unlock the door down to the boiler room. But I soon understood from the heated luxury in which these people seemed to live, by the panelled entrance hall, the thick pink carpet, the deep sofas, the porters ready to carry bags or leap forward to open the lift, and most of all by the tone in which my father spoke of them, that they occupied some plane considerably above the level of the doctor. What plane or level *I* occupied, I hadn't yet begun to ask.

Researching this book, I came upon a curious untitled newspaper cutting in Chelsea Library. Its tone suggests that it is not from the local *Chelsea News*. Perhaps it was the *Daily Mirror* or the *Daily Herald*.

Now at the other end of Chelsea, in green squares, are large mansions left empty – solid houses that stand up (I've seen them) even when bombs drop very near. I made a mild suggestion that someone ought to get at these stately front doors with an axe and make room for those who needed shelter.

That's exactly what they're doing in Chelsea now. They're turning the (vast) basements of these empty houses into dormitories.

'Do we consult the owners?' says the Town Hall. 'We do not. We haven't time.' Lorries are to collect the bedding of those in the small streets of Chelsea's Vulnerable Area and a space will be marked out for Mrs Smith or Mrs Jones every night. The Town Clerk of Chelsea told me this. With a blind eye to red tape he has opened the houses of Chelsea's rich to those of Chelsea who need them.

Two things struck me about the piece. One, that these were the acts of a Conservative council. Two, that the mention of Chelsea's Vulnerable Area suggests the Town Clerk had more knowledge of the Luftwaffe's intentions towards Lots Road power

station than was ever passed on to anybody living in the World's
End at the time.

One morning, a few days before Christmas, we caught the number
11 from Whitelands as usual and struggled off with our cases at the
World's End. My mother talked to another woman while we watched
La-di-dah running about the island like some demented Norman
Wisdom as he sold his morning papers. Walking back towards
Guinness Trust my mother told us about last night's raid. There
would be no more school, she said, at least not at Ashburnham. An
HE bomb had demolished part of Upcerne Road and badly damaged
our school. We were to receive temporary schooling starting the day
after next at Park Walk or St Mark's Elementary. The LCC would
decide which.

    The Luftwaffe, we concluded with the callousness of young boys,
had its uses after all.

The raids continued. Our life of hauling cases, coke-dust, noise, fear
and boredom continued with them. But, unknown to us, some
difficulty with our overnight stays at Whitelands had developed. It
was enough to convince my father that my mother, brother and
myself should leave London. One of the tenants, Captain Fitzgerald,
jauntily elegant, late of the Guards, now bowler-hatted, had seen us
sneaking down to the boiler room and mentioned it to the manager.
In early 1941 we set out on our second, unofficial evacuation. But
this time we were to be going, not to the country suburbs of London
but to the real countryside, to live with an illiterate poacher and his
gypsy wife in deepest Berkshire.

TEN

Royal Windsor

We called it Windsor because the people around us called it Windsor although, in truth, we were seven or so miles distant, and where we were to live was closer to Maidenhead and the riverside village of Bray. Idyllic, you'll say, Olde England. *Three Men in a Boat* territory. And some of it was like that.

Our Auntie May East and her children together with grandmother Eliza had been billeted with a Mrs Keene in Monkey Island Lane in the village of Fifield.

It was of course only twenty-eight miles from the World's End but the sense of entering into real country soon after leaving the great castle at Windsor was immediate and alarming. To begin with there were woods and fields. To continue, there were people working in these fields, men, women and frequently children, digging out and picking up lumps of mud and putting them in sacks. My mother said she thought they were potatoes. There was a bus on which we travelled but it was coloured a green-grey, not London red as all real buses should be. We were used to complaining bitterly about the numbers 11 and 22 on the King's Road if we had more than three or four minutes to wait but these country buses ran *once a day* from Windsor to Maidenhead and back.

I seem to remember we camped with Auntie May at Monkey Island Lane for a few days before my mother was able to make other arrangements for us with the billeting office in Maidenhead. With the limited bus service available this was not easily done but finally her request was accepted. We were to get in touch initially with someone named Dimple Soden and his newly married wife Mollie at a place called Walter Oakley. He would show us the two rooms the billeting officer had arranged for us.

Since it was by the river and was always pronounced *Water* Oakley, I imagined it as a small Thames-side hamlet, a word I knew from the comics. I seem to remember Kit and I were neither excited nor cast down by the prospect of being in the country for a while. The overwhelmingly important fact to both of us was that we had our mother with us. But my guess, too, is that by this point in the war we were all too worn out by our constant evening travels up and down the King's Road, by the dust and sleeplessness of nights in the Whitelands boiler room, and by the emotional onslaught of sudden rushes of fear in London, to be anything but quietly pleased by the prospect of a real bed in a quiet room. For a few days anyway.

Over sandwiches with my cousins I picked up a more informed version of what Walter Oakley might be like. There was, it appeared, a large house more or less by the roadside, the length of five normal houses and shaped, everyone seemed to agree, like a church. In fact, it turned out to be five separate cottages. This setting for our life for the next few months would have fascinated me even more than the prospect of living in a church had I realised that Bray Film Studios and the romantically decrepit Oakley Court, the location of the post-war Hammer House of Horror films, was not more than a hundred or so yards from us down the river lane.

And then there was Dimple Soden. Of course Kit and I laughed a lot at the name. My grandmother Eliza, who was coming with us, said she thought Dimple would be a rich old gentleman with bandy legs, married to the young and beautiful Lady Mollie. 'Ever-open flies,' she said mysteriously, gave us a wink and said they were like that in the country. She remembered from when she was a girl in service.

Dirty business, I thought. Perhaps, at last, I was really going to find out what it was.

There was an important moment the morning before we went to inspect our new Walter Oakley quarters. Important for me because it opened a new door. I had lived all my life in others' company, mostly of course my brother's. Far from objecting to this, I relied on his continual presence as one of the building blocks of my life. I had never had a room of my own, or a cupboard, or even a drawer. Kit neither. We simply didn't understand that other people, including children, could command luxuries which even the adults in our own family lacked. I'm not aware, in fact, of having had any friends who had rooms of their own. Sleeping in the same room as a grandmother was natural enough. Everybody shared.

Lebensraum was not, of course, a term I was yet familiar with, but the idea of personal space, the pre-condition of aloneness, was about to enter my world as a desirable commodity. The eldest of the East family, Margaret (or Peggy to most of us), was at an age just short of call-up and had volunteered for a short period in the Women's Land Army before beginning training in the VAD, a specialist naval nursing unit. Her Land Army assignment had been to the White Lady Poultry Farm at Fifield Corner. Her boss there was a cultured man who, I seem to remember, had suffered some permanent neurasthenic injury after years of trench warfare in the last war.

Peggy herself had suffered an injury as a girl, losing a kidney after a fall down a flight of stairs at Ashburnham, but she had successfully concealed this from the medical board and had been accepted as fit for service anywhere in the world. She was a young woman of strong convictions and determined to play a real part in this war.

For reasons long lost, I went with her to deliver some report on the chickens to her boss the morning before we went to Walter Oakley. He lived in a four-bedroomed, mock-Tudor house built not more than ten or twelve years earlier. He smoked a pipe and wore a long cardigan and spoke in one of those voices we seldom referred to but nevertheless recognised as posh, perhaps not quite Whitelands posh, but posh all the same. He was a kindly man who clearly liked Peggy and he led us through the hall into his sitting room, saying it would be more comfortable than his study.

My cousin and her employer went over the report together at a desk under a bay window while I stood and let my eyes wander. It was the first time I had ever been in a house like this. There was carpet, not lino, on the floor. Carpet that went right up to the walls on either side with no twelve-inch gap. And wallpaper. No worry about bugs here. There were white-painted double doors leading out to a garden with a round table and chairs, and shrubs and bushes bordering a lawn.

The room we were in was the size of four of our front rooms at Guinness put together. It had strange black wooden beams holding up the ceiling, but I was much more taken by a simple fact which I have used to assess the desirability of rooms throughout the rest of my life. Facing the fire was a large pale green sofa with two armchairs set at right angles to it. I'd certainly seen sofas before, though rarely and usually in the form of a Rexine Put-U-Up extra bed as we had at home. This sofa was bigger, grander and newer. But what was most important to me was its position. It stood in front of the fire *but not against the back wall of the room*. In other words, between the back of the sofa and the wall there was plenty of room to walk. There was even a small dark brown table there holding a lamp with a tasselled shade and a picture of a young woman in a silver frame. While my cousin and the man bent over their papers I slowly circled the sofa, trailing my fingertips along its rounded back, across its scrolled arms.

I looked up and saw to my horror that the man had turned from the report and was lifting his glasses high on to his forehead. I stopped dead.

'I'm sorry, old, chap,' he said. 'You've been good enough to come over with Margaret and I'm ignoring you. Now, in the kitchen you'll find cakes my wife made this morning in the cake-tin, and fresh-made lemonade in the fridge. Glass in the cupboard next to it. Help yourself, all right?'

I was struck down with fear. A fridge in the kitchen? I'd never seen a fridge before, certainly never opened one. Whenever Laurel and Hardy did it the whole lot always fell out and shattered on the kitchen floor. And what if I couldn't reach the glass in the cupboard? I couldn't climb up and get it. So I said no, thanks. I said I wasn't hungry. I said I wasn't thirsty. I said five or six other things that probably had nothing to do with the man's kind offer. I wanted to bolt like a frightened horse.

Peggy came to my rescue. She was wearing her Land Army uniform: jodhpurs, Aertex shirt and green sweater. 'Hopping about like that,' she said briskly, 'you want to go, don't you?' She turned to the man. 'Can I show him where it is?'

'Of course,' he said easily and went back to the report.

On the stairs, I hissed angrily at Peggy that I didn't want to go. But she opened a door, said, 'Well, you might as well now you're here,' and pushed me forward, slamming the door behind me.

I had never been in a real bathroom before. It was tiled in white halfway up the wall and contained a long open-topped bath with taps, a basin to match and a lavatory with a white seat. I drew a breath sharply. Standing in the middle of the room, I allowed my eyes to travel slowly over the whiteness of everything, the perfection.

I had no intention of using the lavatory, I would burst before I did. My plan, developed on the spot, was to pull the chain so that downstairs Peggy would hear and not get on to me, asking if I'd forgotten to flush.

I reached up. But there was *no chain*.

There was just no chain. Worse than that, there was no cistern attached to the ceiling. I was baffled. More than baffled. Alarmed. But under the basin there was an empty flowerpot-shaped thing and I had an immediate wheeze which would solve my problem and produce the sound of rushing water for those below. I took the pot and filled it with water from the bath tap and carried it across to the lavatory. Half-way there I learnt that flowerpots have holes in the bottom. I had trailed puddles of water, greenish in colour from some residue in the pot, all over the floor. I was struck by a sense of real disaster. I had desecrated the bathroom of the manager of the White Lady Poultry Farm.

Refilling the pot, this time with my thumb firmly over the treacherously placed hole, I slopped through the water on the floor and lifted the double seat of the lavatory. Hurling the water into it I achieved what seemed a convincing enough sluicing sound, then turned to the problem of the floor. My heart was thudding in my chest. Taking off my grey flannel shirt, I used the shirt tails to sop up the water, wringing it out over the basin. But it wasn't enough. Now I needed a dry cloth to finish it off. Taking off my vest, I got down on my knees, terrified someone would come to the unlocked door. Then sweeping the singlet back and forth across the tile-patterned floor, I took up the rest of the water. For three minutes of panic it wasn't a bad job.

I put the vest back on, cold and wet against my chest. I put the shirt back on, the thick flannel shirt-tails horribly clammy against my waist. I stood for a moment checking that all was as I'd found it. My eyes reached the lavatory. And there, on the side of a boxed-in compartment which must have been the cistern, was a handle. Not a chain, a handle! It took less than genius to guess what it operated but it was all too late.

Looking back on this visit to a middle-class world, it was not my embarrassment at being offered cake and lemonade, or my mad scramble to clear up the bathroom floor, that stays with me most potently. What at least *became* important was the feeling I had had about the positioning of that sofa in the room below. Of course it's possible to say I had been seduced by my first glimpse of gracious living, but I felt nothing as crude as envy. I tried to imagine this man living in this spacious house with countless bedrooms opening off the upstairs landing, three or four at least. And I knew he lived here with only his wife! The kitchen with its fridge, the bathroom and enormous front room with double doors leading on to a sunlit garden – yes, they impressed me. But what I also carried away, however vaguely, was the sense that such space meant freedom. He didn't have to wash in the scullery sink as my father did, with my mother frying kippers in the same room. He had places he could sit in and be alone: the study he had mentioned when we had arrived, the garden. Working-class life is one in which you are always subject to the demands of other people by the simple fact of their proximity. These people may well be people you love, people you couldn't live without, but in that narrow existence they are inescapable. And sometimes we all need that escape, or need to learn the need for that escape. Perhaps the White Lady Poultry Farm manager in his commodious house never achieved those periods of aloneness that I imagined him enjoying. But when we left that day I strongly felt he did. And I wanted, sometime, to be like him.

At eleven years old I left that house filled not with thoughts but images. As Peggy and I walked back through Fifield village to Monkey Island Lane, the principal one I carried away was of the pale green sofa standing free in what was very nearly the middle of the room. That, and the kindness of the man.

It was time to go and see Dimple Soden. We approached Walter Oakley on foot along the mile-long road from Monkey Island Lane. It was, as described by Auntie May, a distinctly church-shaped building set back sixty or seventy yards from the virtually unused main road and approached by a sandy lane which brought you to the far side of the structure. It was not as large as I had thought at first sight but its central point towered like a steeple above its two wings by virtue of a sharply counter-pitched roof.

It was built of aged red brick, with a decoration of Victorian Tudor blue-brick diagonals. It might have housed an Oxbridge college library designed by Waterhouse, Barnes Railway station circa 1899, or an unusually elaborate early water pumping station at Sutton Coldfield. From the front it didn't look too bad. Old-fashioned but exciting.

We approached slowly along the main Windsor Road. My grandmother was suffering pains in her chest and, as usual, passing them off by pretending she needed to take a dip from her twist of snuff or to 'just sit down and rest me legs'. I stayed with her when we found a bit of a wall to sit on. The others (Peggy and another cousin had volunteered to help carry our cases) continued slowly towards the entrance to the sandy lane.

My mother had been saying that the sugar ration was to be decreased and this had clearly turned my grandmother's mind, as almost anything did, towards an incident in the past.

'Sugar.' She shook her head. 'Can't get along without a bit a' sugar in your tea, can you, Dee?'

I was looking round at the wide fields freshly ploughed for spring planting.

'I remember the last lot,' my grandmother mused (she meant the Great War). 'When I worked in Londonderry House for a month or two. On Park Lane, that was. Up West. Piccadilly way.'

I nodded though I'd never been there. 'What sort of work?' I asked.

'At Londonderry House? Cook. No, well, under-cook.' A nudge. 'Quite a way under the cook if the truth was known. More under the butler. Hard to get a job like that those days.' A wink and a pause for a deep sniff of snuff. '1918,' she said, 'March, April. The war wasn't six months off the finish. But nobody knew that yet. And Ole Jerry was giving us the hiding of our life. But we clung on, love. We always do.' She wiped the snuff from under her nostril. Most of it. 'Don't try and muck about with the British, you'd think Ole Jerry'd learnt that by now. You might come off best at first – matter of fact, you *will* come off best at first, look at the last one – but Gawd help you when it comes to the finish. There's a lesson old Hitler's still got to come.'

'So what happened at his Londonderry House?' I pressed, eager for her not to launch into her familiar diatribe against Hitler and his responsibility for us being 'stranded in the middle of nowhere'.

She removed the pin and adjusted her hat. 'That last year of the war, that was a bad year for food. Rationing for most things, and they didn't allow you two penn'orth of anything, anyway. But in Londonderry House they was living off the fat of the land. Had everything down there in the kitchens. Bacon, jam, sugar, lard. In the World's End there was nothing. So what did I do?'

'What did you do?'

'I nicked some.'

'You did?'

'Sugar. There'd just been a delivery from Harrods or somewhere. They had it, you see. And the sack split. I think my friend the butler slipped the ole sharpened fruit knife in. He carried one in the blackout. I think he did it a' purpose. Anyways, whichever way up that partic'lar penny falls, the bag split open and the sugar comes poring out like Niagara.' She winced a little as the angina tightened before it began to fade. Then she smiled. 'I got the lion's share 'cause I'd seen the flicker of the knife. And maybe, truth to tell, I'd had a wink from him just beforehand. Eitherways, I was there with a flour sack scooping up enough for half the World's End.'

'Did anybody find out?'

She paused. 'Well, yes and no. 'S a buggar of a walk, you know, Piccadilly to World's End with a half a sack of sugar on your shoulder. And there was this fog – not so much a pea souper as a spring fog off the river. So I'm trudging along and I'm singing a few of the old favourites to keep my spirits up. *"My ole man said foller the van . . . "* You know that one? *"You can't trust the Specials like the old-time coppers – When you can't find your way home,"* ' she sang. The angina had eased its grip on her chest. Sitting on the wall, she kicked up her legs on the last protracted note.

'Did you think about Jack the Ripper?'

She shook her head. 'That devil was long dead. But sing as I might to keep my spirits up, I still knew you had some bad lots about. Dodging the trenches but still needing to eat. Conchies most of them, I expect. And suddenly, down near the embankment, Cheyne Walk somewhere, not sure where I am, I hear this voice in the fog.'

'Just like when Jack the Ripper called to you?'

'Just like. But he was a big upright sort, this one. Might have been a guardsman when he was younger.'

'Did he ask you what was in the sack?'

'Of course. You don't get many women out after midnight with a weighty sack on their shoulder.'

'Did you tell him?'

'I told him sand. I'd just collected it for my brother who was walling up the family vault in the Brompton Cemetery first thing in the morning.'

'But we don't have a family vault.'

'Of course not. But in this life you don't tell all you know.'

'What did this man say?'

She shook her head. 'He offered to carry the sack. "Charmed," I said. As he took it from me he stuck his finger inside and pulled it out and sucked it, making smacking sounds with his lips. "Little Jack Horner," he says, with a lift of the eyebrows.'

I knew that nursery rhyme.

' "Now" he says, "in the middle of these hard-rationed times where would you be getting a quantity of sugar like that?"

'So I don't know why but I told him straight. Londonderry House, I said. I was cross, you see. I said, "There's no shortage there."

' "I dare say," he says. "For big parties and the like." '

'So he lights his pipe and he's carrying my sack and he walks me back to World's End.'

'Did he try to run away with the sugar?'

'No, love. There are bad men and good in the fog when you're a nice-looking woman. This one hands me the bag back at the end of Upcerne Road and says: "Don't get yourself caught up in any more fogs, Miss." Although of course I'm a Missus but I don't tell him that.'

'And off he went?' I was disappointed.

'Off he went but not before I'd dropped him a curtsey and said, "I'm truly grateful for your help, Mr . . ."

' "Ah," he says, casual as old boots, "Watkins. Chief Inspector Ted Watkins. Never trust a special like an old-time copper, eh, Miss? Gerarrds Row Police Station if you ever need a well-placed friend." '

My grandmother and I approached the bottom of the sandy lane. From the main road we were looking across at the front doors of the five cottages which were clearly never used. There was no path or gap in the fence. No access to them at all. The rest of the party were well ahead and had put the cases down to rest their arms. They were about thirty yards up the lane and staring at what, from their angle, must have been the back of the cottages. It took me a few more paces closer to them to realise that the look on their faces was a mix of dismay and incredulity. I left my grandmother to come on at her own pace and ran ahead to join the others.

I can't easily imagine my mother's feelings. Some might have claimed that the front of Walter Oakley Cottages possessed a certain charm, but the rear view was of rural poverty and privation at their worst. Next to each back door a small section of damp-eaten brick wall joined the cottage to an outside privy. No drainage, no cess-pits. From most of the privies a stream of human waste cut narrow gullies through the cindered mud that made up the rear pathway. A small child of perhaps one or two played among the muck as we walked along the path towards the end cottage. Later we would discover there was one tap in the backus (the 'back-house') reached by the main back door to the cottage. The centre of the backus was occupied by a huge round cement wood-burning boiler, rendering the room unusable for anything but boiling clothes and gutting rabbits. There was no electricity or gas. Paraffin was used for lighting and floor cleaning.

Today no council, no health authority, no social services department would ever tolerate Walter Oakley Cottages as they were then. The farmer who owned this line of tied cottages, and whose company's trucks are still seen on their extensive fields to this day, was at that time a choleric sixty-year-old named Emmet. While we were there my mother got electricity laid on, something 'Old Rommel', as the farmer was to become known, had failed even to try to do before the war. His successors put in mains drainage afterwards but by then, of course, labour was short and even farm labourers' expectations had risen. Or perhaps, and I mean this genuinely, the improvements were the result of simple goodwill on the part of the new management of the farm company.

When Dimple appeared he was no bandy-legged septuagenarian lecher. He was twenty-one and just married to Mollie who, I think, was the same age. They were not, however, a physically well-matched pair. Dimple was short and slender, Mollie broad-hipped and deep-bosomed with several inches on Dimple in height. They were a good-natured couple and very kind, but shy of us as big city folk. In education and understanding of the world they were very definitely out of Thomas Hardy. Like everybody else at Walter Oakley they lived, ate and everything short of slept in their turned-down Wellington boots, their feet inside bound in infrequently changed toe-rags.

Dimple's friend, mentor and protector was the man we eventually went to live with in the cottage next-door. Joe Carey was the unofficial farm manager, the official poacher, illiterate, sly, clever, a bad enemy and the best friend you could have. His wife Jinny, also a farm labourer, was of some sort of settled Romany background, dark-skinned as a North African woman, small, quick, generous, the champion Brussels sprout picker of three counties and undoubtedly the worst cook in the whole wide world.

The billeting arrangements were that we should have two rooms upstairs in Joe and Jinny's cottage for my mother, grandmother, Kit and myself. Since there was no more than one small bedroom fire-grate up there, we would go downstairs to eat. Jinny would cook.

Kit had always been a very robust eater. My mother (and even my grandmother) saw the diplomatic necessity of trying to ignore the problem of Jinny's cooking. But I'm sad to say I was a fairly picky eater. In particular I veered towards vegetarian sensitivities. Although enjoying meat, as I still do, I was loath to see too much of the preparation of it. I don't think it's always necessary to stoke in a boiler room to enjoy central heating. Of course big questions flow from here – but I really am only talking about Jinny's skills.

At over a half century's distance, how can I offer you a true flavour of that cooking? On a normal Saturday morning Kit and I might have been playing by the river at the end of the lane, wondering what the big house was over the wall. Wondering why we had begun to see big black cars run down the drive just a hundred yards along from Walter Oakley. Wondering what those vertically striped blue, white and red flags were on the fenders. Nobody in the area identified the fluttering pennants as French. Nobody realised until after the war that Churchill, with typical guile, had packed General de Gaulle away in mouldering old Oakley Court when he became too troublesome to his London hosts.

On this morning coming back from the river we are both hungry, speculating as children do about what there is for dinner. We know there's always plenty of cheese because both Joe and Jinny get farm-labourers' rations. There could be a piece of ham from a neighbour known as Old Drakey, or fried eggs from Peggy's allowance from the White Lady Poultry Farm. There might even be American dried egg which we like most of all and is just coming into the country as part of Lend Lease.

But none of these is offered today. We come down the cinder track, past the foul smells of the privy and the ferret cages, and let ourselves in through the back door. Now there is another smell, or another mix of smells. We kick off our Wellingtons and open the door of the cupboard where we keep them. And recoil. Joe has been poaching. It is the first time I've seen the evidence. The cupboard is full of rabbits: unskinned with blood still dripping from their noses; or freshly skinned with the fur hanging from their heads. Some think this keeps them fresh. The smell is tangible, a thick stench of blood and guts. I slam the door shut, close to being sick. Kit takes these things more easily.

From the front room comes another appalling, but at least vegetable, reek. Jinny is in there, at the stove, cooking cabbage. It is about twelve-thirty. These days we have cabbage from the fields every day. She goes out for the first session about seven-thirty in the morning, back for breakfast at nine with a cabbage. Trims the cabbage and puts it in water on the stove. Returns at twelve midday. Question – is the cabbage done? Not unless it passes Jinny's test. She lifts the lid, uses a fork to hook up a few leaves, suspends them over the pot. If the leaves don't divide and fall apart under their own weight, she grunts, 'That be not quite done, that cabbage.'

In fact there is little or nothing left of the fibre of the vegetable, only a mess of green sludge in the pot. The cabbage has been reduced to an odour.

It is one of the many distinctive smells my brother and I remember from Walter Oakley: blood, the privy, ferrets, paraffin used every Sunday morning to clean the linoleum. And the deep abiding smell of cabbage.

★

I remember the first weeks at Walter Oakley as really no more than a series of vignettes, new experiences were coming at us so thick and fast. One night we stood at the end of the lane and watched London burning. It was a clear dark night, with of course no street lights along the deserted Windsor Road. Over on our left, way above the rooftops of our decrepit neighbouring mansion, there was a frightening red glow in the sky. Today a young boy used to the setting sun of sodium lighting from bedtime to breakfast time would think nothing of it. But we knew it was our London burning. We had no way of knowing whether it was our World's End, too.

I remember the terrible lump in my throat that made it impossible to talk. 'There she goes,' Joe Carey said. 'There goes that-there Lunnon.'

Jinny was crying when we got back to the cottage. She hadn't come with us but had watched from the front garden. She wasn't crying for London. She had never travelled the twenty-eight miles that would have taken her there. She was crying for all the people she didn't know who were suffering under those huge fires sweeping around St Paul's and through the old city. She was another Mrs Bullen.

Out poaching with Joe was another of those days or afternoons that would live in the memory. Joe had quickly selected Kit as his main man and a more natural poacher than I. I would engage in country pursuits for totally different reasons. I'd climb higher trees than anyone else in the small country school we attended to confirm my status as someone who should be left alone. But also, and very importantly, to put myself to the test. What sense of failure lurked in me I can't guess. In this sense I was not a natural. I never climbed trees because they were there. Later in my life I never joined the Parachute Regiment or decided to try for Cambridge because they were there. It was always more specific than that. Then at some point I stopped putting myself to the test. When, I don't really know. I don't even know if I stopped because it no longer seemed necessary, or because it had come to seem pointless.

Poaching with Joe was an experience which mixed admiration for his skill with distaste for the result. Kit had none of the same qualms and went out with Joe far more than I did. He was a boy who could take a rabbit from a snare and kill it with one blow to the back of the neck. I couldn't.

Joe Carey's poaching skill had been learnt over a lifetime. He was not a very tall man, and he was heavy from bad cooking and the extras that came from poaching and knowing men like Mr Drake, the local pig-keeper ('That old Drakey's killed a pig agin'), but he was unbelievably light-footed. His poacher's gear was his twelve-bore shotgun, of course, and his worn flat cap which he would often turn so that the peak pointed backwards. I think this gesture, and the grin on his round, ruddy face that accompanied it, was somehow the equivalent of putting two fingers up to the world: I'm only illiterate Joe Carey but I can do such and such better than any of you. Another indispensable item of his working clothes was an oversize suit jacket with the sewn-in long pockets where he could conceal a broken twelve-bore or, after the hunt, a hare or half a dozen rabbits.

His technique was not immediately remarkable. He would stroll soundlessly in his Wellington boots along a path through a copse, unworried it seemed by the noise I was making crashing after him. Sometimes he would talk about the news as if he had read the paper from cover to cover that day. In fact most of his information came from the BBC, his illiteracy and his poaching successes being the only things he was anxious to hide. Then, as we walked, there'd be a flicker of his eyes towards the field beyond.

'That there old hare thinks he's going to be waiting us out, young Dee.'

'What hare?'

'Don't turn your head. Use your eyes. We'll get past and he'll up and lope off, soon as we do.' Joe would all the time be very quietly loading cartridges and clicking in the oiled barrel of his shotgun.

And I would walk, stiff-legged, terrified for the hare, terrified too that I would scare it out of range. Then the movement of both animal and man would overtake me. The hare would speed past us maybe fifty yards away. The stock of the gun would seem to fly up and rest couched in Joe's shoulder. When he fired the hare would leap and tumble like, I suppose, a March hare. But a dead one.

Rabbiting was even more disagreeable to me because then I had to carry the bag of ferrets. This bag was of canvas, tied at the end. Inside, the two ferrets scrambled ceaselessly and gnawed at the top, at your hand in fact, to get loose. You could shake them down every few minutes but this would so infuriate them that they would fight each other to hurl their way back up at your hand, and Joe would glance over and say: 'Stop bothering them there ferrets, young Dee.' And wink and grin because he knew how alarmed I was by their great sharp teeth.

Joe himself was completely unconcerned by the idea of receiving a bite. When he had set the snares round a chosen burrow he'd take the bag from me, drop his hand in and pull out a ferret. He might have got the odd nip but I think the skin on his hands was too rough and scarred by a hundred ferret and rat bites (he was also the local rat-catcher) for him to suffer anything more than a scratch. Did he have tetanus injections? God knows, but I can't imagine it.

When he introduced the ferrets to the burrow the noise below was indescribable: the thumping of the rabbits' feet, their terror of the ferrets communicated through eighteen inches of earth – and then the moment when they came bursting from the ground into the nets. One . . . three . . . five. Some would streak past their brothers rolling in the snare, others would have chosen an exit that Joe had not covered. Then suddenly all would be silent. Joe would pick one out of the net, wondering casually if he could hear how far his ferrets had got, stretch the rabbit by its ears and hind legs, chop it once across the neck with his heavy hand and, without a glance, drop it into the pocket in the lining of his jacket. Sometimes then we would have to dig out one of the ferrets that had caught up with its prey in the burrow.

The night of the Dornier is a night my brother and I still talk about. My grandmother had not been well again and it had been decided that she would have one of our two rooms and my brother and I would share the bedding roll my mother had on the floor. I remember the details with great clarity. Kit and I were in bed awaiting two treats. The first was some cakes that my mother had mixed by breaking up some Australian fruit cake, a gift of the people of Sydney, and stirring it into a wartime cake mix. Since we lacked any kind of oven, this was fried in a pan on the small bedroom grate. While waiting we were listening to our favourite BBC comedy-quiz programme, *Can* you *Beat the Band?* There was a raid on and Jinny had asked us to come downstairs where it was felt to be safer, but straight from the blitz we really weren't worried about the distant throb of aircraft leaving London and about to turn south for France.

Then, as we listened to the wireless, with Old Ebenezer the Night Watchman's story just about to begin, my mother's face changed. After a few moments she said, 'Turn if off, Dee.'

We groaned, but we understood she had heard something. I turned off the wireless. 'There's a plane circling,' she said. 'A German.' She got up and brought my grandmother in from the other room, wrapped in a blanket but still wearing her hat, of course. My mother told us to get up and put our trousers and sweaters on. They sat in the two chairs and we lay back on the mattress, listening to the slowly swelling sound of a low-flying German aircraft.

In the last year I had become an 'expert' in aircraft recognition. It was no more than a boy's collecting mania, in fact; instead of collecting fag-cards I had chosen to 'collect' planes. My bible was the *Penguin Book of Aircraft Recognition* and I soon learned the vital statistics of every aircraft in it, Japanese included. My principal interest, of course, was in the ones I might see – RAF fighters – or hear – the Luftwaffe medium bombers that had been ruining our sleep for the last few months in London. I persuaded myself that I could tell the difference between the two 1580hp BMW 801 engines of the Dornier 217 bomber, straining under a bomb load of 8,818lbs, and the Heinkel 111's two Junkers Jumo 1200hp plants. Of course I couldn't, but it gave me the opportunity at least to seem knowledgeable. This plane, moving in ever-tightening circles above our heads, I identified as a Dornier 217E2.

My mother, uncharacteristically, paid no attention to my feat of aircraft recognition. I looked at her face, the way her mouth had tensed. My grandmother was white and trembling. Kit and I sat cross-legged on the bedroll on the floor, holding hands, I think, as the circles tightened overhead. Whatever the make of its engine, the throbbing of a German bomber was unmistakable. Even my grandmother recognised the insistent thudding above our heads. 'It's not one of ours, is it?' she whispered.

My mother shook her head, listening intently.

Kit leant towards me and whispered so our grandmother couldn't hear, 'I think it's landing.'

It was certainly getting lower with every circuit. I tried to imagine the interior of the plane, its pilot and crew. I tried to guess what they were doing. Was it possible they had German parachutists in the plane, lined up in their menacing steel helmets ready to jump, the spearhead of the invasion force we'd heard so much about?

At that moment Jinny's voice came from downstairs. It was half-strangled by fear. 'They Germans are landing,' she said hoarsely from the bottom of the stair. 'Joe's out there. He's taken his shotgun.'

We bundled downstairs. My mother helped my grandmother down. Fear had brought on another wave of angina. The Zeppelins in the First World War had never been anything like this. We could none of us reckon altitude but I would guess now that the plane was not much more than three or four hundred feet above us, the engines no longer throbbing. As they came over the cottage roof they were growling wildly, unevenly.

In the front room Joe and Jinny's brass double bed took up half the space. My grandmother sat on it, my mother next to her. As the bomber's engines faded we breathed in slowly.

'It's going away,' I said.

It wasn't. It was describing its final circle.

'Joe's out there,' Jinny whispered. 'He'll be all right. He's got Dimple with him.' The idea raised a sickly smile from all of us, even Jinny herself. Even at that moment we all knew Dimple wouldn't be much of an ally.

'Put out the light, Jinny,' my mother said. 'See what we can see.'

Jinny turned out the paraffin lamp and pulled open the blackout curtains. There was some moonlight. The fields, divided by Bluebell Lane leading up to Braywood School, were sinister shades of grey. The sky was lighter, full of roaring noise now. Then as the sound approached again and the engines, or perhaps just one single functioning engine, screamed in a frantic effort to clear our rooftop, we lifted our eyes to the sky. From the direction of the river behind us the German bomber appeared, at no more than tree height as it banked over the cottages, one wingtip spitting long sparks as it touched the road just in front of us, the other wing sharply angled up, hanging there, it seemed, in a crescendo of engine noise until field, lane and hedgerow were drowned in a massive explosion of magnesium-bright light.

As the ball of white faded to yellow, we crowded to the window. Silhouetted against the light of the burning bomber not sixty yards from us we could see men in the road. They were taking the weight on their back foot, necks craned back, looking not at the burning plane but up into the sky. One or two lifted shotguns . . . And as it came into silhouette against the burning aircraft we too saw what they were aiming at. A pale parachute floated down, a German airman's canopy umbered by the light of his blazing plane, a black figure dangling from it.

Young Jack Emmet, Old Rommel's son, was there with his car. As the German hit the road, he was surrounded by farm labourers with shotguns levelled at him. The Dornier, for a Dornier indeed it would turn out to be, was a mass of crackling ammunition. Tracer ripped haphazardly through the night air, incendiary bombs popped and hurled quantities of white flame. We half crouched in the darkened room, the light from the burning bomber, white one moment, yellow the next, flickering on the ceiling.

Not long after, Jack Emmet's car drew away with the German and an escort. We heard Joe's voice outside and Jinny, who had locked a door for what was probably the first time in her life, ran through the backus to open it. Joe was smiling, shaking his head. 'Young fella he was,' he said. 'Broke his ankle when he came down. Spoke the King's English, though. Eighteen, he said he were. Frightened out of his wits with all those shotguns pointing at him. Then young Jack Emmet's wife comes up in her car. "Poor little sod," she says. "Fancy a cup of tea, do you, Fritz?"' Joe laughed as he took the orange cartridges from his shotgun, snapped it shut and stood it in the corner.

'What you got to laugh about, Joe Carey?' Jinny said crossly. 'There could be others out there. We could been murdered while you was out there.'

'Don't worry,' he said, turning his cap back to front. 'I left Dimple guarding the plane.'

None of us knew whether or not he was serious.

It was Jinny who started laughing first. 'You left him out there all by himself? That young Dimple?'

'I told him to hide in the ditch for fear of the bullets exploding all over. That there Dimp's crouched down there now with his hat over his eyes.'

Before Jinny could become serious again, Joe straightened his cap, a sign that *he* had become serious. 'Excitement's over,' he said. 'Home Guard's just coming. They'll have a thorough scout around. That there young German fella said two others jumped while the pilot was circling. He were the last.'

'And what happened to the pilot?' my mother asked.

Joe pointed through the still uncovered window to the burning plane. 'He can't feel anything anymore.'

Kit and I stared out across the road. I don't know what he was thinking. I was thinking that a man could still be dying out there. I imagined I saw a shadow moving inside the blazing aluminium skeleton that was all that remained of the Dornier, but I thought better of saying anything. I knew only my grandmother would have believed me.

ELEVEN

In absentia

The Dornier was an exception. For the most part, deep in the country we heard little more than the low rumble of the wider world around us. Our upstairs part of the house was freezing; the stench of dead animals and unemptied buckets inescapable. The walk to the bus stop was a mile every frost-bitten morning and a mile back every dark winter afternoon. School was grim, and the other children unfriendly. The war seemed to have lasted for ever.

My father came down for the occasional weekend and I would collect news of the war's progress from him. My mother would sometimes try to explain the course of events in North Africa but we'd laugh after a few minutes, both recognising that she was without my father's understanding. So I turned to Joe.

At Walter Oakley there was the nine o'clock news but I was mostly in bed by then. There was also the *Daily Mirror* delivered every morning, a very much more literate newspaper then than it is now. It tried gallantly to make the war in North Africa comprehensible to Joe and myself. But given the complexities of the fighting, our shaky sense of geography, and Joe's illiteracy which I was not, of course, supposed to be aware of, we didn't make the sharpest analytical team.

Early 1941 had seen the beginning of striking British successes against the Italian armies in Libya. Bardia was captured in January, Australian troops took Tobruk as the month ended and stormed Benghazi in February. These were North African coastal cities which were to become household names. In February 1941 the Desert Rats cut the coast road and forced the wholesale surrender of an entire Italian army. Two British Empire divisions had defeated ten enemy divisions and taken 130,000 prisoners. We began to see Italian prisoners working in the fields in their dark brown uniforms with their identifying circular patches cut in the back of their jackets. They were friendly, cheerful and seemed genuinely pleased to be out of the war. The way things were going in the desert we expected more to be on their way to work in the fields soon.

Then in March an unknown German general, Erwin Rommel, came to the rescue of the remaining Italian forces. Taking the offensive almost immediately, he re-took Bardia and was besieging Tobruk by early April. It soon seemed that wherever Rommel thrust, the British front buckled. Immediately Joe christened Farmer Emmet 'Old Rommel', and Old Rommel he remained until at least the end of the war.

While we struggled with the news pages of the *Mirror* there were other items of the sort I was finding increasingly diverting. Beyond the news pages the paper also carried a strip cartoon entitled *Jane*. Jane was a young blonde member of the WAAF, the women's RAF, and achieved the loss of, or the necessity to change, most of her clothing (falling into ponds, catching her skirt on the bumper of a fast roadster, being sprayed with mud, getting covered in oil, or just idly chatting to an equally half-dressed girl-friend) pretty well six days a week. Joe and I were very keen on Jane.

'Let's just see how that-there Jane's lost her skirt today, Raz D,' he'd say, opening the page and scanning the cartoon with no need to read the caption. Kit and I were always Raz K and Raz D to him. *Raz* being some Arabic title or form of address which Joe had picked up from the news during the successful British spring invasion of Iraq.

Over a half century later 'Raz' still springs easily to the lips when I
phone my brother.

But the most exciting moment, and the most frustrating, of this
year's war news was the landing of Rudolf Hess in Scotland. The
BBC was utterly unforthcoming. The government was leaning
heavily on journalists and broadcasters not to speculate. Churchill
had been quick to see that the arrival of Hess could blow up into a
major crisis. The Prime Minister was mortally afraid that the
American people would think that Hess had arrived *by British
invitiation*. He was after all the deputy leader of a Nazi state pledged
to fight us to the death. The PM's fear was that the American press
and people would conclude that if he, Churchill, had invited Hess,
the British were clearly on the verge of surrender.

My interest survived the years and (much later) I wrote a book
about the landing, *Shadow of the Wolf*, which offered a fictionalised
account of Hess's mission. There was still, even in the 1980s, enough
interest in the strange journey of Rudolf Hess to put the book into
the *Sunday Times* best-seller list. Today, if asked, I would say that
there is ample evidence that Hitler, planning his attack on Russia for
later that same month of May, would have welcomed (if no longer
believing possible) an 'honourable' peace with Britain. This he had
undoubtedly stated several times to his inner circle. Now add this to
the fact that Hess was, despite his Deputy Leader's title, losing
ground to both Goering and Bormann and it's possible to see the
landing as the last desperate throw of a pathetic sycophant hoping to
regain Hitler's favour. Not a conspiracy theory in sight.

But in 1941 I was as baffled as everyone else. Perhaps familiarity
has dulled the melodrama, but that May I couldn't talk about it
enough. There were pictures in the *Mirror* showing Hess making the
warm-up speech for Hitler at a Nuremberg rally. But what was the
truth? I was obsessed by the mystery. Had Hitler sent him? That
seemed then, at least, a certainty, although it was not in fact the case.
Did it mean that Hitler wanted to surrender? The very idea

generated a rush of pure excitement. Had *Hess* thought Germany should surrender and was he defying Hitler? Or was he a British spy bringing secret information? I developed theories with a wild tinge – although not as wild as those which have been developed since. The *Daily Mirror* was not informative enough. To learn more I even tried to read other newspapers, upside down, in Maggie Mole's shop in Fifield. A form of literary shoplifting, I suppose.

Most of my theories, I tried not to admit, were less than plausible. Kit, I believe, was bored to the bone by Hess. Joe was no help when I put the big questions to him. 'Onpossible,' he said (his rendering of impossible) about most of my theories. 'You can count on it, Raz D,' he said mysteriously, pulling his cap round back to front, 'that that-there Rudolf, he do know which side his bread's buttered.'

I can hardly suggest to you that the life we lived at Walter Oakley was the unbridled life of the mind. Joe was illiterate, my grandmother over-fanciful, my mother too busy making life tolerable, and Kit and myself too young. Furthermore the village school we attended at Braywood was for the most part designed to produce the same-again farm labourers their fathers had been. And in the house there were of course no books. For Joe, what would have been the point?

I suppose, up to this time, I had never read a book. I don't know how much I missed by never becoming familiar with Beatrix Potter or A. A. Milne or Kenneth Grahame. I don't say it with pride but until I began this book I might well have guessed that it was Milne who wrote *Wind in the Willow* and I still have only a hazy idea of its anthropomorphic cast. What surprised me when I first joined the army (I was drafted into the Greenjackets, a notably upper class-leaning brigade as far as its potential officers went), and later when I got to university, was the affection with which my comrades and friends would quote from their childhood reading. No mention of growth or augmentation was ever allowed to pass without an obscure reference to Topsy who, it seemed, 'just grow'd and grow'd'. I was left baffled, but then I had never read *Uncle Tom's Cabin* either.

But we did have comics. I have no idea how widely they were read by upper-class children. They were, I suppose, our television. My mother (with the help of my grandmother's pension) was extremely generous with our weekly comics. She would bring them back from Maggie Mole's on Friday evening after school, sometimes with the meagre monthly ration of chocolate we were allocated. My favourites were *Champion, Wizard* and *Adventure*. Brian Magee, the former MP, has included an account of the importance of comics to him in his memoir of a Hoxton childhood and I recognise every word. These were not illustrated stories, not remotely connected to the American funnies or to the *Beano* and *Dandy*. Our comics, designed for older boys, contained mystery, adventure and war stories.

My favourite character, or the one I remember best, was the macho boxer-fighter pilot, Rockfist Rogan. He dealt with the Nazis in a pleasingly brisk manner. The old one-two. Right hook or close burst of his Spitfire's 20-millimetre cannon. But often enough there was an underlying, more civilised element. In one story Rogan, shot down over enemy-occupied territory, is challenged to box by the champion of a competing crack Messerschmitt squadron, the prize if he wins to be his liberty. It was the age-old clash of the champions, and it illustrated the existence of good decent Germans even in the midst of Nazism. There were stereotype Nazis in the comics, of course, plenty of them, but not all were stereotypes. So much for government manipulation and censorship of the comics, an accusation which has come up from time to time.

I also remember Wilson, the athlete from nowhere, dressed in black Long Johns and capable of running speeds and distances which modern athletes would use as training schedules but were then remarkable. I remember the serial mystery of the assassin with the disappearing bullet – I think you've got it, it was made of ice – and I remember Colwyn Dane. He was a detective of the old school. A gent, I think, so maybe a private detective. The single illustration to each episode showed him in tweeds, countryman's hat, well-cut suit and pensive look. I've just realised (never having read Conan Doyle in my youth) that, apart from the deer-stalker and Ulster, he was a direct steal from Sherlock Holmes. We all do it.

But one sentence in the Colwyn Dane series stayed with me and I think of it as my first introduction to literary criticism. Any off-camera clue, so to speak, usually something barely more subtle than a blood-stained dagger wrapped in a monogrammed handkerchief, would always elicit the same reaction: 'Dane's eyes narrowed'. This telegraph was enough to set your heart thumping. My God, what had he seen that I'd missed?

This pregnant sentence usually came at the end of a story. The following week we would discover what Dane had seen. But as I grew a little older I began to see and then dislike the repetition of the narrowing eyes, the tediousness of this single reaction to what could clearly be a clue of some significance. The writer, of course, was creating a cliff-hanger for the next issue. But even for children (especially for children as we'd all automatically and meaninglessly add today?) you have to work harder than that.

Nevertheless these comics played a big part in my life. Country children, I noticed, seldom read them. My scattered London friends did, whenever they could lay hands on them. When we all trickled back to the World's End in 1942 the stories were part of a common currency we used to restart our friendships.

We saw my father every two or three weeks at this time. He quickly formed a friendship with Joe, appreciating the goodwill that flowed from both him and Jinny, and was characteristically intrigued by the whole new field of country expertise he had never before encountered.

Mostly he rode an old bicycle the twenty-eight miles down from London but on a few special occasions he took a train to Windsor and the country bus out to Walter Oakley Cottages. The special occasions were usually when he had somehow acquired a black market bag or two of sugar from Mr Jones the grocer at the World's End or a piece of beef from one of the American diplomats or journalists who lived at Whitelands. This weekend, as we were to discover, it was a leg of lamb *and* some sugar and margarine from an unmentioned source.

He arrived at Joe and Jinny's on Saturday morning carrying a suitcase and looking particularly pleased with himself. My mother kissed him, looked down and asked him where he'd got the suitcase.

For a moment he was baffled. 'What do you mean? It's ours . . .'

Slowly she shook her head.

I watched as his expression changed. With five of us looking on he dropped on to one knee, sprang the catches and threw open the case. Inside there was a bundle of greasy overalls, some tools, an old shirt or two. 'Stone the crows!' he said. 'Stiffen the Prussian Guards! I've got the wrong case!'

My mother looked at him, eyebrows raised in horror. She didn't need telling what he might have had in the case. And buying on the black market was a prison offence.

There had been two suitcases in the luggage rack of the bus, he remembered. The owner of the other case had got off near Bullock's Hatch. My father borrowed Joe's bicycle, balancing the suitcase on the cross-bar. Kit and I jumped on our bikes and we all pedalled like mad down past the entrance to de Gaulle's house of exile and arrived a few minutes later at Bullock's hatch. There were very few houses there in those days. Taking a deep breath, my father began knocking on doors. My brother and I cycled up and down the road in the boyish hope of picking up a clue.

Kit saw him first. A man leaving the Nag's Head carrying an old suitcase. My father was on to him in seconds. The man's face showed his astonishment. He'd not realised. Which meant he had not opened my father's case. 'I thought it was a bit heavier than when I started out.'

'Schoolbooks,' my father said before the man could ask, and nodded towards us. 'They're just down from London.'

'Quiet enough round this way,' the man said. He handed back the case. 'Schoolbooks. Bet you boys wish you'd never found it again, eh?'

Smiles all round. The cases were exchanged. And half a crown which sent the man back into the Nag's Head for another couple of pints.

I asked my father why he hadn't given him a bit of sugar. Or maybe a half-pound of margarine. He looked at me, shaking his head. 'Use your intelligence, Dee. Give him half a crown, he's grateful. Give him a packet of margarine and he thinks the story's just begun. I'd as soon have let him keep the whole caseful.'

Our days were spent in the village school, a single large room with a sharply pitched roof, one teacher fits all, and a playground we called the grassy at the back. There was bullying – and bullying had to be fought. I had several battles in the yard outside the blacksmith's smithy; after I left the village school, Kit became the champion and led Freddie Coco and the small group of Londoners against the country boys.

There was bullying on the grassy – but away from school there was play too, mostly beside the River Thames as we always had done in London.

But this was not a River Thames we were at all familiar with. No black mud, no coaling ships dropping anchor to supply Lots Road power station. No old engines stuck in the mud, no interesting driftwood that we could try to sell for firewood until we realised what everybody else knew, that it was too sodden to burn. No pair of sunken barges, the subject of a thousand Sunday painters' views from Battersea Bridge. The Thames at Bray is beautiful but it had yet to be made exciting.

What transformed it was the discovery of a spy in the village. I first became aware of the possibility when I noticed, crossing a field that led down to the river, that I was by accident following a trail: a succession of black crow's feathers mostly sticking upright in the soft, damp earth. Colwyn Dane's eyes would have narrowed. Perhaps mine did too. There was no doubt that it was a clever ruse. Who would pay attention to a scatter of crow's feathers? Most people would see no more significance in the feathers than the idea that some farmer had shot a crow. But if you continued on across the field you saw, if you were looking hard (and I was), that they were placed *in an unmistakable line*. A trail.

I thought immediately of those two missing members of the German aircrew who had parachuted from their crashing plane. Of course, in Berlin German airmen would be given prearranged escape routes which, if they were forced to parachute or crash-land, would direct them to a house of safety. Somewhere remote, quite big obviously, big enough to house several airmen while they awaited secret transport back across the Channel. A house, furthermore, obviously equipped with a long-range radio to call Berlin for orders. My first thought was, Old Rommel's house. I thought that if young Jack Emmet was in on the plot he might have taken the German rear gunner who had broken his ankle on the road outside Walter Oakley to Old Rommel's house *en route* to Germany.

But that didn't fit. Too many people knew that Jack Emmet's wife had offered the German a cup of tea, and besides the Emmets would have been found out pretty quickly if they hadn't handed their prisoner over to the police or Home Guard. With reluctance, because I had no love for Old Rommel (especially when later that year he paid me only fourpence a day to top beans in the school holidays, and sacked me for daydreaming at the end of the first week), I dismissed the Emmets as major suspects.

I tried to grasp the scope of the operation. In the *Champion*, Rockfist Rogan had already escaped twice after being shot down in Occupied France. He was helped back to England by an underground French Resistance organisation. And what was a Resistance organisation if not a whole bunch of spies? That was just a story, but this was *fact*. When I thought more about it I realised there would have to be a network of spies across the whole of southern England, possibly the entire country. The enemy airmen would have to be provided with civilian clothes and papers. We already knew, from what Joe had told us about the man who had come down by parachute, that German airmen were taught to speak the King's English. It was probably part of their training in case they were shot down. All very likely, but none of this provided me with any further clues. There was only one thing to do: I followed the trail of feathers.

It led to an island in the river. At least it looked very much to me as if that's where it led. To Monkey Island, before the war the scene of expensive high jinks according to my cousin Peggy, its banks now overgrown with shrubbery apparently out of control, its roomy hotel deserted . . . *or having that calculated appearance*. Quite clearly there were leads here that had to be followed up.

None of this happened straight away, of course, and I seem to remember a pretty heavy cloud of suspicion settled on the Braywood blacksmith when I found another trail of crow's feathers leading straight towards his smithy. But his bona fides were established when we heard he had won a medal fighting in the first war. I quietly allowed my suspicions of him to subside and Monkey Island to recover pole position, difficult as it was to get at for a thorough investigation.

The recruitment of a team to help me – I would have said 'gang' at the time – was more of a problem. Kit was not wholly convinced of the importance of my discovery but was always ready for an expedition. The country boys were not readers of the *Champion* and thus had no belief in spy networks which spirited shot-down airmen back to their own countries. But one of the country boys from school, whose name I now sadly forget but whose nickname was Towser, was impressed by the way I could tap my fingers, index to little finger giving a more even rhythm than the more normal vice versa. (I was later told that this was a basic first test for identifying a psychopath – but no matter.) My finger-tapping made Towser a firm adherent and he agreed to join us.

One dark late-February afternoon we stole down our lane, past the Emmets' farm to the river. There were two boats moored there, a short flat-bottomed punt and a strange aluminium boat with seats and high sides. We chose that one. I knew perfectly well what my mother would have thought if she'd seen us. But this was, in my eyes, an important mission. Fritz (we had already awarded him a code name) might even now be finalising preparation for the two German airmen to be spirited back to Berlin this very night.

We hugged the bank, paddling silently. There was not a soul to be seen as we approached Monkey Island. I had already given Towser a probable description of Fritz closely based on the Luftwaffe pilot Rockfist successfully fought for his freedom.

We landed a few moments later, allowing the boat to snuggle its way into the reeds and shrubs by the water's edge. We stowed the paddles. Jumping on to fairly dry land, we moved forward crouched over, ready for anything. Our first big moment was the discovery of a radio mast cleverly concealed in the trees. It was made of metal, about twenty feet high, and had a strange windmill-like top-piece, presumably designed to pick up a wide range of foreign wavelengths.

We pushed on. It was getting very dark by now and behind me there was a general sentiment expressed in favour of going home to tea. But I was betting my pride on a discovery. We lay in the long, wet grass on the edge of the unkempt lawn. The house was in front of us, the old Monkey Island Hotel. Somewhat bafflingly there were no lights, no German pilots studying road-maps by the light of shaded torches on the lawn. No sign of Fritz the master spy . . .

As leader of a schoolboy gang you have a keen nose for mutiny. It's never far away. And that evening it was at my shoulder. It was time to take a risk.

We've lost them,' I said, standing up in full view of the house.

Towser tried to pull me down, the remnant of his belief in the theory remaining as caution rather than real fear. 'They'll see you,' he said. 'They Germans could be hiding behind a blackout curtain.'

'No.' I shook my head. 'They've got away. At this moment those two Jerries are on their way to Berlin. Not got far probably. Windsor, perhaps . . . Slough. They have smoke screens there, remember.' Which indeed they did, with great steel drums on the street corners full of oily rags which the ARP burnt on the nights of the worst London raids, presumably on the basis that industrial Slough would be an overfly secondary target for the German bombers.

'The two of them could easily escape into the smoke,' I said. 'Probably already have.' We turned back towards the boat.

Fortune sometimes favours the wilder reaches of imagination. We heard next day that the two airmen who had parachuted from the Dornier had been arrested . . . just beyond Slough. At school that Monday Towser spilled the story around the class: they Jerry airmen who were caught at Slough had been set on their journey by Fritz. Fritz himself had then disappeared into the mist, probably to a new safe house. We'd been just one step behind them, Towser was convinced. I'm far less sure about Kit.

Very slowly I began to appreciate the Thames at Bray. It would never be the Thames at London and there was no point in pretending otherwise. But as the summer of 1941 came upon us I began to learn something about birds and their nests. There would be a competition, mostly with other London boys, to climb for the highest though we would not have interfered with a swan's or a wren's. I came to take a delight in the blue flash of a kingfisher, not that uncommon along the high-banked creeks that led down to the river. And Joe once dug up a strange coin, bronze, dated 1327 in flowing numerals, with a ship of sorts on one face and a head on the obverse. I lost it, of course, but it served to excite me with the idea of buried treasure. Little did I know that at Bray a promising Saxon dig had

been abandoned as the war began. I would have been down by the
water digging the riverbank away if I had.

But the river can be a place of tragedy as well as pleasure for small
boys. There were three brothers we saw from time to time playing
not far from us as the summer came on. They used to shout at us
when they heard our London accents, but then so did most country
boys. On any hot day the brothers would be in the water. The eldest
swam well, very well even, the middle was less skilful in the water but
knew enough not to get himself into trouble. The youngest barely
swam at all. They were aged between eight and thirteen.

At Bray the river is not, of course, tidal and on a calm warm day it
flows smoothly down from somewhere in Oxfordshire, its glassy
green surface, no more than forty or fifty yards across, ruffled then at
least by no more than the occasional wake of a crew sculling past
from Maidenhead School.

We were down there one day in June playing on the river bank
with Billy, the son of Mrs Corfield who lived on the top floor of our
block at Guinness Trust. He was on holiday from his evacuated
London school and his mother had brought him down to Windsor
for a week to keep him out of the bombing. The three brothers were
there, the elder swimming across to the far bank, the middle brother
sitting in an inflated car tyre inner tube. The youngest was drying
himself on the bank, shivering I remember despite the sun, his own
inner tube dripping water from its liver-red sides.

What our game was I can't really remember but we were running
in and out of the bushes on the Bray bank when we heard the
youngest brother yelling to the others that he was going home. He
was fed up. They wouldn't play with him. It was late. The sun was
going down. He was getting cold.

The other two weren't anxious to go home yet. One was
swimming, diving under, kicking his legs in the air. The other was
hand-paddling around in his inflated inner tube, skidding across the
water like a moorhen.

When I was next aware of looking, the youngest had stopped drying himself. He had hauled his red inner tube back to the water's edge, launched it in and splashed out to clamber into it. He must have been out of his depth in a matter of minutes. He lay back and paddled like his brother, skidding gracefully across the calm water.

Our friend Billy Corfield decided he'd had enough for the day. He started to towel himself dry. Billy, Kit and I stood around, idly watching the antics of the three brothers, listening to them shouting amicably at each other. They were fairly close together, in a rough equilateral triangle each thirty or so yards apart from the other.

Then disaster struck. The youngest brother yelled as he slipped through his inner tube. The others laughed watching him dog paddle back to the rubber ring although, from our angle on the bank, we could see the effort he had to put into keeping afloat. Puffing and spitting water, he reached for the tube. Stretching for it, his fingers slipped as he grasped the wet, smooth rubber and the inner tube skidded away from him, almost playfully, a few yards across the river's smooth surface. The others laughed. We all laughed as he dog paddled towards it again. Suddenly the mood changed. We could see the boy's desperation now. Fear that his strength would fail. He tried a few over-arm strokes, reached the inner tube again, grasped too hard for it . . . and screamed as it skidded away again across the surface of the water.

Who was first to understand that he was going under? The middle brother, I think, the one paddling his own inner tube. He turned it round skilfully and paddled to the rescue. The sun dipped behind some thicker cloud and I suddenly realised how dark it was getting.

The middle brother slipped out of his rubber ring, one arm hanging over it for buoyancy, scooping water with his other to bring him closer to his brother. It was the first moment we on the bank realised that he too couldn't swim.

The sun came out. It was a cool summer evening on the placid Thames. Then, quite suddenly, three young boys died. The youngest brother sank below the water. The rescuing brother grabbed at his arm, missed it and lost his own hold on his rubber ring. Flailing at it with his free hand, he made the same mistake as his young brother and the inner tube skidded away. There were suddenly two boys floundering helplessly without the support of their rubber rings

Our friend Billy, nearly a year older than me and a far better swimmer than Kit or myself, ran for the water's edge. The eldest brother suddenly realised the danger, turned and swam towards his brothers. Only one was now visible. When the eldest reached them, the water thrashed white in a tight circle around him. One, from just below the surface, seized him in panic and held on to his legs. Within seconds, the third brother too was drowning. The thrashing stopped, the water's empty surface rippled in the setting sunlight. The rubber rings bobbed innocently upon it, testimony to the tragedy.

When Billy Corfield reached the spot where the boys had disappeared he dived three or four times, a brave effort for a boy of thirteen. For a few moments he was able to locate one of the brothers. He snatched at his hair and tried to haul him to the far bank, but exhaustion was dragging them both down. We saw the moment when the boy slipped from his grasp, saw the heave of Billy's shoulders as he was relieved of his burden, saw a moment's hesitation as he asked himself whether he could go back – then saw him strike out the last twenty yards for his own life and crawl exhausted up the far bank.

As darkness fell the police boats arrived. I suppose today they wouldn't dare, but we were asked by the river police to go out with them in their narrow boats, the sides just a few inches about the water-level as the heavy chains were dropped over the side. On the end of the chains were big blunt-ended grapples like massive curved garden rakes, long enough to roll a man along the bottom until he was lifted in the steel fingers. With a drowned boy it was that much easier. Billy's boat found the boy he had struggled to save without much difficulty. He was close to the bank in quite shallow water.

The inner tubes were of no help in locating the other two. They had long ago bobbed away with the gentle flow of the river. Heavy police lamps were shone into the depths as it grew darker and colder, and we trawled back and forth across the patch of river where we felt sure the other two boys had disappeared. We were cold and drenched by the splashing of the chains as they were dropped again and again into the water. Then, after about an hour, each boat found a boy at more or less the same time. I won't forget the tightening of the chain, the muffled exclamation of the policeman holding it, the sense of a body being rolled across the bottom below us, and the brisk nod of the sergeant with the lamp as the curved hooks finally engaged.

He was drawn up slowly, his head cradled awkwardly in the steel arms of the grapple, his thin legs hanging over the side. In the lamplight he looked blue, sleeping rather than dead.

TWELVE

1942

By the middle of 1941 the devastating months of the blitz were over in London, although nobody on this side of the Channel was yet aware of it and heavy isolated raids continued on the capital and on ports like Glasgow, Plymouth and Liverpool. My father had been promoted to become one of the six uniformed porters at Whitelands (although he still did much of the stoking) and lived five days a week in a small service room he had been allocated there. These were maids' rooms, each originally owned by an apartment in the main part of the building, but now under a process I didn't understand had mostly reverted to the owners of Whitelands.

Throughout London, Air Raid Wardens' posts, often staffed by women, were now situated in basements to monitor the progress of raids or call for medical or rescue support. Light Rescue units had been formed to deal with minor incidents. Heavy Rescue teams utilised cutting and earth-moving equipment to dig out people buried under their homes. The Local Defence Volunteers, or Home Guard, the much derided Dad's Army of later years, was also formed. The invasion scare was diminishing – somehow the country understood (and was immensely proud of the fact) that Hitler had shot his bolt across the Channel, and it had fallen short. There would be other battles now, long grinding battles in North Africa, terrifying battles against the wolf packs of U-boats in the Atlantic, before any military return to Europe was even remotely possible. 'Hard pounding', the Duke of Wellington would have called it. By the early summer of 1941 Britain was settling in for a long war.

With the beginning of hostilities, some parts of Chelsea had been slow to join the surge of determination that characterised the rest of the *communitas Angliae* as the old documents had it, the whole British community as it was now. This reluctance was, for the most part, over marginal issues. One such was the question of donating cast-iron railings to the war effort. In the summer of 1941 *The Times* reported that unlike the rest of London, and indeed the whole country, Chelsea squares had not yet given up their railings for war scrap. St Luke's Church, the newspaper announced, was the only donor (60 tons of never-to-be-replaced early nineteenth century railings). *The Times* completely ignored the equal quantity of less impressive railings from Guinness Trust. In a letter to *The Times* one of the far-seeing residents of the squares explained that to surrender the railings would result in a decline in post-war property values. Certainly the council had great difficulty contacting the garden committees of the various squares, all members of which had to give their permission before the railings could be taken. Other squares, in other boroughs, surrendered their railings with notably more good grace than Chelsea. But this was only a token reluctance by local residents to support the war effort, a certain sense that the leeway they had enjoyed most of their lives should continue to be recognised if only in this small area. Many of the residents of Chelsea's squares were, of course, already in the forces or engaged in valuable war work.

Chelsea's bohemians initially showed rather more reluctance to join the war effort. But then bohemians, whether in Prague or Paris, were often strangely slow to sense or understand the nature of real political danger, even when it was in the process of taking military shape. Many certainly began the war as they had ended the peace, in a state of heightened anguish about possible damage to their way of life. Admittedly, Chelsea's bohemians might have been somewhat different from others: younger, closer to bright young things than real bohemians perhaps but still often absurdly prepared to believe their modest efforts with the paintbrush justified their withdrawal from the war. Perhaps this confidence derived from the fact that a few shillings a week would buy you the teaching of the really talented, like Henry Moore, teaching at Chelsea Polytechnic at the time.

Richard, surname no longer remembered, lived next to my father in a room on a Whitelands maids' corridor rented from wealthier relatives in an apartment somewhere above. He was a very young (as I see now), over-confident youth who claimed to have a studio somewhere near Redcliffe Gardens. I only met him twice and he had no interest in speaking to me, for which I don't blame him. But he was insufferably rude to my father, demanding attention and service on the grounds that he was a tenant and my father an employee. My father, as ever preoccupied with losing his job, felt he had no choice but to comply with his neighbour's wishes. Drunk, Richard would change tune and offer to share a bottle of beer and sit on my father's bed in the small room and talk about his painting. Looking back on it I can see what an intolerable, self-satisfied bore my father must have found him.

Richard had money, though not much, and no responsibilities. He also had a 4F medical grade. In 1940 he had regarded the war as an empty example of pointless physical courage between a generation of German and British youth, nose-led by their capitalist (Jewish?) masters. Russia, he believed, had done the right thing in encouraging Germany and Britain to fight to the death. Later, when Germany attacked Russia, though seeing himself as a left-leaning thinker rather than a Communist, he dramatically changed tack to follow the Communist Party line.

*

This, of course, was my father's account of the information he had gained after Richard had spent a late night at the Pheasantry Club – my father's description filtered through the nib of my own pen. It is probably no more than roughly accurate. But the point I'm making is that the whole country did not hurl itself into the war at the starter's gun in September 1939. Of course I'm not suggesting that Chelsea artists did not go to war. They did, for the most part like millions of others, but there were marked exceptions.

People who thought like Richard were not the unquantifiable group of Fascist-leaning mandarins, peers and junior ministers (even, as we know, occasionally admirals) who originally supported peace at almost any price that someone else was prepared to pay. They were not members of 'The English Mystery', that secret society of far Right aristocrats. The Left-leaning Richards were the obverse of the coin. Their theoretical justification for their view of the war (a healthy capitalist v. capitalist struggle) only held up, however, as long as Adolf Hitler played along.

As June 1941 burned itself away and the raids on London almost ceased, another great move in what was rapidly becoming the world-wide game of chess was being prepared in Berlin. It was a move which would bring massive relief to many (and of course in the thirties they were not just bohemians) who had found themselves bewildered and deeply pained at the thought that the Soviet Union was an active ally of Adolf Hitler. A hundred excuses had been manufactured. But Stalin *was* active. He *was* supplying oil and grain and metals in huge quantities to Hitler's armies. The Left-leaning world knew in its heart that Russia was no longer on the side of the angels. The far-Left continued to believe the Soviet Union planned a dramatic change; the dilettante Left like Richard and his friends preferred to make love and jokes and continue to *hope* Russia planned a dramatic change. Russia, as we now know, had no plans in that direction.

When Hitler invaded Russia the shock to what remained of

bohemian Chelsea was profound. Did this mean that, for Richard, since capitalism was no longer the primary issue, since Fascism had to be destroyed first, he (having obtained exemption from the army) would be volunteering for munitions work to aid the Soviet Union? No, it meant he was making family arrangements to develop his painterly talents somewhere in Canada or the United States.

Nobody in Whitelands House was sorry to see him go. The heat of my feeling is in direct proportion to my belief as a small boy and indeed to this day, that the war against Fascism was worth winning, that the sacrifices Britain was making were worth making.

And yes, since you mention it, I do still have a problem with the ambiguity of my own father's conscription status.

We returned to London at the end of 1941. The World's End looked not much different from the last time we'd seen it, even more drab perhaps. But La-di-dah was on his island leaping from one tied bundle of newspapers to another, Perry's the fish and chip shop still fried and, bad luck for us, Gus the one-legged barber in Langton Street, still chopped hair.

I think his shop must have been the dirtiest in the World's End. I sincerely hope so. I think my father sent my brother and me there quite simply because it was the World's End barber that everybody used. The shop had two small rooms, one with a barber's chair, the other a bedroom. I assume there was a shared sink and lavatory somewhere in the small yard outside. You came off the street into the hair-cutting room, a ten by twelve area with patchy lino floor covering. A very narrow seat ran along the side wall of the shop and this was normally strewn with newspapers open at the racing pages. The floor would be thick with hair interleafed with week-old copies of the *Sporting Life* and crushed out cigarettes. Two or three men would normally be sitting waiting. They were in all likelihood known to us, which would somehow increase our embarrassment and distaste for what was to come. The talk was entirely about horse or

dog racing, about winners, prices, fancied runners, missed opportunities. We would sit silently, apprehensive that Gus talking casually
to one of his cronies over his shoulder, would clip our hair down to
within a quarter inch of the skull.

Most of this was tolerable if you didn't peek into the back room.
This was difficult to avoid though, because Gus kept the connecting
door open all the time. A large brass bed filled the room, a tumble of
unclean sheets and blankets. Again it was only visible under folded,
crushed or crumpled copies of the racing papers. The other furniture
was one hat-rack on which Gus hung his clothes. The floor was
boarded. From time to time, particularly when the front door opened
on a windy day, a wave of cut hair and racing papers would lift gently
into the bedroom.

Gus was quick, rough and never talked to us when it was our turn.
All we heard above our heads was the clip of scissors as he offered his
predictions to his customers for Stamford Bridge or Harringay for
that evening's meeting. Gus himself laid his bets with Alf Gordon the
local bookmaker or with his runner (later to be my colleague at the
race track), Fatty the Yid. When Fatty the Yid came in there was no
room for his huge backside on the narrow shelf-like seat so he would
discuss business from inside the back room perched on the bed
which would creak and bend under his enormous weight.

Gus himself seldom went to the track, even to Stamford Bridge.
His pleasure was taken once every month or two when he would
dress up in a, no doubt seedy, dinner jacket and go 'up West' for
some entertainment of his choice. When my father told me this long
after the war, I had the utmost difficulty in imagining Gus at a table
in some nightclub playing Champagne Charlie to an admiring ring of
showgirls. But clearly the Cremorne traditions of the World's End
were not quite dead.

Gus's barber shop is now long gone, of course. I'm surprised it
never burnt down with so much combustible material floating in and
out of the two rooms and cigarettes habitually crushed out on the

floor. Today the shop's part of a smart Italian fish restaurant where I used to meet my agent to be given an update on book sales.

We celebrated Christmas and the New Year at home in number 3 Guinness Trust, though unknown to us the coming year would not offer very much to celebrate. Pearl Harbor had brought the Americans into the war together with, for us, an enormous burst of confidence that Hitler would now be quickly beaten. Yet the first months of the New Year brought grim news from the Far East, both for Britain and America. I remember the sinking of the battleships, the *Prince of Wales* and the *Repulse*. The loss of Singapore and the Philippines became just part of a long depressing catalogue of Japanese victories. My father cheered me by saying that everybody knew that it would take some time for America to fight back. She had an army to build, factories to turn to the making of planes and guns, warships to launch. There weren't going to be any quick victories.

In fact, I think the year 1942 can easily lay claim to being the darkest of the twentieth century, possibly even the most hopeless in human history. In January a secret conference took place in the Berlin suburb of Wannsee. During the course of that day, it was efficiently decided how many German policemen, French gendarmes, Ukrainian auxiliaries, locomotives, cattle trucks, kilometres of new railroad, poison gas supplies, trained Allgemeine SS guards, rolls of barbed wire, posts, staples, planking and a thousand other items needed to be assembled to achieve the extermination of European Jewry. Throughout the year the horrors of arrest and transportation taking place on the continent were matched by the barbarities of the fighting in Russia and the wholesale murders being committed behind their own lines by the SS and the Soviet NKVD. The German Army had picked itself up after the Russian winter had all but destroyed it and, as SS Reichsfürher Heinrich Himmler put it, 'the Goths were moving East again'. This time Hitler had decided to strike not at Moscow but south-east towards Stalingrad.

As spring arrived, hope for an allied victory, even for the human race itself, could hardly be more remote.

Early in this year daubed whitewash lettering began to appear on the sides of bombed houses: *Second front now – Summer 1942!* I took very little notice until early summer. We were now going to school at St Mark's just opposite Stamford Bridge Stadium. Our short journey took us along Hortensia Road where Harry Veitch of the Exotic Nurseries had once had his top-hatted floor walkers showing customers the remarkable blooms. Now the site was occupied by the gutted and half-collapsed Hudson's depository that had been fire-bombed last year, and on the other side of the road, still unfamiliar to me at this stage, a building called the Sloane School. We usually hunted around in the blackened wreckage of the depository on our way to St Mark's in the hope of repeating a find I had made last month, one whose renown had travelled like news of a major archaeological discovery and had kids coming from all the sur-rounding schools to dig away in the ash and brickdust on Saturday mornings. It was a purple velvet scabbard for an Italian stiletto (no sign of the dagger itself). The inside lining was of leather and the rim where hilt met scabbard was of real silver (although not much of it). Nevertheless word spread: there were treasures to be found at Hudson's Depository. The scavengers were out.

I was one of them on my way to school when I first saw the huge dribbling whitewash letters on the blackened far wall of the Depository: *Make Britain do its bit – Second Front now!'*

I thought whoever had written that had a real nerve. We'd won the Battle of Britain. We'd survived the blitz. The man who painted that ought to have slept nights in Whitelands boiler room and woken with mouth, ears, eyes, clothes, full of coke dust. The lettering was too high and far too big for me to climb up and rub it out but I was late for school that morning trying to throw handfuls of damp ash at it in an unsuccessful attempt to obliterate it.

*

That night at tea I told my father about the slogan on the wall of Hudson's Depository. Who would do that? Who could think Britain wasn't doing its bit? It had been doing its bit longer than anybody else. He was trying to read the *Sporting Life* as he ate his liver and bacon but realised that in my indignation I was going to give him no peace until he explained.

'Most of the people in this country think the same way about the war,' he said laying aside his paper.

'How do they think?'

'More or less as you do.' He smiled. 'More or less.'

'But some don't?'

'That's right.'

'Spies?'

'Well, I wasn't thinking of spies,' he said. 'I was thinking of members of the Communist Party.'

I'd heard of them, of course. 'They used to fight the Fascists at the World's End?'

'That's right. They look at the world in a very different way. They're difficult people to talk about because they're not all the same. Many of them honestly think their way of arranging things will give workers everywhere a better chance for a decent life. And these people are prepared to give time and money and sometimes their lives to achieve that. That's more or less your Uncle Bill's way of looking at it.'

'Uncle Bill's a Communist?' This was news to me. Bill was married to my father's sister Nell. I didn't know him very well because they lived miles away in Streatham.

'I don't think he's planning to give his life for the workers,' my father said. 'But he's a Communist, yes.'

A frightening idea came to me. 'Are you?'

He laughed. 'I'd lose my job tomorrow if I were a Communist.'

That was a relief.

'But there are other members of the Party who don't think the same way. They're not really for the workers, as much as they're for Russia. They're for the system. They believe in that more than they believe in anything else. Do you understand me?'

'No.'

'For them, Russia, the Soviet Union, has become more important than people. Some of them would be willing for us to lose at the front door if it saves Russia at the back.'

'And they think we're not doing our bit?'

'As far as they're concerned nobody's really doing their bit except the Russians. But don't forget, Dee, it is true that the Russians have far more soldiers fighting the Germans than anybody else.'

'But they're still losing.'

'They're not doing well at the moment, true, which is why the Communists want us to cross the Channel and invade France now. Open up another front. A Second Front, as it's called.'

'Good idea.'

'Not if we get such a hiding when we do that we can't go back there for years. It's like a bully at school who's bigger than you. You know you've got to fight him sometime but best to wait until you're a bit bigger and stronger before you take him on. Make sure you give yourself the best chance of beating him.'

At school I explained the situation to Bobby Cooksley and John Knewstub. The Communists were spies who wanted to get us to attack France before we were ready. Some of them were known to be hanging round the World's End in the blackout. I didn't mention Uncle Bill.

John Knewstub looked disbelieving. 'In the blackout?' he said.

First chance I had I pointed out the big whitewash message on Hudson's Depository's blackened wall. 'Who d'you think did that, then? And when? You think they did it in their dinner break?'

Bobby Cooksley said they definitely didn't. That was good enough for John.

I listened to the news regularly now. Sevastopol and Rostov fell to the Germans in July. For a few days I even noted down the progress of the German advance in an exercise book. By the end of that month German troops were leading camel trains through the Caucasus, their objective the rail and river junction of Stalingrad which would isolate Moscow in the north. Everybody said things looked bad. My father said America had a powerful enemy on its hands in Japan and was already fighting naval battles in the Pacific. It would be some time yet before American soldiers could be spared for Europe.

Then on August 19 the news burst upon us: the Canadians and British had invaded France. I couldn't hear enough. I raced home from school and began to quiz my mother who had heard the news. It was too early to say how things were going but apparently thousands of Canadian and British soldiers had landed on the beaches at Dieppe. They had taken tanks with them which everybody on the news had found very significant. The Germans were falling back and the French people were warmly welcoming the Canadians who spoke their language. But I should wait until my father came in. He would know more about it.

My grandmother was doing some darning in the front room. I went in to ask her what she thought. She put down her work on the table and helped herself to a pinch of snuff. 'It could be the finish for the Germans,' she said, drawing out her hat-pin, holding the hat steady and then plunging the pin back in.

'Unless it's spies that've led us up the garden path. Communists,' I said. 'They'd sooner we lost the war than the Russians.'

My grandmother frowned at me and prepared another pinch of snuff. 'I dare say,' she murmured. 'I dare say they would.'

I can't remember how many days it took for the bad news to start rolling in. A German counter-attack had begun. The Canadians were fighting fiercely, but taking heavy casualties. And then it was over. All our troops had been killed or captured. I went out into the yard and walked around by myself. In a sense, you could say the Communists had won.

It was also a time when I couldn't forget my father's prediction: the war to last two years and Britain defeated.

When I thought of these things I became miserable. I went down to the river by myself and cried a bit. The war had been going on for three years now and all my main memories were of events since it had started. Although an incurable optimist, even I knew that it hadn't been going well. Britain had held off the Germans in 1940 and 1941 but this year was dogged by bad news. More than that, it began to seem that the war could go on for ever. It took quite an effort even to imagine living in peacetime. Of course I realised sweets would be off the ration then and pomegranates back in the shops (although I couldn't remember what they tasted like), but I was mostly thinking that when the war was over I could have a pair of white running slippers because they wouldn't be rationed either and I was aware my father was making more money now than he used to.

When I came back from the river it was with a new resolve. This was not the time to be miserable about the loss of Tobruk, the defeat at Dieppe (that'd show the Communists), or the German advance on Stalingrad. Something had to be done. I thought of forming an army of boys from the Guinness yard. We could even let those from round the Hundreds join, if we had to. We'd need helmets and armbands . . . Where from? I put that idea aside for the moment. I had to do something practical to contribute to the defeat of Germany. But as yet, I couldn't think of anything that might tip the scales.

In the end, my first venture was to run a raffle, the illicit proceeds of which I sent to the Minister of War. My father, who'd warned me raffles were illegal, laughed when he saw the official envelope delivered a week later and said it was probably a summons. But in fact, when I opened it, it was a letter of thanks from the Minister himself. This was to be the first of several such schemes to aid the war effort throughout 1942, some considerably less successful than others. Later there would be more ambitious undertakings, even involving a difficult degree of negotiation with Chelsea Police Station.

And I had not given up my idea of forming an army, but that was for later in the year.

THIRTEEN

Land of Opportunities

The 1940-1 blitz on London and the far less frequent air attacks that continued into 1942 destroyed over a million houses and damaged, in some degree, hundreds of thousands of others. It was normal in London (and I'm sure many other blitzed British cities from Glasgow to Plymouth) to see streets of abandoned houses or gaps in terraces where two or three homes had been demolished by a smaller bomb. Most of the damaged houses were very quickly made safe by the Heavy Rescue Units and a triangle of thick timbers propping up the side wall of a terrace became another of the everyday sights that people in bombed cities took for granted.

To boys of my age the bombing had opened up a vast and varied new playground. Within a few hundred yards of Guinness Trust there were literally hundreds of abandoned houses. We had always had the river to play along but now we had an extraordinary selection of dens or camps in which to set ourselves up. No cramped potting sheds in the back of our own suburban gardens for us, no damp spot in the shubbery where you ate sandwiches and were always at the beck and call of your anxious mother. We were free.

Saturday morning was prime time. The gang comprised boys from Guinness and others like Bobby Cooksley and sometimes John

Knewstub from St Mark's where we were currently at school. Where exactly they lived I never knew, and it never seemed important. This was time of our own, time completely cut off from our parents' concerns and worries. On Saturdays both my mother and my father worked all day, she from nine in the morning till nine at night in Hunt's the haberdashery where she had started before the war. I wasn't really aware of it at this time but my father was now working Saturday evenings at Stamford Bridge dog track for Alf Gordon, the biggest bookmaker in the World's End. Kit and I were therefore nominally in the charge of my grandmother who gave us both a fair amount of rope. When I asked my mother in later life what she thought I was doing then, she normally shuddered and said, 'I hate to think.' I'm sure she had in fact heard enough to mean this literally.

What we did was more or less what all boys of that age enjoy doing. We explored. We established camps or dens. We played games of German spies and British Army. But we did all these things in surroundings most boys never have the opportunity to play in.

To do this we climbed tumbledown garden walls and ducked under shattered back doors to enter a dusty, cracked and broken-windowed wonderland. We wandered though enormous houses on Redcliffe Gardens or the empty flats in Ashburnham Mansions behind Guinness Trust. Empty of people, that is, but not of objects. I think now that many people must have taken the opportunity of the bombing to leave behind some of the junk of empire inherited from fathers and grandfathers who had once ruled a quarter of the globe. We found rooms with lop-sided antelopes' heads mounted on the walls. We found military portraits and racks of ancient gramophone records, piles of books, comfortable, though battered cane arm-chairs, hammered-brass Arab tables . . . We shuffled through old secretaires, sometimes collapsed by blast or split by a flying splinter of metal, and found old letters tied in bundles with silk ribbon. There were browning photographs too: of men on hunters toasting the photographer with their stirrup cup, cool muslin-dressed women holding tea parties on spacious lawns, or perhaps a young Indian boy in turban and white robe standing next to a regimental sign at the entrance to some summer camp in the hills.

There was no need to force doors or damage locks. Each Saturday morning we were presented with an *embarras de richesses*. Other gangs roamed the ruins too, and rumours passed back and forth among us about finds of particularly unusual bombed buildings or abandoned contents. Riley's Gang was our main competitor and word was out that he had found a Chinese den with silk robes and magnificent curved swords (I think we were thinking of Japanese swords), and Chinese writing on scrolls and opium pipes.

We were particularly keen on the swords and opium pipes and we hunted for clues Saturday after Saturday, planning the swoops on Riley hang-outs from our operations room on the top floor of Ashburnham Mansions, trailing Riley and his known associates all over the World's End – and even once trying to install a mole in his gang. But if Riley's Chinese den ever existed we never found it. Last time I saw Riley was about thirty years later. He was a conductor on a number 14 bus, swinging out with his arm hooked round the pole as it cornered into the Chelverton Road bus garage at Putney. I swear he gave me a wink.

Ashburnham Mansions was one of our favourite sites, an upper-middle-class block with more in common with Cheyne Walk than the World's End. Moving into a new headquarters which for some reason we did quite frequently, we would get to work with brooms and dust-pans all of which were to be found in the building. We would move dusty rugs and favourite furniture in from another flat and would each choose a room in the new one for a personal 'office'. All our offices were bigger by far than the rooms we shared with brothers or sisters or aunts or grandmothers in Guinness, or wherever Bobby Cooksley and the *outlanders* lived.

I suppose there were (and still are) fifty or more flats there, which offered plenty of choice as long as we kept to the upper floors out of sight of patrolling police. This, I admit, was a problem for me because I saw myself as a law-abiding citizen and always impressed on the boys that we were borrowing these flats and weren't here to do any more damage than Hitler had already done. But all the same we knew that what we were doing was not approved of. Indeed there were fading ARP notices on many of the buildings we explored warning that entry could be dangerous. We were therefore always on the look-out for the police and had an established routine to abandon ship via the expanding fire escape which ran down the blind side of the building. This we practised doing just once, a frightening experience, and discovered we needed the weight of two boys to get the iron ladder moving smoothly down to the garage roof below. From there we could jump free with the special parachute jump we had perfected for emergencies.

In fact we never used the fire escape for real because our only major scare was when, to our horror, two policemen were spotted, one climbing into the ground-floor window of the mansions while the other positioned himself outside where he could watch the fire escape. Obviously we had been seen moving in front of one of the broken windows. There were only Bobby Cooksley and myself at home at the time, the others having all been detailed to follow Riley or stake out his house in Lots Road. We crept to the edge of the stairwell. Down below we could hear the policeman making his way up the stairs, slowed down fortunately by the clutter of broken doors, shattered window frames, and everything else the bomb blast had thrown there.

Then we heard his voice: 'Come down here, lads. I know you're up there.'

We were trapped. What our punishment for this might have been from police or parents I don't like to think. There was only one remaining escape route. We ran back through our flat to my office, the balconied rear bedroom overlooking the communal lawn five floors below. It had been chosen because it was light and airy, because none of the windows was broken, and because it was large enough to take the sofa we had struggled up five floors with from the basement below. This sofa, it will hardly surprise you to hear, was placed facing the fireplace with ample room to move round behind it. It was rule number one, however, to consider a line of retreat, however fanciful, when choosing a den. In this case, Bobby Cooksley and I had both agreed that a climb over the balcony and down the back of the building was perfectly possible if we were blocked from reaching the fire escape. One glance out of the window now, however, with the policeman's voice echoing up the stairwell, and the prospect of a Lone Ranger-style escape bid was daunting to say the least.

It was five floors down. Each balcony was supported by two cast-iron poles. You could, in theory, swing out over the balcony rail and slide down the pole to the balcony below, swing over the rail again, slide down, and so on to the ground. But it meant that every time you swung out over the rail and dangled your legs to catch the supporting pole below, you hung over a sheer drop.

Only a floor below now, I could hear the policeman shouting to us. Bobby and I looked at each other. There were only seconds left to decide.

We did it in nervous unison. Mostly I kept my mind on the green-painted balcony support. I looked down only once, terrified myself and didn't look again, arriving at the last balcony shaking with triumph. A grinning Bobby made it down his side. Then with one well-practised parachute jump we were sprawled safely on the overgrown lawn.

Getting to our feet, we twisted our heads once to look up at the high building above us then ran crouching across the long grass, through the hole in the nearest garden wall, on through the bombed wreck of Mrs Quinn's house and out on to the river end of Edith Grove. We always called it Mrs Quinn's because we found some bones buried in the garden and a tattered photograph of a Mrs Emily

Quinn and were convinced Mr Quinn had done for her. Sometime we intended to report the matter to the police.

From Edith Grove we sauntered back through Guinness Trust to warn the other boys when they returned from Riley-watching that the rozzers were on to us. Positioning ourselves behind the ruins of a fire-gutted St John's Church, we saw that the two policemen were just leaving.

After that we favoured the garage at the bottom of Ashburnham Mansions as our den. It was a large glass-roofed structure with a few pieces of machinery for repairing cars, but behind the main court were a pair of windowless offices. It lacked the middle-class comforts that we were accustomed to in the flats above but it did have tins of white distemper which we used to decorate the main office. More astonishingly it had electric light. Although electricity was familiar from school and shops and even some people's houses in the World's End, it was still a particular wonder to us to have electricity in our office since we had none in Guinness Trust. That, a gas ring and running water, made the garage one of the best-appointed dens we ever had. There was a telephone on my desk but sadly it didn't work – although who I might have called I can't imagine. We got to work on the garage that same morning, painting and selecting furnishings. Our best furniture was hauled down from our old top-floor den to the second floor of Ashburnham Mansions and lowered by ropes through the reinforced glass swing-window of the garage roof. We were soon comfortably installed and could have made tea on the working gas ring if we'd had any.

But we were still no nearer finding Riley's Chinese den.

Another problem however now began to preoccupy us. In one of the Ashburnham flats we had found a locked wooden box, perhaps a foot long and six inches wide. It had some sort of brass inlay on its curved top *but no visible means of opening it.*

This presented us with a real difficulty. It was obvious that the box contained something mysterious or at least special. We could hear paper fluttering about inside it. Bobby Cooksley thought it was five-pound notes. I wasn't so sure. I suggested we ought to take it to Chelsea Police Station just up the King's Road and maybe say we'd found it outside in the street.

Nobody was in favour of this course of action – and the truth is I wasn't really myself. But I had a reputation to maintain. Having maintained it, I conceded and Bobby Cooksley got the big screwdriver from the tool-box.

Turning the darkwood box over in his hand, he pointed to four brass screws on the bottom. 'I knew they'd have to be there,' he said. His father was a carpenter before the war so he knew about things like that. Selecting a smaller screwdriver, he unscrewed each corner in turn. Then, shaking the box in one hand, he dislodged a series of wooden compartments which dropped out into his hand. The box had contained an old pen set with two glass bottles stained with dried red and black ink.

But that wasn't what we were all looking at. In Bobby's hand remained the contents of a *secret* compartment.

'Jumping Jehozaphat!' he said. We got this from the comics.

Underneath the pen set was hidden a small wad of slim yellow booklets, a dozen at most. And they were printed in German!

This clearly called for action right away. German documents in secret compartments . . . But there were problems. We had roamed through so many flats that none of us could any longer remember where exactly we had found the box. Then there was the other problem that some of the others weren't at all sure it was actually German writing on the yellow booklets. They needed a swastika or a picture of Hitler before they could believe we had unearthed a nest of spies. I reminded them all of the flashing lights many people in Guinness claimed to have seen the night St John's Church and the Mansions were bombed.

John Knewstub was sceptical. 'Why would the spy signal bombs down on his own head?'

I pointed out it was an obvious mistake. There are always mistakes in wartime. People think war goes smoothly, but it never does. My father had told me that. Obviously the spy was signalling the bomber towards the power station and the pilot mistook the signals. Quite normal in war, I assured him. No, the police had to be informed. One of these booklets should be put in an envelope with a letter.

'A letter has to have a stamp,' Knewstub said.

I gave him a pitying look. 'Bobby and me'll pay for it. Ha'penny each. OK, Bob?'

Bobby nodded reluctantly.

'And I'll write the letter,' I said.

We were not short of writing paper. In fact I think we had printed letterhead from almost every flat in Ashburnham Mansions. But we still didn't know which flat the box came from. And we didn't want to give the police any false leads, or accuse any innocent former tenant of betraying his country, so we carefully cut off the flat's number before I sat down at my desk to write.

It came out something like this;

TO THE POLICE.
There is a spy in Ashburnham Mansions. We think he lives in number 47 but it might be 22. Remember the one who was signalling with a torch the night St John's Church was bombed? Well then.
  P.S. He doesn't live there any more but this German message will give you all the clues you need to find him.
  Signed, HK (The Hooded Knights)

We stayed away from Ashburnham Mansions for some while after the letter was sent, but we kept the entrance under what we considered close, if in fact cursory, surveillance. Our field of interest had, as it happened, moved down to the river again so that the loss of our Ashburnham Mansions headquarters was less telling than it might have been. What puzzled us, however, was that the police had not swooped immediately, in large numbers, on what we believed to be a German spy nest using the mansions at night when we weren't there.

The answer, we realised, must lie in that yellow printed booklet.

It did. Some six months later, by which time I had been transferred to the local version of a grammar school, I asked the German master if he would translate the yellow booklet. By way of explanation I said no more than that it had been found hidden in an old box.

Fortunately, I did not tell him of my suspicions that it was a top secret spy document. He mused over it for a moment or two, turned to the back page and lifted his eyebrows promisingly.

'Is it code?' I asked him.

'No.'

'It's German, though?'

'Of a sort. A Swiss hotel menu and brochure. For businessmen. Unusual in that it offers a night-club with what appear to be scantily dressed dancers to entertain the male guests.'

Much as we enjoyed the bombed houses we never entirely deserted the river. We mostly went at low tide when we could run along the shingle which was still visible in those days and do a bit of beach-combing in the mud. One really adventurous day we climbed through holes in the wire netting under Battersea Bridge's spars, waved off the flapping pigeons and clambered through portholes in the curved steel girders until we reached the first stone buttress.

A small stone archway tempted us, set like a medieval doorway in the top of the buttress. A short but dangerous step from the girder across the void, with the river flowing thirty feet below, would take us into the mystery of the middle of the massive bridge support. It was quite possible that nobody had been in there since the bridge was built. Who knows what the old navvies might have left? It was one of the silliest and most dangerous things Bobby and I had ever done.

When we dared to make the step we had no idea how we might get back to the girders, and our chances of calling for help from under the bridge were close to nil. Worst of all, of course, was the possibility of a fall into the river below. I took a deep breath and made the step. Bobby followed behind almost immediately.

Inside the central bastion there were dark passages leading to an enormous stone cavern. Excited as we were, we were by now seriously frightened that we would not get back. As each short passage opened into another bare stone cavern it was almost pitch black. At the end of the very last passage there was an iron ladder. I climbed it, felt a trap-door above my head and worked the iron handle. It was too heavy for me to move. Bobby climbed up the ladder and positioned himself beside me, both of us sharing the weight on our backs. Using all our strength we heaved it up to the sudden rush of light and traffic. An inch or two further and we saw we were in the middle of the pavement with adult legs, male and female, passing back and forth. Relief merged with a blast of fresh air from the river. We ignored the bewildered glances of passers-by as we scrambled up on to the bridge, dropped the trap-door back into position and ran for the safety of the familiar World's End riverside.

Most of our time spent by the river was at low tide. I had once been told at school of the sacking of John of Gaunt's riverside palace and the hurling of all his coins and weapons into the river. The possibility of some of his great treasure having been washed up at the World's End never ceased to intrigue me. Spies and buried treasure were our twin obsessions.

High tide was not really interesting to us and if we were there then it was more or less by mistake, or perhaps inspired by one of the sporadic rumours that a dead German airman was floating down towards Chelsea in his Mae West. Somebody's dad would have seen him at Putney and if we hurried we could beat the outgoing tide and drag him out of the water at Sir Thomas More's mulberry tree which grew, and still grows, just next to Battersea Bridge. We were after his medals or anything that might have a swastika on it.

Responding to one such improbable rumour we ran down to the bridge one Saturday morning and climbed the mulberry. No sign of a dead German pilot – but a coaler had anchored off Dakin's Yard. It was about a hundred feet long and we could clearly see the double Bofors gun on its deck.

It was a squally day with sudden short bursts of rain, not enough to wet you through but enough to leave your woollen clothes damp and uncomfortable. We were about to turn for home when we saw six or seven Merchant Navy men begin to climb down the rope ladder to a long wooden rowing boat bucking on the heavy swell.

We hung about watching them row the heavy boat to the steps just below us and called down a few questions to them about how many times they'd fired their gun at German planes or E-boats. At the steps six of the sailors left the boat. There was only one man remaining now, much older than the others, and it was obvious he was going to have trouble handling the heavy boat in the fast-flowing tide and gusting wind.

The others had disappeared. We watched the old man's struggle with the oars, seeing the front of the boat turned by wind and tide every time he tried to drive it out towards mid-river and the anchored coaler.

After about ten minutes he lowered the oars and let the tide bring the boat back alongside the steps. We hung over the wet granite of the parapet.

'You boys,' he said, 'you look a strong coupla lads. You want to give me a hand with this? I'll pick up someone aboard to help me row you back.'

We were down the steps in a matter of seconds and clambering into the boat. The man set us both on one of the seats so that the two of us could handle one oar while he looked after the other.

'When I say heave,' he said, 'give it all you've got.'

We spat on our hands, rubbed them together and waited for the word.

'Now, *heave!*'

We dug the oar into the water and heaved.

I'd never thought for a moment it would be like pulling through treacle. I looked at Bobby to see if he was pulling his weight and saw by his puffed red face that he was. The second or two when we lifted the oar out of the water allowed a blissful relaxation for our muscles – but only for a moment.

'Heave!'

The old man kept us at it. I suppose it was only eighty yards to the ship but rowing there was the one totally exhausting experience I remember from boyhood.

'Heave . . . heave . . . heave . . .' the old man shouted rhythmically. The rough wooden planking under us lifted and fell, rocking from one side to the other so that the oar was nearly wrenched from our hands. And because our backs were to the ship we had no real idea, after we were clear of the steps, how much progress we were making across the water.

When we finally bumped against the hull and the old sailor grabbed the rope ladder, I thought my arms would be too weak to carry me up. But there was an insistent note in his voice that drove us on. I went first. The side of the ship seemed to go on for ever – rusting, peeling paint and a burnt smell like a dozen steam trains. The wind carried smoke from the funnel down to us, a thick choking cloud with pieces of grit in it big enough to sting your cheeks.

When Bobby and I reached the deck we were a forlorn pair. We looked round for the old man who had pressganged us and found he had already disappeared. Then everything changed. Another man came out of one of the steel cabins and on to the deck.

'Trust old Jock to pull a pair of lads in,' he said. 'You did a good job there, boys. You'll want to have a look over the ship, am I right?'

Calling through a voice-pipe he ordered up two mugs of tea. And most important of all he asked us if we wanted to have a look at the Bofors gun.

Striding the deck with the first mate, mug of tea in our hands, we felt like kings. Each of us was given a go in the Bofors seat, working the controls that trained the gun. I aimed it at the river side of Lots Road power station, making *chu . . . chu . . . chu . . . chu . . . chu* noises to imitate the sound of a rapid firing Bofors. It was a standard shot in films and newsreels so I knew all the moves.

Soon it was time for us to go home. Bobby Cooksley's mother never seemed to expect him back at any time but my grandmother was making dinner – and more to the point my father had said he would be home in the afternoon. The first mate called up the old sailor we'd helped and he came on deck, grumbling and tying his raincoat with string. One of the young cooks would take the other oar. Bobby and I would sit in the back of the boat and be rowed across. We were just preparing to face the rope ladder down to the rowing boat when that familiar sinister hollow howling seemed to rise from the depths of the river. An air raid.

On deck a dozen men appeared at once running to their action stations, clapping helmets on their heads. The young cook disappeared. 'I've really got to be home,' I appealed to the old man.

'Admiralty orders,' he said, not without some satisfaction. 'All ships to weigh anchor during an air raid.'

'What does that mean?'

'We're moving.'

I could see we were moving. 'Where to?'

'Depends how long the air raid is. Nine Elms, Tower of London maybe . . .'

I was furious. 'I wish we'd bloody well not helped you now!'

The first mate came running past. 'Don't worry, son,' he said, stopping for a moment. 'We'll be back here in no time.' He eyed the old man. 'Take them into the galley. Get 'em a corned beef sandwich.'

We pulled out from Chelsea Reach and steamed down river. With our sandwich and another mug of tea we went back on deck. There was quite a lot of gunfire ahead but it wouldn't have been easy to see German planes in this murky weather even if they'd been attacking our ship. To our intense disappointment the Bofors gun was never fired.

I was very late back. My grandmother was obviously a lot more worried about my father's imminent return than she was about where I had been. I had my dinner quickly and spent the rest of the afternoon worrying about whether to tell him. I knew he generally thought it was a good thing for us to roam about and have adventures. But he would come down hard on Kit or me taking a stupid risk. The trouble was it wasn't always possible to guess what he'd think *was* a stupid risk. With my mother it was easy. She didn't fuss and she wasn't overprotective, but as far as Kit and I were concerned no risk was worthwhile. She didn't have my father's obsession with preparing us for the harsher aspects of life, especially the physical ones.

I remember once climbing up into a forbidden high cupboard in the scullery. I must have been six or seven at the most. I reached for the top shelf, scooped for something there and pulled down a cut-throat razor, the blade opening as it fell. It slashed my knee before it hit the ground and blood ran freely. My grandmother, who was looking after us as usual, tore off a piece of pillow case, wrapped my leg and set it up on another chair while feeding me sausage sandwiches. I looked down at the impressively wide bloodstain on the strip of pillow case with some satisfaction and waited confidently for my mother to get back from work.

My father arrived first. He listened to what had happened. 'He's got a bad cut on his knee,' my grandmother said.

My father looked down at it as she peeled back the bandage. 'So he has,' he said. And turned and left the flat.

At the time I was shattered by the callousness of it – much later I discovered he'd met my mother from work and warned her to try and modify her sympathy. It was the only way to teach me a lesson.

On the day of our visit to the coaler he sat down at the kitchen table, nodding as I recounted the fight we'd had to row the boat against the Thames tide and the scary climb up the rope ladder. I thought all the stuff about the Bofors gun would interest him enough to change the expression on his face, which seemed to me to be neither approving nor disapproving. When I had finished he shook his head slowly and I realised he was having difficulty knowing how to respond. This was unusual. His reactions were usually quick, often alarmingly so to Kit and myself.

I decided to ask him outright. 'Should we have said no when the sailor asked us to help row the boat across?'

My father lifted his eyebrows. 'All's well that ends well,' he said. 'All the same, this is one thing you'd best not tell your mother, at least not for a few days, or she won't be so keen on letting you get up to your Saturday tricks.' And he went back to his *Sporting Life*.

I was surprised to discover that even my father could be unsure about which side of the line to stand.

Throughout the summer of 1942 the news from the Western Desert continued to be bad. The port of Tobruk was mentioned daily as was the German everybody was talking about – General Rommel.

Facing him in the defence of Tobruk in June 1942 was General Sir Neil Ritchie, commanding the British Eighth Army. Ritchie's misfortune, and that of his army, was that he had little experience as a field commander and was up against one of the most innovative generals of the war. Perhaps the result should not have been difficult to predict.

Most people in Britain did not realise how complete was Rommel's victory over Ritchie at Gazala where the British general squandered his superior tank force in a series of disjointed and unsuccessful attacks. But the result of the defeat, the fall of the fortress of Tobruk and the British headlong retreat to the Egyptian frontier, was a bitter blow to the home front. At number 3 Guinness Trust we had an unusual insight into events in the Western Desert. General Ritchie and his wife were tenants of an apartment at Whitelands House and my father quite accurately computed the ebb and flow of the desert battle from the degree of solace Lady Ritchie sought in the gin bottle. His calculations were, admittedly, supported by the comments of General 'Boy' Browning, later famous as the 1944 parachute commander at Arnhem, who also lived at White-lands. Unlike his disagreeable wife Daphne Du Maurier, Browning was quite happy to pass the time of day with my father, who had by now been promoted to the position of second porter. Perhaps 'Boy' Browning hinted too much about his fellow general's plight in the desert, but the fall of Tobruk was certainly less of a shock to my father than it appeared to be to many at a quite senior level in the government.

FOURTEEN

Goodbye, Bobby Cooksley

The unusual building of St Mark's Elementary School still stands, a small prep school now, not far from the gates of Stamford Bridge Stadium, although the previously grey brick has now been cleaned to a dramatic yellow. When Kit and I were there the grimy octagonal building contained, as far as I can recall, two junior classrooms downstairs and a senior classroom occupying the whole of the upper floor. From this senior classroom children took the eleven plus exam. Those who passed went to Sloane School for boys or Carlyle School for Girls, by then standing together on Harry Veitch's old Exotic Nursery patch on Hortensia Road. Those who failed moved into a building just behind the octagonal. There they would remain for another two years until, at the age of fourteen, they were released from school to become shop-assistants or errand boys, apprentice tradesmen or Watney's Brewery girls.

My chances of passing the eleven plus were not high. No genetic thread bound Kit or me to my father's extraordinary quickness with figures. While my English was satisfactory and expected by the teacher, Miss Perkins, to pass muster, nobody seriously thought I could make it through the arithmetic. My problem was that I never understood what any of it was for, beyond addition, subtraction, multiplication and division.

I don't know if this ignorance of the purpose of mathematics bothered me more than most other children in the class, but I think it probably did. I remember vaguely even now that the problem of percentages was not, for me, a simple school exercise. In our arithmetic book, to add to its allure, the problem was framed under the heading 'Stocks & Shares'. Nobody I knew, including Miss Perkins, knew what a debenture was, or what 3% Great Western Railway Debenture Stock maturing in 1951 meant. Or what BATS or preference shares were. Miss Perkins had the answer book which gave her some advantage but it didn't help her or us to know what we were doing. We simply did not come from the social class which held debenture stock. Mortgage calculations presented a similar problem. In a community where *nobody* had a mortgage we were presented with questions couched in terms of repayment or endowment mortgages that unnecessarily obfuscated the real mathematical issue. I am not, you understand, claiming that an arithmetic test book written by someone from our own background would have enabled me to pass the eleven plus. I doubt it. But it might have helped a lot of children who were more borderline than myself.

I failed.

I didn't at the time realise the significance of failure. I would be staying at St Mark's with Bobby Cooksley and John Knewstub and other friends. I wouldn't be going with those who had passed from St Mark's to Sloane School. I had no sense of disaster.

I know now how much of a blow it was to my father, although he contrived to keep it from me. He was determined to do all he could to help his sons up the ladder. The sad thing was that he could easily have taught me the arithmetic I lacked but he lacked the temperament to be a good teacher. He simply could not understand how anybody could fail to grasp the process of solving a maths problem with the same lightning speed he did. I was equally incapable of keeping up with the steps he took or of following the numbers that whisked before my eyes.

I'm not sure how my mother took my failure. Her natural role was to offer infinite support without any pressure to Kit and myself. My father could also be described as supportive – but with a strong element of additional expectation. My mother didn't blindly believe we could do no wrong, but I think she felt we had a war to survive and life was pressurised enough. Perhaps this was because we had already shared so much more together than the average pre-war family, during the blitz, trekking to Whitelands and staying at Windsor. But it also stemmed from her natural protectiveness which extended even so far as to modify the ambitions of my father. She was undoubtedly the one who held the centre of the family ring, the balance. With my father's full agreement, we lived by my mother's rules of sense and survival.

The simple concept of respect was at the core of her philosophy, as I believe it must have been for her father, Jesse James Toop. It was a respect she naturally accorded my father, my brother and myself. She knew its importance because it was a respect that she herself evoked naturally throughout her life. The result was that when, in later life, my father died and the family roles changed, with Kit and I now looking after *her*, it was a natural process involving no painful cession of authority. It's true this was not unaided by the fact that she somehow contrived to be the easiest possible person to get along with, and although never educated beyond fourteen years of age and in no sense an autodidact her advice continued to be sought by an extraordinary range of our more educated, but often troubled, friends. Few people have that classless ability to draw people to them. My mother was one of the few.

There was life after the eleven plus. Kit became more and more immersed in his football, playing for the school on the neighbouring St Mark's College pitch, the first time he had ever played on grass in his life. I pursued my own extra-mural activities with increasing energy.

The desperate state of the war news in the early autumn made me determined to act. The Germans seemed poised to gain knock-out victories in North Africa and at Stalingrad in Russia. Studying the atlas, I began to feel that it was reasonable to think in terms of a revival of the invasion threat of 1940.

It was time, it seemed to me, to abandon the Hooded Knights, or rather to convert them into a working army. With the help of Kit and Bobby Cooksley, I set up a recruiting office in the yard. I had done a bit of drilling in the Church Lads' Brigade and we soon had eight more or less willing recruits. Field training took place on Putney Common, reached by a bus ride to the end of the 22 route on Saturday morning. Everybody held rank. There were lance-corporals and sergeants and a privileged few were officers. I decided to appoint myself Captain and took a long-term loan of a khaki officer's cap Kit had bought for sixpence from Clarke's Marine Junk stores opposite St Mark's School.

For reasons I don't clearly understand, the army became a great success. Most gangs at the time had no more than four or five members with the loyalty levels of Renaissance Italy's *condottieri*. Gangs would form and re-form under new leaderships and with different memberships. This army was different. First, its member-ship was relatively stable. Second, at its height it boasted twenty boys, and two girls as nurses. Most important it was joined not just by boys from our two blocks but by others from the other two Guinness blocks which we called 'the Hundreds'. Usually they didn't play with us.

And along with the Hundreds we soon had boys sidling in from Dartrey Road down by the river, and Meek Street and Lots Road. Riley came round once with his gang but it was clearly on recon-naissance. I wasn't surprised to hear next week that he'd formed a Lots Road Army himself.

Discipline in our army was not easily maintained. We had neither carrot nor stick beyond promotion or demotion. My mother told me afterwards how much she and my father had laughed at the constant process of shifting ranks which was necessary to keep the Dartrey Road kids in line, or punish a breach of Army Regulations by the Meek Streeters.

With Bobby Cooksley as sergeant-major and threats and promises abounding, we just about kept order. Indeed, our disciplined marches to the 22 bus stop for field training attracted the attention (I now realise it was the amused attention) of a good number of people in the World's End.

One day as we were lining up at the 22 bus stop two Air Raid Wardens with officers' tabs stood watching and as the bus drew up they invited me to come to the Wardens' Post in Redcliffe Gardens later that day. There they proposed that we should use our army to form the nucleus of a Junior Fire Service. We would be supplied with helmets, armbands and badges of rank. We would receive training twice a week in First Aid and stirrup pump fire-fighting. A small corner of the post would be assigned to us as a JFS office.

This was heady stuff. Official recognition. An identity book with our JFS ranks and personal details. For the first month it went well. We would parade in enormous grey steel helmets and arm-bands and the Chief Warden would inspect us. But I could feel the other boys didn't really take to it. Fewer and fewer attended parades. I suppose whereas before the army had been fun with lots of time spent practising crawling through the barbed wire on Putney Common, doing the Assault Course on Wimbledon Common and generally bucking for promotion by the threat of quitting and taking others with you, the Junior Fire Service, despite arm-bands and helmets, was too staid. A month later I was down to ten members . . . the following week it was just the five regulars from our old gang.

A man's reach should exceed his grasp. Mine had, and I'd fallen flat on my face. We were soon back to the Hooded Knights.

I remember this period, my last year at St Mark's, as a time of patriotic activities interspersed with stark efforts to make some money. The opportunities were there given the effort. First there was winter. All fires were coal-burning but coal was rationed. Coke, however, could be used to supplement the ration although its stinging, eye-watering smoke meant it had to be used sparingly. Many people in the Buildings were good for a small bag at about this time of year. We could buy it from the gasworks on the other side of Lots Road for fourpence a bag and deliver it in our home-made cart for sixpence. This was hard work when there could well be four floors of stairs to climb with a bag of coke too heavy for any of us to carry alone. But it was profitable, especially if we combined it with a waste paper collection from our coke customers – waste paper could, apart from providing some previously unread comics, be sold near the Riley Street fairground to a rag and bone man who gave us a fair price.

We also used the cart for our patriotic work. In even the most stripped out bombed houses and flats we had played in over the last year there had been sink fittings and very often disconnected gas stoves. At this moment the government was making appeals for scrap iron for rebuilding the merchant fleet whose ships were being sunk by the U-boats in the Atlantic almost faster than new ones could be launched. It seemed to us that the enormous quantity of scrap iron standing unused in the kitchens of those bombed houses must be put to use. A 1940s kitchen stove was several times the weight of its bigger modern brother and there was no question of our carrying the complete stove out of the house. Nor was there any chance that the cart would support its weight all along the King's Road to the red-painted Scrap Metal for Victory shop which the WVS ran. In the window it had aluminium saucepans, several coils of old electric copper wire and a few sections of lead flashing. There was, it is true, no sign of anything like a cast-iron gas stove. But the government had spoken. Scrap iron was needed for the war effort. The Hooded Knights would do their bit.

We learnt to demolish gas stoves. Handles were removed, doors, grills, the insulating panels of the oven itself. Before long we could strip down most gas stoves to twenty parts, convenient for loading on the cart and, with an old blanket over them, unlikely to attract unwelcome attention.

What was this unwelcome attention? Well, it's true that although we were convinced of the patriotic importance of our activities, we weren't quite so convinced of their legality. So delivery to the WVS shop was in their lunch hour or even before they opened at 9.30 in the morning. The cart was pushed into the deep doorway, the blanket whipped clear and a stove or a stove and a half of scrap would be dropped in front of the door. I think I can now more accurately read how the WVS received this weighty manna than I did then. Every delivery was the result of no small amount of organisation, from selection of the stove or stoves to be dismantled, to the plotting of a series of back-streets to take us as close to the WVS as possible, to the final emergence on to the King's Road and the heart-stopping journey for four or five hundred yards along crowded pavements, pushing the wooden cart with its four pram wheels and rudimentary steering.

Then one day it happened. The central plank of the cart broke under the strain of the twentieth or twenty-fifth stove. The cart tipped over and several identifiable pieces of gas stove slid across the pavement. We were no distance from the end of World's End Passage where the big Sergeant used to harry Alf Gordon's runners collecting bets over the backyard wall. As a matter of fact we were no distance from Chelsea Police Station as it was then situated on the bend in the King's Road. This was a police station we enjoyed visiting (on the outside) because its cell windows, barred and only a foot square, sat at pavement level and on Sunday mornings you could taunt the Saturday night drunk and disorderlies then race down Milman Street before anybody came out of the station.

But I had no thought of drunk and disorderlies now. Instead I saw myself in one of the cells looking up at the ankles of the people passing down Milman Street. I was staring up at the shadow cast over me. The fearsome Sergeant, a big sixteen-stone officer, was looking down. 'You're Bob's son, aren't you?' were his first chilling words.

His instructions left no room for manoeuvre. Return the stoves to wherever they came from and report at eleven o'clock to Chelsea Police Station. With an adult member of the family! He didn't seem to be too worried about Bobby Cooksley who didn't actually live in the World's End. I think he just told him to make himself scarce.

I had to confide in my grandmother. There was no other way out. I told her it was like the way she felt about Ladysmith when we had defeated the Boers. What I'd been doing was like all those posters that told us to *Dig for Victory!* or *Buy National Savings!* I'd been following that other poster that said: *Throw Us Your Old Scrap Gas Stoves!*

She said she didn't know that one. 'This morning,' she said, 'your father opened the last tin of Spam. Big Spam fritters for dinner.'

This would normally have had the saliva glands trickling but today I was much more concerned about the Sergeant. 'He wants us to go up to the station,' I said. 'At eleven o'clock.'

My grandmother drew out her hat-pin, held her hat on with the other hand flat across the top and stood thinking.

'Will you come with me?' I asked her.

'To the station?'

She drew in a breath through her teeth, circling the point of her hat-pin in the air. she was a lot more worried about doing something without telling my father than simply going up to the cop-shop to tell a few fibs. The truth was, so was I.

'Will you?'

She drove in the pin and nodded, eyes raised to the ceiling.

The Sergeant was strict about it. He said he understood what we were trying to do but we were causing a lot of damage doing it. Most importantly, we were playing in very dangerous places. In later years I came to know him well because his son became my best friend at school, but this time I got off lightly, I suspect, because he already knew of my father and his connection to the Gordon brothers, the best-known bookmakers in Chelsea.

Gambling and the policing of gambling went hand in glove in the 1930s and '40s. I speak here only of the World's End but I suspect that other poor districts in London were little different.

First, gambling whether on horses or greyhounds was illegal unless money was handed direct to bookmakers on the track, or the Tote, also situated at the tracks, was used. This meant that the gambler had not only to find the money for a bet on a horse but also the price of an afternoon at Epsom Races or further afield. If it were dog racing the tracks were usually closer home. In the World's End itself we had Stamford Bridge. Even so women, a sizeable minority of the gambling public, would not dream of going alone or even in pairs to the dogs. Since these factors affected everyone who gambled in the World's End, a furtive acquaintanceship with the street bookmaker was the only way for most people to place a bet. The law, as frequently happens, had made the growth of illegal street bookmaking inevitable.

Secondly, gambling was the only way that poorer people saw of making enough money to lift them from out of their present troubles: arrears of rent, debts to the tally-man, shortage of money to feed the family. Needless to say only wins were remembered, the steady drip, drip of losses ignored. Unlike drugs today in London and many other big cities, supply and demand formed a network between police and bookmakers and police and public that remained for the most part friendly and involved no more than minor bribery. A few drinks at the Conservative Club opposite the station was about as far as it normally went.

My father, unusual in this as in so many things, I realise as I write more about him, was passionately addicted to horse and dog racing – but was not a gambler. There were plenty of people in the World's End who didn't gamble (although I never actually knew any) but he was one of the few who would bet rarely and then never more than he could afford. He was in fact a natural *bookmaker*. But to be a bookmaker you needed experience and a reasonable amount of money to fund the enterprise. You also had to decide whether you were going to be a legal, licensed track bookmaker or an illegal street bookmaker – or like almost all of the small bookmakers then, both track and street.

Almost anybody could do the job of a bookmaker's runner, collecting a housewife's sixpence wrapped in the details of the bet as she threw it from the window or palming a bet in a pub under the eyes of the local off-duty P.C. None of this was difficult. But the only way to gain experience at the track was to work for a bookmaker at his stand. This meant working as a tick-tack man, signalling the prices in your 'ring' while 'reading' the movement of prices in a more expensive ring across the track. All this information, and it had to be strictly accurate, was conveyed by a complex system of hand signals, usually executed by a man wearing white gloves or waving a rolled newspaper.

For the unusually gifted there was the job of bookmaker's clerk. This required a calculator in the head. You stood beside the bookmaker. At enormous speed you were required to record each bet and to calculate how that altered the balance of the book – what the sixth dog would win or lose the bookmaker at any given moment of the betting, taking the success or failure of the other five dogs into account. On this basis the bookmaker decided whether or not to lay off some of his potential losses at the best price his tick-tack man could find him. It was a nerve-wracking business as time slipped away towards the beginning of the race and the clerk was warning that the 'book' was dangerously top-heavy with bets on one dog, and no suitable lay-off price as yet spotted by the tick-tack man.

I don't know how my father met Alf Gordon but at some time in 1943 Alf asked him if he'd like to try his hand at clerking. This was an offer my father couldn't refuse. He would be there in the middle of the game, responding to just the sort of challenge he loved, in the knowledge that few people could calculate half as quickly or predict danger spots so accurately. Apart from which he would receive £6, nearly twice his Whitelands wage, for a good evening's work at Stamford Bridge.

In appearance, the men Alf Gordon led from the Weatherby to the Bridge on Saturday evenings were an ill-assorted team. Alf was probably in his forties, Jewish, thick-set and dressed, I have to admit, as many would have expected a World's End bookmaker to dress, in a dark, wide-striped suit and fawn Homburg hat. He was self-confident, good-natured and generous if the book had had a good win that night. His number two was Fatty the Yid, frequenter of Gus the barber's shop and Alf's tick-tack man at the track. He had thick black hair and pale white skin and weighed over twenty stone. How he managed in an era of clothes rationing I do not know. His black suit certainly took twice the cloth of an average man's. When I knew him he was putting on even more weight, and always walked, head back, with his vast double-breasted jacket open, his enormous belly protruding almost a yard in front of him and the fingers of his white gloves, the proud token of his specialist trade, flapping out of his side pockets.

Alf's runner was a new arrival, a dark-skinned ex-boxer, middle-weight I would guess, named Darkie Evans. His face was of a generally European cast but his pale brown skin and flat, crinkly hair signalled some distant Caribbean origin. He was a quiet, reserved man whom I never really knew well though we were to share an odd sort of friendship. My father was the fourth member of the team, always wearing a suit, white shirt and tie, standing slightly apart from the others as befitted his status as clerk.

*

One day my mother called me in early for tea. My father was sitting at the scullery table and I sat down opposite. I could always tell by his face if he had something important to say, something that was about to alter our lives.

'I want to talk to you about going to another school, he said. 'Your mother's been to see Miss Perkins and she believes you should go somewhere else, a school where you can stay on until you're seventeen or eighteen.'

The idea of staying at school until I was that age was a shock. I knew some of the boys at Sloane School were really big, almost like men. But I'd never thought much about what would happen to me when I was 14 and ready to leave St Mark's. I'd never imagined being a plumber or stoker as I almost inevitably would have been. I didn't think about my adult future because I was still a child. Still felt like one. If I had any ambition at all it was probably to become someone like Rockfist Rogan. But I suppose the fact that I was even conscious of childhood hinted that another of the ages of man was approaching. All this was the first intimation that my childhood was ending.

'Why do you stay at school until you're seventeen or eighteen?' I asked my father.

'It's the only way you really get on in the world. I would never have been a stoker if I'd stayed at school until I was eighteen.'

'Why didn't you?'

His mouth twisted. 'I had the chance, as a matter of fact. But . . . you can guess what your grandmother thought about that.'

'So some people stay at school till they're grown up?'

He nodded. 'And then they go on to universities like Oxford and Cambridge.'

'I'm Cambridge,' I said automatically.

'There you are then. Sloane School. Then Cambridge. What d'you think? Do you want to go to Sloane?'

'But I failed the eleven plus.'

'You can still go, I've been making some enquiries. Apparently Sloane will take a few boys, if they think they're suitable. You have to pay.'

That was another shock, the idea that you should pay for something as generally disagreeable as school. 'How much?' I asked him.

'*You* don't have to pay. I've saved a bit working for Alf Gordon. It costs twenty-four pounds a year for you to go to Sloane. We can do it. And we can do it for Kit too, if it comes to it.'

I said yes because I knew he wanted me to say yes. My father showed me a piece of paper with the subjects I'd study written on it. Our lessons at St Mark's were in reading, writing and arithmetic, sometimes with a bit of additional scribbling on newsprint that was called art. I couldn't imagine what it would be like learning chemistry and physics and French and Latin. Obviously my parents couldn't tell me. I turned to my grandmother who had always claimed to be able to speak French. This was on the basis of a proximate osmosis with her husband Jesse James who, I'm prepared to believe, spoke something of the language from his summers in France.

She pointed out that French was easy. It didn't have many words and a lot of these you could learn from songs: '*Mademoiselle from Armenteers, parlez-vous? Mademoiselle from Armenteers, parlez-vous? Mademoiselle from Armenteers, we haven't been here for a thousand years, inky-pinky, parlez-vous.*'

Only this time, despite being given an opportunity to dance around and sing, I noticed she stayed in her chair. When she'd finished she was grey-faced. 'Here,' she said, 'hand me that twist. Helps me get me breath back.'

She had moved back in with us again by then, occupying the one bedroom. My brother, my mother and myself slept on the Put-U-Up in the front room. My father sometimes slept in the scullery, but mostly at Whitelands where he had persuaded the management that it was in their best interests for him to occupy the first of what would become several rooms (some of them simultaneously) over the next twenty years, rooms which he used for his own obscure but, I'm sure, profitable purposes.

Sometime about now I began to realise that my grandmother was very ill. The heart trouble that she'd suffered from early in the war was obvious in her drawn face. She became bent and stopped often between the bedroom and the scullery, straightening and trying to catch her breath. Sometimes my mother wouldn't let us have the wireless on when we got into bed in case it woke my grandmother in the bedroom. Then, on other days, she would be laughing or telling a story just as she used to and I'd feel a surge of relief, suddenly sure she was going to get better.

My father took me see the headmaster of Sloane School that autumn. Reverend John Kingsford was a retired Latin master, recalled to duty as more and more younger teachers were called up for the forces. He was a frightening figure straight from the comics: tall, grey-haired, and dressed in a dark suit and long black gown with ribbons that wafted from his shoulders in the draught from the door. He presided over the school which we called Sloane but whose official wartime name was the West London Emergency Secondary School for Boys. The pupils were, in truth, a motley lot. There were seven schools represented and seven very shabby uniforms thronged the corridors, from the red and green of Wandsworth to the blue and yellow of Clement Danes and the gold and black of Westminster City. Sloane boys wore a black jacket. Some even had a badge.

Once seated in his huge leather armchair, Reverend Kingsford seemed barely awake. He glanced at the letter Miss Perkins had written, curled his lip as he flicked it aside and nodded his long chin terrifyingly in my direction. I was in.

My mother was waiting for us outside. We stood in Hortensia Road, looking up at Sloane. 'It might not seem it yet,' my father said, 'but this is one of the most important days of your life.'

I had no real idea what he was talking about. But I saw, as he looked up at the school, the glitter of tears in his eyes. My mother had seen too. She put a hand on his shoulder and he held her round the waist.

'Just think about the life your grandmother's had,' my father said. He meant Eliza. 'Half the time she's not been able to afford a doctor, never been able to buy new clothes, hardly has a few pence for a pinch of snuff.'

My mother shook his arm. I think she was trying to stop him. I was on the verge of tears myself by now, but not entirely sure why.

'If it wasn't for your mother and your Aunt May, she would have been in the workhouse when your grandfather died.'

If it wasn't for you, too, I thought. *You'd never let her go to the workhouse.* But I was too moved by the emotion I could feel in him to say anything.

'Anyway,' he reached out and cupped the back of my neck, 'you have to get back to school now. We'll have a talk later.'

I walked slowly back round the corner to St Mark's thinking about what he'd said but not getting much further. My father hadn't been to Sloane and *he* wasn't going to end up in the workhouse. Yet, on some deeper level, I did understand what he was saying. He was talking about the sort of lives lived by the people whose big houses and flats I had roamed through, every one of which had space behind the sofa, every one of which had bedrooms to spare. He was talking about the tenants of Whitelands House, some of whom deserved their wealth, some of whom were simply privileged by birth.

At St Mark's the kids were pounding out. I saw Bobby Cooksley waiting by the gate.

'How did it go?' he asked.

'I got in. Didn't have to do anything. Man in a big black robe said, "You'll do." And that was that.'

'Easy then.' Bobby grinned his big-toothed grin. I knew he was forcing it.

'Yeah. Easy.'

'When d'you start?'

'He said I could start next week.'

He shrugged his big shoulders. 'So that's it, then. Goodbye, Bobby Cooksley.'

'No, Bob. We'll meet Saturday mornings. What's different?'

'They play football Saturday mornings. I seen 'em catching the 14 bus up to Roehampton Field.'

'Nah. Nothing's changed.'

'We'll see.'

But of course he was right. Almost from my first day at Sloane, everything had changed. It was, as he'd said, Goodbye, Bobby Cooksley.

I had joined the Air Scouts, the 20th Mohicans at Walham Green, a number 11 bus ride to the church at Dawes Road and a short walk from there. We wore grey shirts and black shorts and a chocolate brown neck scarf. Our headgear was totally unlike all other Scouts'. We wore a seamed black beret with an eagle-wing badge. I was immensely proud of the badges of merit I was able to acquire, my aircraft recognition almost immediately scooping me that particularly sought-after shoulder badge. One of the two Assistant Skippers was an amiable pederast who had been banned from taking boys on Scout camp. From time to time there was a minor incident (laughed about by the boys) when he invited a few Scouts round for tea but there was no element of compulsion and I myself never went – or possibly was never invited.

Helping others was part of the Scout credo and we would, on occasional Saturday mornings, go from house to house offering to do odd jobs. One Saturday I mounted the steps and knocked on the door of a house in Fulham Road, a few yards from the corner of Edith Grove. An old lady came to the door and I offered to carry out rubbish or cut the grass. She invited me in with alacrity. She was, I only slowly realised, all too ready to exploit my Scout's goodwill. I worked all that morning in the garden and when I told her I had to go home for my dinner, she insisted that she needed me back in the afternoon to finish off the work. The truth was that by this stage I liked what I was doing. By now she had got me polishing furniture and I enjoyed seeing the size and comfort of her house. Behind the sofa there was a good six feet of space, the fire surround was marble and carved, there were French windows looking down on to the garden. There were books too on long shelves. I would like to claim, as so many memoirists find themselves able to, that I was immediately drawn to the shelves and began to read promiscuously: Kant, Hegel, Plato, Shakespeare, Goncharov, Racine. But it was not, of course, the case. What attracted me rather more was a slender young woman with a baby who appeared to live in the basement below and would, from time to time, walk in the garden rocking the child, before she went back inside. What most attracted me was that the baby was on her naked breast.

I volunteered to come back the following Saturday and the old lady, who told me she was called Mrs Featherstone, smiled her gratitude and gave me a list of tasks. For days before Saturday arrived I was thinking only of the young woman. I knew well enough what was happening to me but found it difficult to bear the heat that even thinking about my next visit inspired. When the day came I presented myself in my uniform at the front door and rang the bell.

There was no answer. Again, the intensity of my disappointment could only be expressed in terms of heat. Heat and a sort of sickness in the stomach. I pushed the bell once more and examined the front of the house. From the steps up to the front door I could see into the front room (the old lady called it the drawing room) window. No sign of movement. The blackout curtains were drawn in the basement.

I was about to go when I heard a noise inside. Someone coming up the basement stairs. When the door opened the young woman stood there, head cocked. She wore no shoes, a white muslin dress or maybe nightdress that divided above her bare knee. The top fell about her shoulders so that even in these few seconds of silent confrontation she was hooking it over her shoulder with her thumb. When it slipped again, and was replaced, it revealed a rounded arm, a deep armpit and swelling breasts, pale, almost bluish in the overcast autumn light.

Perhaps I spoke a few words of explanation. She nodded and pulled open the door to the old lady's part of the house. 'You'd better come in,' she said.

It was true that she was barefoot and I was wearing shoes, but nevertheless her blue, slightly staring eyes were on roughly the same level as mine, or maybe a fraction below. I was taller than she was. Perhaps this idea made me flush, I'm not sure. Truthfully, I was sure of very little.

'Are you coming in or not?'

I entered the dark hall. She closed the door. Long, low book-shelves, the top shelf displaying funny pottery dogs jostling with old-fashioned sailors, crowded the corridor and made us bump thigh against thigh.

'When you've finished up here,' she said, 'if you feel like a cup of tea . . .'

'Yes,' I said. 'Thank you. Yes, please.'

She smiled. 'Call down,' she said. She had a faint cockney accent and for a moment I thought she had said, 'Cool down.' Sweat ran down my cheeks.

I worked away for a good half an hour, washing up and cleaning windows. From the French windows at the back of the drawing room, steps led down to the garden where I was to sweep the terrace. Working there I was on a level with the basement flat and when I looked up I could see the young woman smoking a cigarette, leaning against a door jamb, staring at me.

I had promised Mrs Featherstone I'd dust the bookshelves and the china ornaments as part of that Saturday's bob a job. The week before she had shown me how to use the vacuum cleaner. With only gaslight at home we had never had any of these domestic appliances of course. As a matter of fact, I think that was the first time I had ever used an electric plug. I switched it on and, turning the vacuum head, ran it along the lines of books. The dust of decades lifted from them. Within seconds I had tackled the second, then the third, shelf. On top were more ugly spotted dogs, sailors in bright blue ballooning trousers and Shire horses with huge black hooves. The sort of thing you got from a fairground coconut shy it seemed to me. And all of them covered with dust.

I was skilled now with the vacuum, convinced of the power of its draw. I swung it round to run it across the front of the ornaments. But the tube had a snake-like life of its own. It jumped from my hand, the head leapt at the dogs and sailors, two, maybe three, crashed to the floor. A Shire horse toppled and dropped, losing its hind legs to a shattered dog.

I collected up the pieces. Mrs Featherstone had so many ornaments, there must have been thirty or forty along the tops of the bookshelves. We had two at home that my father had won at the Riley Street Fair. Matter of fact, I'd seen similar ornaments to Mrs Featherstone's in the pawn shop window for sixpence each. I put the pieces all together on an empty space on one of the shelves. I was worried by what I'd done, but not overly anxious. I could take them to one of my cousins who was very good at sticking things together or perhaps old Mrs Featherstone had so many she wouldn't worry about three less.

I finished my work upstairs and called over the basement banister, softly in case I woke the baby. The young woman appeared almost immediately.

'Come on down then,' she said, and waited as I began to descend the stairs. 'I'm Pam. The old trout calls you Dee. Is that your name?'

'That's what a lot of people call me.'

'How old are you?'

'Fourteen,' I lied.

She turned down her bottom lip approvingly. 'Wish I was fourteen again.' There was a soft, grumbling cry from the bedroom. 'Then I wouldn't have this bloody kid.'

She sat me down opposite the sofa while she went into the narrow kitchen to make the tea. 'His father's in the Guards,' she said, bobbing her head out of the kitchen. 'Somewhere in the desert. We got married a week after we met.' Her head disappeared.

Seconds later she was looking round the kitchen door. 'I told him, who knows whether I'm pregnant or not? But I wasn't going to struggle bringing up a baby without a married allowance from the army.'

She brought the tea out. 'So he said yes. And as luck would have it, bad luck, I *was* pregnant. And Old Mother Featherstone's always one to pick up something for nothing – like having you here.' She winked and leaned down to hand me the cup of tea, causing a billowing rearrangement of the dress covering her upper body. 'So she has the best part of my army allowance for these two rooms, and I can't even choose how I have them. Look at all those books of hers and her stupid china ornaments I have to have down here. Staffordshire, she calls them . . . as if they're worth a small fortune just because they come from Staffordshire! And look at the damp up the wall there. Bloody disgrace! She's a greedy old cow.'

She sat on the sofa, legs crossed to the thighs. She knew I was looking. And I knew she was teasing me. She made me think of the girls from Watney's bottling plant. But she was older. And I didn't know where she would stop. As she moved her legs about she was smiling all the time.

'Something went down with a wallop when you was hoovering upstairs. Heard that all right. Nothing broke, I hope?'

I shook my head. 'Are they really valuable, the dogs and things?'

'So she says. Her husband collected old things, books and china. That's why she's got so much of it she has to dump it on me.'

'How much?' I said.

'What?'

'How much are the ornaments worth?'

'She's never said. A fiver at least the way she speaks. Catch me paying her a fiver if I happen to knock one off its perch! You mind if I feed the baby? Won't embarrass you, will it?'

I got up. 'I've got to go.'

'Hold on.'

'No, I've finished upstairs. I must go.'

'Here,' she said, smiling. 'It's me feeding the baby, isn't it? It's that that's worrying you. I could wait till you've gone. You haven't even finished your tea.'

She stood close but didn't touch me.

'Say I'm sorry to Mrs Featherstone,' I said. By now I was thinking only of fifteen pounds worth of ornaments. Fifteen pounds! 'Say I'm really sorry.'

'Sorry? What for? You don't have to run off like that,' she said. 'The baby can wait. We could put another record on. Dance music. Here, you're big enough. I could teach you to dance . . .'

I shook my head.

'She never comes down here, you know.'

'All the same,' I said, grabbing up my beret, 'I have to go.' Adding, as she looked at me with doubting, pursed lips: 'Scout's Honour.'

We buried my grandmother in Brompton Cemetery next to Jesse James in October 1943. My clearest memory of this is of my mother's distress. After the war when I was a senior at Sloane I used regularly to walk in the cemetery, the entrance to which was just opposite the back wall of the school, and visit her grave. It was not much more than a hundred yards from the prefects' room. From the window I could see the rather tattered shrubbery that surrounded that part of the cemetery, could almost hear my grandmother's music hall songs, almost see her Eliza Doolittle hat with its limp cloth flowers, the famous hat-pin . . . She had passed through the World's End from child to grandmother. On the way she had suffered extremes of poverty, never imagining she deserved better than Jesse James could provide. She'd treated my father as if he were a being from another planet, perpetually astonished by his unfailingly positive approach to life and his uncanny ability to earn extra money for his family. In the year before she died he slipped her five shillings every Saturday.

When I was in the sixth form at Sloane memories of her came back to me more strongly than in any of the intervening years since her death. Once, walking there with me, one of my friends asked me why I didn't at least tidy up the grave. But she was too Victorian to have a neat white headstone. I saw nothing wrong in the faded wooden crosses that marked the plot where she and Jesse James lay. You can't thank those who play so big a part in forming you. You don't leave flowers.

FIFTEEN

Seven to one bar

I'm not sure how I started going to the race track at Stamford Bridge on Saturday evenings or what my father's purpose was in taking me there. It certainly wasn't to make a gambler of me. But the book-maker Alf Gordon would give me a shilling or two to fetch and carry for him, run messages, set up the stand and attach the leather money bag with his name painted on it in red and white. Now that I think about it that was probably all my father intended, that I should grow accustomed to the idea of earning some money when chance offered.

So Saturday night, still barely a teenager but one of those boys who do their growing early and in their teens are always considered big for their age, I would pass through the Stamford Bridge turnstiles masquerading as a fourteen-year-old, looking ridiculous in a flat workman's cap and thick muffler. Inside I'd set up the bookmaker's stand on the rail above the track and make sure there were plenty of chalks for him and pencils for my father in case he broke one in the middle of a rush to get bets on in the last moments before a race. Meanwhile Alf and my father would exchange tips or fancies with the other bookmakers and their clerks to either side of us. Fatty the Yid would don his white gloves and take his binoculars to locate his opposer in the more expensive ring across the stadium, and Darkie would bounce around on the balls of his feet. When I'd finished setting up he'd spar with me, lightning fast and quite prepared to give me a barely pulled thump in the ribs from time to time. Sparring like this he was most truly himself, his fists moving faster sometimes than I could follow, the fierce snort of air coming from his nostrils like an angry horse. But there was no trace of anger.

Then the time for relaxation was over as the first race approached. The race card consulted, my father would draw up his big folded accounts book which he balanced on his arm. Alf would be taking wads of pound notes from his inside pockets and counting them into the leather bag, reeling off the amounts in ponies and monkeys to my father. Fatty was all prepared with binoculars resting almost flat on the jutting prow of his great belly, both thick hands grasping the rail in front of him; Darkie keyed up to check the odds offered by neighbouring bookmakers. I myself was free to wander for a few minutes before the recorded trumpet calls announced the first race.

There were a lot of soldiers on the terraces in those days and, wandering through them, I enjoyed seeing how many uniforms I could 'collect'. 'Norge', the red shoulder flash of Norway, or the Dutch 'Nederland', the strange pom-pom beret of the Free French Navy, the diamond-topped caps of Polish officers, the flashes of Canadians, Belgians, a rare South African or Australian because they were mostly fighting in the desert or the Far East, and increasingly the big, bold flashes of American soldiers. What was immediately apparent to my emerging teenage libido was that the Americans always seemed to have the prettiest girls with them: British WAAFs in RAF blue, ATS, or even occasionally, if the American was an officer, a WREN, a member of the Women's Royal Navy, who in her trim blue-black uniform and black stockings was generally recognised as being an upper-class sort.

The races themselves I found stultifyingly dull. The fanfare of trumpets, the parade round the track of the white-coated, bowler-hatted trainers with greyhounds on the leash. The locking of the dogs in the long white kennel. The electric hare racketing round the track until it reached the start line, then the urgent screech of the bell as the kennel gates flew up and the dogs hurtled out.

It was all over in seconds. Losing tickets would be torn up. Winners would surge round the bookmakers. My father would be reeling off the figures for Alf. Fatty would check the tickets. Darkie would spar against the barrier.

At one point, probably at the end of 1943 or early in 1944, I began to ask Fatty about the meaning of the signals. I liked the terminology of gambling better than any other part of it. Two at fours (the number two dog at four to one) involved theatrical sweeps of the hand from nose to out beyond the shoulder. Seven to one bar one (all dogs priced at sevens bar the hot favourite) had its own peculiar romance. I already knew a few of the more obvious moves when Fatty began to teach me the full range as we walked up to the Bridge or perhaps back to the World's End (where I, of course, was not allowed to take part in the one-for-the-road at the Weatherby which was part of the race-night ritual). Fatty couldn't walk that fast and puffed horrendously so that Darkie, carrying the stand and bag, and I used to walk slowly along with him while my father and Alf bustled on ahead, analysing where they'd succeeded or miscalculated in laying off the loss in the four race or the six race. Bookmaking is not a matter of luck, or of odds fixed against the punter. Successful bookmaking is mostly a matter of laying off potential losses, leaving the book exposed only to the possibility of small losses against substantial wins. It is, of course, closely connected to stock-broking – but considered far less respectable. It was an article of faith among the bookmaking fraternity in those days that you stood more chance of getting swindled in the City of London than you did on the average race track – and today I certainly believe it.

It's hard, in our politically correct culture, not to ask questions about racism in those days. I have no doubt that there were plenty of denizens of the World's End who believed, despite the evidence of their own eyes, that the Jews were behind the black market or that they were not pulling their weight in the war effort. But there was never anything comparable to my appalling mother-in-law's casual comments about 'that filthy Jew shop on the corner' – and this twelve years after the Holocaust.

You'll perhaps question my calling Alf Gordon's tick-tack man Fatty the Yid. For me and my father at least it held no racial connotation. It was the way that Alf (Jewish himself) always referred to Fatty in his presence. It was the way he would buy him a drink in the Weatherby: 'A brown and mild for Fatty the Yid.' It was the way he was known throughout the World's End. I suspect he was more concerned by the forename. If he suffered from his name, it was likely to be from this constant public acknowledgement of his obesity. It's almost impossible for people today to accept that the racial terminology was probably less important to him. But of course, at that time, although the horrors of the Holocaust were engulfing Europe, few people in Britain knew about it.

Darkie Evans was both shy and aggressive. I didn't know him well enough or know sufficient people of mixed race at the time (indeed, he was the only one) to make any useful comment now on how he accepted his allotted role in Alf Gordon's team. I do know that people of little or no learning like Darkie felt a respect for others, even those barely more than children like me, who had or were having some sort of education. It's also true that Alf Gordon gave me more responsibility than he did Darkie, and there was perhaps a degree of discrimination in this. But Darkie shied away from responsibility, and I didn't. However much it terrified me, I felt the need, from vanity, pride, call it what you will, to accept whatever was offered me. Much of this attitude derived from my father's Whitelands experience, his discovery that in day-to-day terms the tenants he served there were no more competent, mostly much less so, than he was himself. Of course, he was well aware there were other dimensions to life than mere mechanical competence and that education was the key to most of them. But he had also learnt that what the world believed about you, or was prepared to accept on the slender basis of dress, mannerism or accent, was often as important as what in fact you were. At Whitelands he had struggled to acquire self-confidence while moving among another social group. And as I have said, except in certain specialised encounters, he achieved it. In ten years he advanced from stoker (a dweller in the depths, not to be seen by the tenants) to manager of Whitelands and two smaller blocks, dealing with a whole range of problems and requirements. It was a considerable achievement for someone who was, at heart, constantly fighting a sense of his own social inferiority.

But then, he had my mother's backing.

By the beginning of 1944, we all knew that the war had turned the corner. People were tired but had confidence in the result of the coming invasion. I no longer feared my father's prediction that we would lose. The end was not yet in sight but was no longer entirely out of mind. I used to think about what it could mean but got no further than an amorphous feeling of rightness. That the right thing was about to happen. That until it did the world could not go on. Go on to where? I hadn't thought. We still took for granted that when we grew up we would be soldiers, or sailors, or in my case, I thought at that time, an airman. Somehow the idea that the war would end was not allowed to affect our eventual participation – and with National Service to come, how right we were!

By now war seemed to be all I had ever known. I think this simple fact had a decisive influence on me and all the big city children of my generation. We lived in a grey world. A world of battered buildings, of overcrowding on dimly lit trains and buses, of uniforms everywhere, of rationed cheese and meat and sweets, of worn clothes, of something close to a total absence of consumer goods.

Into this world the American cinema elbowed its way. It was an essential diversion for children and adults like. But it was more than that. The gloss that Hollywood put on living contrasted powerfully with the reality of war-time London, but it also speeded the process of the Americanisation of the British working class. The American cinema encouraged aspiration in a way the British social system or even socialism just didn't. At Whitelands my father had met American colonels who treated him as an equal, who didn't feel entitled to judge him purely by his job or accent. It was the same message that Hollywood was offering Britain. And it was being listened to.

The year just past, 1943, had seen a long succession of victories. In Russia it had begun with the German surrender at Stalingrad. Kit and I followed the battlefield maps as the Red Army began its two-year fight back against the Wehrmacht. The tide had begun to turn against Hitler at the very end of 1942 with the Eighth Army's victory at El Alamein and the Anglo-American Torch landings in French North Africa. Churchill summed it up as concisely as ever: 'Before El Alamein we had barely a victory. After Alamein we had barely a defeat.' In the air the RAF night attacks on Germany were reaching devastating proportions and would soon be joined by the USAAF. Few people apart from Bishop Bell in the Lords considered how much they really contributed to the war effort, or debated the morality of area bombing. At sea the U-boat stranglehold on Britain was gradually loosened and finally broken.

During 1943 an Allied army invaded and fought its way up the spine of Italy. One of my greatest disappointments, still vivid in my mind though I have had, of course, to check the date, was on September 8, 1943 when Jumbo Chandler came racing round from the Hundreds yelling, 'It's over! The war's over. They've surrendered.'

I can almost retrieve in memory the unbelievable surge of plain wonderment I felt finding myself on the threshold of the long-awaited new life. It was over! The Germans had surrendered!

Peace.

I rushed indoors to tell my mother. She looked at me for a moment and put her arms round me. I felt quietness settle round us. 'It's only Italy, Dee,' she said. 'I just heard it on the news. We've still got a way to go with the other lot.'

As an adult, I've often wondered what being at war really meant to us at the time. To Kit and myself for example. There was, of course, always that extraordinary consciousness of it that filled the nooks and crannies of your existence. The war was always with us. 'Don't you know there's a war on?' people said, as if we needed reminding. There was always that overriding imperative which put your own wishes, or juvenile ambitions, into a certain perspective. This was especially true during the blitz or when Hitler's VI and V2 Revenge Weapons, the flying bombs and rockets, began. I'm jumping ahead now to late 1944, but back from school then would involve a quick supper and homework if you could find the time to do it. Our family system was for my mother and Kit to spend the night in the depths of Lancaster Gate tube station and my father and I to go to Whitelands where he was on fire-watch duty. These nightly movements involved an immense amount of carrying of blankets and pillows, sandwiches and thermos flasks to the tube station. As the war went on, we were, I sense, more like Elizabethan children, children truly without childhood, much more deeply involved with the lives and fortunes of our parents and families than the children of the remaining half of the twentieth century would ever be.

We had kept in touch with Joe and Jinny in Windsor through the presence of my Aunt May and the East family in the area. Life was beginning to change for Joe and Jinny too. When we were last there, my mother's efforts had gained electricity for Walter Oakley Cottages. Almost as big a change was the arrival of an enormous camp of American infantry at Hollyport, a village no distance from Walter Oakley Cottages.

Around the Christmas of 1943 we spent frequent weekends with

our aunt who had much the same air of relaxed generosity with her
time and effort as my mother, though not so much of her will to
effect change. Auntie May was renting with the aid of the billeting
allowance an unused wing of the large vicarage of Braywood Church
from the vicar and his wife. It was a mile walk up the vicarage drive
but ideal for her and her very large family.

There was, however, one drawback to what might have been an
idyllic setting on the edge of Windsor Forest. Sadly, Christian charity
had not yet reached this small corner of the Anglican world. And the
Reverend Daniels conducted himself more like some eighteenth-
century incumbent than the sort of vicar desperately needed with a
Barnardo's Home near by. The man's lack of charity was sufficient
to drive even my devout cousin to worship some miles away and the
time the Easts were at Braywood was peppered with petty examples
of his ill-will. In particular, he considered Sparborough, the sprawling hillside field in front of the vicarage, an extension of his own
garden. He showed his disapproval of the local Scout troop camping
among the huge clumps of blackberry bushes and elm trees that gave
the hillside its character, by refusing any co-operation. Luckily the
Scouts had Auntie May on their side. When they were camping there
one night in a thunderstorm of truly biblical proportions, the
Reverend Daniels refused them shelter. Again, Auntie May brought
them all in to dry out. They were profuse in their thanks to her but
they never came to Sparborough again.

The issue had become complicated by the fact that nobody was
quite sure who owned Sparborough. I think it very likely that the
answer was, however apparently improbable, the Belgian Embassy.
In the later nineteenth century the Belgian government had built an
enormous country house called New Lodge in which to conduct its
weekend entertaining. This was suitably close to Windsor Castle and
Queen Victoria, Belgium's Royal Protector under the 1839
guarantee. For the benefit of Protestant servants working in New
Lodge a church was built at Braywood together with an attractive

vicarage. At some point in the thirties New Lodge was sold to Barnado's and the living abandoned to the tender mercies of the Reverend Daniels. My guess is that Sparborough always remained outside the reversion. Had it been included, Daniels would have forbidden anybody, including Auntie May's family, the pleasures of an autumn afternoon spent picking blackberries on the secluded slopes.

Daniels was never known to visit a member of the parish and his sneering comments on the orphaned status of the Barnado's boys ensured that the head of New Lodge refused to take them to the church any longer. This may well have been Daniels' objective. Locals like my cousin had long since ceased to attend. He had therefore achieved the remarkable feat of reducing his congregation to one – his wife – and his work-load to virtually zero.

Until the point in the war he had won most of the petty battles. At least, that's the way I think he would have seen it. He was, after all, the vicar, a local authority figure though an idle good-for-nothing one. He made us all think fondly of eccentric Mr Newson, curate in the World's End, who carried coal up to old people living on the fourth floor of the flats and was always there when the bombs were dropping. The Reverend Daniels was more inclined to support the Christian war effort from behind a newspaper in his secluded study.

But he was about to be challenged from an unexpected quarter. On a night we were staying with my aunt a few days before New Year 1944 when the silence which was normal up there (we were after all on the very edge of Windsor Forest) was shattered by the clatter of engines, the crash of vehicles through the rhododendron shrubbery, the shouts of soldiers and the hooting of horns. A fifty-vehicle United States Reconnaissance Unit had arrived on Sparborough *to camp*.

The vicar stumbled out in his dressing gown, waving his arms at the lead vehicle and angrily informing the officer in command that he was not allowed to bring his vehicles on to Sparborough. In an unhurried Texan drawl the officer told him, very courteously, how sorry he was. But the war came first – and his orders were quite explicit, down even to map references. With that he waved his unit through, drivers greeting the scandalised cleric with a 'Howdy, Reverend' as they passed.

Within days, our lives became bliss and the Reverend Daniels's life became hell. A baseball diamond was marked out on the flattest part of Sparborough. Jazz from the unit loudspeaker system played much of the day. Trees were looped with telephone wire. Jeeps churned up the muddy shrubbery path of the drive to the vicarage. The smells of the sumptuously provided field kitchen floated across the vicarage. And worst of all, Mrs Daniels reported, girls from the local villages had been seen on Sparborough. There was corroborative evidence of the activities she was suggesting when the litter of Hollywood chewing gum packets was joined by empty condom three-packs.

Slowly the Reverend Daniels and his wife began to retire to the vicarage to be seen occasionally peeping out impotently from behind the curtains at some new iniquity the Americans had wrought. My mother and aunt once met him skulking in the shrubbery of the back garden. I was reminded compellingly of Rupert's Brooke's 'sly shade of a rural dean' when they reminisced about the incident years later. They were returning to the vicarage at the time with a pound of fresh butter, some bacon and a dozen C-ration tins of cheese the American cook sergeant had given them. The vicar (emerging from the shrubbery) began to complain bitterly about the Americans. Their commanding officer had just called on him to say that a good number of his men were Episcopalians and, instead of their chapel-tent, they would welcome the opportunity to pray Sundays in a real English church. Did my mother and aunt not think that was the limit Daniels demanded? They sympathised. My mother hitched up her heavy bag of American provisions. But we all had to pull our weight, she added. 'There is, after all, a war on.'

SIXTEEN

The Little Blitz

Fatty the Yid was ill. It looked likely he would be away for two or three weeks. Crisis in Alf Gordon's small team. My father proposed me as a substitute tick-tack man. Alf produced a pair of white gloves from somewhere.

'Learning Latin, are you, son?'

'Yeah.'

'Goin' to be a doctor?'

'I don't know yet, Alf.'

'Think you can manage the tick-tack?'

I was sweating with fear. 'I think so. Fatty's been teaching me.'

'Could cost me a lot of money if you get it wrong.'

'I know.'

'I'll pay you properly. Not what I pay Fatty, but he's got a wife to support. You'll keep an eye on him, Darkie?'

'Got it,' Darkie said, executing a neat side-step and clubbing me a right hook to the upper arm.

So I was hired. Promoted. Was I scared? I was scared. I knew what a mistake could mean. I knew if I read the wrong odds from the bookmakers across the track, Alf would adjust his prices and my father's book would be sent all askew. This was winter 1944, freezing cold and for once justifying my disguise of flat cap and muffler. My father's technique for getting an underage boy through the turnstile ratchet was to give me a fiver, a big, black and white five-pound note, a week's money or nearly two for many workers, to hand to the man behind the ticket grille. While the cashier concentrated on changing the note, he automatically pressed the foot button. The turnstile revolved and carried me through as I scooped up the change from the counter.

That first race was a searing experience. Activity began as usual with the recorded trumpet call and the parade of dogs. Money was being thrust at Alf, he in turn was calling each bet to my father. Cold as the night was, sweat was pouring down my chest. I felt I wanted to double-check every call. I don't remember the details now, only that I never once felt with absolute certainty that I was transmitting the right odds, although Darkie was at my shoulder murmuring constantly, 'That's it, boy. You got that one . . .'

If I actually made any mistakes that evening my memory has obliterated them. But when I heard the amount of money going down on prices I'd called I felt sick to my stomach. Somehow we reached the last race. The book had had a good night. Alf and my father counted through. Darkie snapped the red and white-painted Gladstone bag shut and gave me a grin and a wink.

I felt the cold again. And the rain. Both were refreshing. My father nodded, just once. The usual neighbouring bookmakers bustled around, asking each other the same question; 'Good night, Harry?' 'Done yourself a bit of good, have you, Tom?' 'How'd it go, Alf?'

I felt an extraordinary sense of relief. Of achievement. Through the wet camelhair coat's sleeve, Alf's hand came out.

'Well done, boy. Stick that in your back pocket, Dee.'

And he pushed two one-pound notes into my hand.

Growing up is hard to do. It's the astonishing unevenness of the experience that baffles young people. I was learning Latin at school

with a master who flicked you under the nose for every trivial mistake
– yet on Saturday nights I was working for Alf Gordon at the dog
track at Stamford Bridge. On my word real money could be made or
lost. More than that, I was already aware that, when the twilight
groups gathered, a girl in the Buildings named Kathy Davis would
stroll over and talk to *me*. And that the Watney's girls no longer
thought they could frighten me with the offer of a jump round the
bike sheds.

Nevertheless.

I still had a long way to go.

Peggy, Aunt May's eldest, the Land Girl at White Lady Poultry
Farm in 1941, had become a fully qualified nurse in the Naval VAD
and had been posted out to Colombo in 1942. She was a highly
committed young woman prepared to work all hours with the naval
wounded as they were brought in. In addition, she still managed to
keep concealed the fact that she had only one kidney.

At home, in the vicarage at Braywood, my Aunt May received a
telegram from the hospital in Colombo, via the Admiralty in
London, with what was obviously thought by the sender to be good
news. It read: *Naval VAD Margaret East. Crisis past. Near miraculous
recovery. Margaret to be evacuated home soonest.*

The family was stunned. Miraculous recovery from what? These
were days in which further information was not easily obtained. But
before my aunt could even begin enquiries, another telegram arrived.
This one read: *Naval VAD Margaret East. Deepest regrets. Margaret's
condition declining. Regret, prepare for worst.*

Prepare for worst. While the shock was being absorbed, my aunt
looked yet again at the telegram. And suddenly she saw the date. It
was dated the day *preceding* the first message. It must have taken her
minutes to work out what had happened, minutes more to assure
herself that her daughter was not about to die. Read in the right order
the telegrams said Margaret was no longer on the brink of death. She

had been, but had made what even the Navy called a near miraculous recovery. And she was on her way home!

Peggy, or Margaret as she now insisted on being called, came home by ship and air and was admitted to the Naval Hospital at Gosport. My father and mother and I went down to see her. She was, I remember, sitting in a rest room with three other servicewomen from the Far East. A month had elapsed since she had nearly died and she was looking very well, I thought. More than that, the three other young women with her seemed to me particularly attractive. Sun tans were rare indeed in England at that time. I'm not sure how many real tans I'd ever seen. These young women all looked as if they had been exposed to a foreign sun for months. In an attempt at teenage courtliness, I tried to compliment them on their tans. They all stared at me, biting back their laughter.

I was baffled. I thought I'd handled the compliment with aplomb. Then one of the girls could hold back no longer and burst into laughter. I looked in panic towards my cousin.

'The tan,' she said crisply. 'It's jaundice. You're in the jaundice ward, you fool.'

All three girls were now grinning broadly.

Growing up is hard to do.

In January 1944 the raids had begun again. In Germany the revenge weapons were not yet ready. The V1 flying bomb was being tested but was still unsteady on its launch rails. The V2 rocket was many months off the first faster-than-sound air offensive. The Luftwaffe, with its bomber units now technically inferior to the British defence with its nightfighters, flak and radar, was ordered to gather together all serviceable aircraft to attack London.

By day school continued pretty much as normal. Most air raids were carried out by night. There were a few daylight raids which sent us to the shelters but nothing like the non-stop V1 attacks of later in the year when Latin and French gave way to developing skills in card sharpery as we spent much of the day playing our begowned masters in the shelter.

For the moment our days were fairly uneventful. To say that the West London Emergency Secondary School for Boys (alias Sloane School) was slack is among the richer of understatements. During what later became known as the little blitz of the early months of 1944, attendance was voluntary (although it's true that throughout, it was well over ninety-five percent every day) but many of our masters were just marking time for their second retirement to begin with the war's end. Standards, it's fair to say, were pitifully low. I remembered more of the stinging pain of Mr Colon's fat, white finger flicking me beneath the nose than any of the Latin declensions he imagined he was teaching. French was taught by Harry Little whose Commando French Course never seriously advanced our knowledge of the language but whose black-market visit to Paris within months of the war ending netted the boys a good return – and himself a handsome profit, as well as renewed acquaintance with his good friends the night-club hostesses of Pigalle.

If days were fairly normal in the World's End during the Little Blitz, nights were becoming sleepless again. My cousin Margaret had recovered sufficiently from her near-death experience in Colombo to return to duty at a London Naval Hospital but was unable to serve as a VAD overseas again. Her evenings off were spent with us at number 3, and at night, because we were so short of space in our flat, Kit and I would go with her 'round the Hundreds' to number 84, Auntie May's empty flat, to sleep there. It was quite common in wartime London for sleeping arrangements to be shuffled around. Of course, for adults, there was often an accompanying heightened sexual charge but it basically stemmed from the mobility that war demanded – part of the ceaseless search for safety. To young people of my age and Kit's it was just a normal life.

*

Auntie May was always ready to see us at Braywood Vicarage. My mother and her half-sisters could not have been closer friends. As the night raids increased in ferocity, we took more and more to spending the weekend at Braywood. My father stayed in London to clerk for Alf Gordon on Saturdays. My first short spell as a tick-tack man was over. I was no longer needed once Fatty the Yid came back.

Returning to Windsor was a chance, too, to see Joe and Jinny. It was strange how they-there Yanks had now become a big part of their lives. Joe would be down at the White Hart in a miraculously quite clean shirt, probably fresh in the last two weeks anyway, where he and his 'old friend' the American Commanding Officer of the regiment at Hollyport would trade hares from deep inside pockets for packs of cigarettes.

A smile always lit Jinny's dark-skinned, black-eyed face when the Americans were mentioned. A local girl of just fifteen who lived quite close to us was known to be 'going with the Americans', and Jinny and Joe, alone of everybody in the cottages, actively approved. Although they never went to the cinema and consequently knew nothing whatsoever of Hollywood values, I think America, or Americans, had already begun to mean something liberating to them. They saw a chance, and were too generous to begrudge it, for young girls in the area to break out of the slavery of agricultural life, of tied cottages without sewage, of backus boilers and brass beds in front rooms because the stairs weren't wide enough to permit a double bed to pass. Of course not all girls who 'went with the Americans' married GIs. When we last heard of our village girl, Shirley Rickman, she was married to a salesman, living on the new estate at Deadworth. At least they had mains drainage.

On the night of February 19, 1944, Kit, my mother and myself had just arrived at Braywood for the weekend. My father thought it a good thing for us to be out of London whenever possible at that time. He was proved right.

That night the Luftwaffe assembled the planes to mount a major raid against the capital. Given the strength of the London defences at this stage of the war, the odds on German pilots returning to base in Belgium or the Pas de Calais were not high. Nevertheless, that night they broke through the flak and nightfighter defences to drop a higher tonnage of bombs, mostly aimed at government buildings in Central London, than had been dropped in any one night since the blitz. Civilian casualties were 216 killed and 417 seriously injured.

I vividly remember returning to London on Monday. There had been bombing over the weekend just west of us, probably the dumping of a light bomb load before the plane turned south to try to make it back to the coast. A florist's shop was destroyed in Fulham Broadway (Walham Green as we called it then), our Scout church burnt out beside the bus stop in Dawes Road. One of my friends had been bombed out and was commended by the sleepy Reverend Kingsford for having come to school that Monday morning. The siren went before break heralding Focke Wulf 190s from SK Geschwader 10, as I now know from Luftwaffe records, the Fighter Reconnaissance squadron at Amiens. The school retired to the shelter to play cards.

I have no difficulty in remembering how I felt about being away in the country that weekend: I had missed something. All the rest of my class had stories of bombs dropping or incendiaries blazing. I could only talk about a part of the world they'd never seen and many of them would never know. They just weren't interested.

But I could interest them easily enough with stories of the games we were playing in the yard at Guinness Trust. It was February and darkness fell early. The system was that the porter would come round as it got dark and call 'All up'. This was not of course the Superintendent, Mr Caple, in his orange rough tweed suit and bowler hat. On a normal duty night he was far above ensuring that all the children were out of the yard. This was the under-porter, Jock. 'Aal-op!' was the cry that echoed through the gathering darkness. 'Aal-op!'

It was an opportunity and a half in the blacked-out yards of Guinness Trust. By slipping through the shadows, pressing ourselves into corners, hiding in the darkened entrances to the four separate blocks (two entrances to a block), we were able to avoid detection until Jock decided he had done his bit and went back to his own flat.

Then we would play black-out touch. Same rules as a game of touch the world over – except that this was played in guaranteed, legally enforced darkness and the players were all in the hormonal range twelve to fourteen.

In one dark doorway Kathy Davies touched me. In that same doorway I first kissed a girl. Thereafter we never played without quickly seeking each other out. She was fair-haired, blue-eyed and already beginning to lose the straight slenderness of a young girl. I was breathless with excitement as I kissed her.

For some reason on Tuesday February 22 we were not able to play. Perhaps, after all, Superintendent Caple had come down to the yard to see that Jock had not abandoned his duties too early. Perhaps Jock's 'Aal-op' had been unusually effective, I no longer remember. But I do remember that the prospect of the next night, Wednesday, was in the forefront of my mind. I had early Scouts that evening and would be back just after 'All-up' time. Kathy and I had never spoken a word to each other of what we did in the darkened entrances to the flats. But she knew I went to Air Scouts on Wednesday. And I knew she would hold herself back from the game until then.

SEVENTEEN

Target for Tonight

Kesselhaus & Maschinenhalle, Lots Road

The raids which had begun sporadically after Christmas had, in the last weeks, acquired a pattern. We now know that code-breaking at Bletchley was, by early 1944, producing the fullest information of Luftwaffe intentions. What had emerged was a German plan to launch a series of heavy attacks, initially on London but later on other cities, while the V1 flying bombs and V2 rockets were being readied for use against Britain later in the year.

Bletchley provided the Air Ministry with considerable detail. The Luftwaffe had codenamed the campaign *Operation Steinbock* and appointed Oberstleutenant Dietrich Peltz as *Angriffsfuhrer England* (Attack-leader England). Peltz's orders were to concentrate on ports and government and industrial centres. He was to be given a substantial force of 524 bombers, of which 460 could be expected to be serviceable at any one time. The squadrons allotted to *Operation Steinbock* were mostly Dornier 217s (of the type that had come down earlier in the war at Walter Oakley Cottages) and Junkers 88. Peltz had decided that most of the bombers should be based in Germany and Holland but were to be forward-based just before a raid, at northern French and Belgian airfields at

Coulommiers, Laon, Melun, Amiens and Mondidier. Target marking with coloured flares was to be undertaken by special Reconnaissance squadrons of Focke-Wulf 190s and Junker 88s. In West London the prime target was marked *GB 503 Kraftwerke, Kesselhaus und Maschinenhalle*, (Boiler House and Turbine Hall) Lots Road power station.

As Wednesday February 23rd 1944, dawned, I awoke tired but was quickly enlivened by thoughts of games of touch and kiss after Air Scouts. I found an increasing amount of my time was taken up thinking about these games, or to be more accurate, with wondering whether Kathy Davis would be among the dark figures running through the shadows that night.

We had had an air raid, perhaps even two, during the previous night. Some people at Guinness had started going down to the communal shelters again but, now that my grandmother was no longer with us, we thought we could stick it out in the flat. Mrs Corfield from the top floor would usually come down during a bad raid and my father would be there, of course, if he wasn't fire-watching at Whitelands.

Tonight would be different, though, because my cousin Margaret was to have the night off duty from the hospital. As usual that would mean that Kit and I would stay with her over at Auntie May's empty ground floor flat at no 84, round the Hundreds, in the third of the four Guinness blocks.

The day was the usual winter overcast, no sign of snow, no more than a damp bite in the air. I was sleeping in the bedroom with Kit again, our parents together on the Put-U-Up in the front room. I got up, dressed and went into the scullery to wash. My mother had the gas-light on making the scullery hiss warm and yellow. She warned us we were going to be late.

Kit was already up and having breakfast. I expect we talked about football. He was already playing for the St Mark's First Eleven. I myself was no great footballer but not quite as bad as my younger brother insisted, and later when we played against each other took delight in demonstrating.

We walked to school together, me stopping at Sloane, Kit continuing on to St Mark's. At Sloane a boy named Arthur Revell was one of the monitors on the gate. He took my name for being late but since buses couldn't be relied upon to run on time after a night of air raids, punctuality wasn't enforceable for most boys and the name-taking was no more than a formality. In any case, I knew Revell. He lived in Guinness, round the Hundreds at number 88, just above Kathy Davis. He wouldn't have handed my name in if there was any chance of real trouble.

I can't remember too much about that day. The usual attempt at lessons, I suppose. Most of the boys were sleepy at their desks although it was wonderful to see how they perked up at break and went out into the playground to play football or to swop souvenirs of the previous night's raid – a particularly vicious piece of shrapnel or the tail fin of an incendiary bomb. I think it might have been that day that I was wearing a new pair of boots. Reluctantly wearing a new pair of boots.

Growing fast as I was, I needed new shoes fairly often. But under the clothes rationing scheme, a pair of adult-sized shoes was heavy on ration coupons. My father had therefore acquired, how I'll never know, a pair of soft leather black 'U-boat commander's boots'. Their size was no problem since my feet were growing as fast as the rest of my body. In a period of rationing my father saw procuring an extra pair of shoes as a triumph. These were ankle-length but could be slipped under the bottom of my long trousers. They would look, he insisted, like any other pair of shoes.

My mother had more understanding of what I might feel about the boots. In the sixties they would be called Chelsea Boots by the fashion magazines. In 1944 it felt worse than wearing any sort of cast-offs. But we had no ration coupons left for a new pair of shoes for me, so U-boat commander's boots it had to be, although I'm now very sure that my boots had never been to sea in their lives.

At school they were spotted almost immediately by my friend Norman Chapman. Norman had and has an exuberant personality and a voice loud enough to accompany his incorrigible cheerfulness. (He was, incidentally, the son of the same police sergeant who had chased Darkie Evans down World's End Passage in the past). 'What are *those*?' He grabbed at my foot and tugged it up in full view of Form IIA.

'U-boat commander's boots,' I said.

He looked sceptical.

My grandmother must have been looking down on me. 'From U 231, as a matter of fact,' I said. 'Brought to the surface by depth charges in the North Atlantic last month.'

'Wow! Come and look at these!' he invited the whole class – and my boots were from then on seen as an object of very pleasing envy.

Perhaps it wasn't that very same day, but it might well have been. Or it might have been the day Ted Simon, now a well-known traveller and author of *Jupiter's Travels*, took me back to his house in the dinner hour, a 31 bus ride up to Notting Hill. His mother was to me an exotic figure, a dedicated Communist but also, perhaps more interestingly at that time, a German. Indeed, Ted himself had been born in Hamburg.

I remember two things from my first visit to their house in Notting Hill Gate. The first was the extraordinary way in which books lined the walls in a room painted predominantly deep red. They were books in which the names Stalin and Lenin appeared frequently in the titles. In fact, it was from these shelves, a few years later, that I acquired the book that first sparked my lifelong interest in Russia. Alexi Tolstoy's *Road to Calvary* charts the incredible suffering of its people and, although it was a Stalin Prize-winning novel, their dawning awareness of the horrors of Stalinism and the monstrousness of the man himself. *Road to Calvary* was, too, the source of the three

Vadim novels I have written in the last few years. I have Ted to thank
for it.

The other thing I found remarkable about the house was the line of
coat hooks in the hall with children's names below them. Ted had not
told me that his mother ran a nursery school. I don't think he'd even
told me that she was German. He certainly hadn't told me that all the
children were *foreign*. They were all Natashas and Dashenkas and
Galinas and Anoushkas. The Tower of Babel had been reconstructed
in that house in Notting Hill Gate. I had never before seen foreign
people *en masse*. Of course they were very little people, mostly rather
pretty girls, but it was my first meeting with foreignness in any
number. I found it embarrassing, mildly irritating that they couldn't
answer me, frustrating that they didn't respond in the same way
British children did. Was it from arrogance? Something constantly
underlined their difference from me. They seemed to exude a childish
sense of superiority. Was it because they were Russian Embassy
children, as several were? Was it the result of some sense communicated to them by their parents that they, the Russians, were doing
most of the fighting? Either way, their manner was not at all what I
would have expected from the inhabitants of a country where, Ted
told me, everybody was equal. Their manner was, I decided, not so
very different from some of the little children at Whitelands in the way
they spoke to my father. I knew no American children, but grown-up
Americans weren't like that, nor were Canadians, Australians, New
Zealanders. They were different from us, of course, indeed many of
the American soldiers by 1944 were black. But they weren't different
in the same way that these children were different. So was it just a
question of language? I couldn't escape the impression that it was
something more. That these little people thought they came from a
superior part of the planet. Further than that I could not go.

In all likelihood it wasn't that day that I first went to Ted's house
or had my strange boots held up for public execration by Norman
Chapman. But it would have been in the days or weeks just before

that day. So, as on dozens of similar days, at 4.30 the bell rang for the end of school. It was already dark outside as we asked each other about homework, packed our books, said our 'See you tomorrows' and left the school. Boys set off in the black-out for homes mostly scattered around the World's End area.

Very few thought about the danger from the skies.

I hurried home and changed into my black shorts, grey Air Scout shirt with badges and brown neckerchief. The U-boat boots were a problem and very obvious in shorts. But after my success at school I decided to bluff it through at Scouts. After macaroni cheese for tea, I was ready to leave. As I was at the door my mother promised to make some shortbread for a snack to have with Ovaltine if we were kept up by the sirens that night.

Scouts was always enjoyable, and always fairly brief in the winter so that boys could get home before any air raids were mounted. Courtly, friendly and a most open pederast, our Assistant Skipper stood at the door as we left, inviting boys to come round to his house in Earl's Court for tea and cakes on Saturday morning. Most of them just laughed. He laughed with them.

I ran down North End Road and caught a number 11 back to the World's End. It was late and I thought there would be no one playing. The 'All Up!' had been shouted by Jock nearly half an hour earlier. Then, as I jumped over the stunted wall where the railings had once been, I saw two figures flit from A entrance in our block to D entrance in the second block. Rolling my beret into my shoulder strap, I joined in the game.

It was only minutes before Kathy and I were running together. Little more than that and we were squeezed into a doorway as close as we could possibly get. I kissed her and she laughed. Then I kissed her again and she kissed me.

We were cuddling closer when a torch beam fell upon us.

'Aal-op, you two. Away you go now, Kathy,' Jock the porter's rasping Scottish voice said, the torch beam flicking impatiently in the direction of the entrance. 'You too, me lad.'

In those days you didn't argue. Kathy ran off without a word, round to her flat in the Hundreds. I went into number 3 where homework awaited me.

Kit's day had been mostly taken up with football. There had been a St Mark's match that afternoon and my father had got time off to go round and see him play. After the match Kit had played football until dark in the yard with his friends, Ronnie Howes from round the Hundreds and Ginger Green who lived on the corner of the King's Road and Edith Grove. They were too young for games of touch and kiss.

Indoors that evening Kit was drawing, my father was home and listening to the wireless, and my mother was in the scullery making the promised shortbread. By nine o'clock, sitting at the glass-fronted thirties display cupboard, its flap down to form a desk, I had finished my French homework. It was then that I remembered I had a history essay to do for the next day on Mary Queen of Scots. This was really a problem because I had not brought my history textbook home from school.

As ever, my father could help. It was one of those coincidences that seemed to occur remarkably often in his life. He knew nothing about Tudor history but he had brought a pile of books home that had been 'abandoned' by someone in Whitelands. He'd wondered if they'd be useful to me. Didn't he remember that one of them was by a woman named Margaret Irwin – its title *Mary, Queen of Scots*?

Some time about now Margaret arrived in her VAD uniform. She had dropped in during a break between shifts (I seem to remember they called them watches, they were naval VAD, after all). A heavy raid was expected and she had been assigned an emergency night watch. It meant she would not be sleeping over at number 84 that night after all.

That also meant Kit and I would sleep at home. Neither of us was sorry. It was always cold in the East family flat because no fire had been lit there since the beginning of the war. The place had a damp, dismal feel. And in any case we preferred to be with my parents during a raid.

A few minutes after Margaret left there was a knock and my mother answered the door. A moment later she came into the front room with the Corfields from upstairs. Mr Corfield, a Leading Aircraftman in the RAF, was leaving to go back to West Drayton airfield after forty-eight hours' leave. Mrs Corfield would come and sit with us for an hour in case there was an early raid.

The room was too small for all of us to sit comfortably. I had a seat because I was copying out chunks of Margaret Irwin into my exercise book. Mr Corfield stood smoking, leaning against the wall in his Air Force uniform, Mrs Corfield sat on a chair in the doorway to the scullery. My mother, waiting for the shortbread to cook, had the most comfortable seat, a heavy imitation Louis XV boudoir chair which my father had acquired, probably as a throwaway from Whitelands, the silk back quite tattered and the gilded legs scratched by cats. Kit and my father sat on the Put-U-Up in front of the stove.

Many years later I checked the Warden's reports. It was 10.07 p.m. I had just returned to my chair at the drop-lid desk and opened the Margaret Irwin when I felt everybody rise fractionally in their chairs behind me. It was that chilling moment when the sirens seemed to take a deep intake of breath before they began to wail. My mother went into the scullery to make a cup of tea.

EIGHTEEN

World's End

By eight o'clock that evening, under cover of darkness, Oberstleutenant Peltz had brought his pathfinder and bomber formations
forward from their Dutch and German airfields. At Belgian and
French forward stations, Mons, Montdidier, Melun, Amiens, the
crews received final briefings while their aircraft were loaded with
flares and high-explosive bombs.

Ronnie Howes, Kit's footballing friend, went to bed early. By ten
o'clock he was tucked up in the bedroom he had occupied alone
since his elder brother had been called up. Now that elder brother
was on embarkation leave, drinking tea in the front room with
Ronnie's grandmother. Their father was firewatching on the roof of
St Stephen's Hospital in the Fulham Road and had left instructions
for the elder brother to get Ronnie out of bed and dressed if the
warning went. You never knew when you'd have to run like mad
down to the shelter, although by then it was usually too late. The
Howes lived in number 111, on the third floor of Block 3. Their
staircase was approached by F entrance, the further of the two
entrances from the King's Road.

My Aunt May's flat at number 84 on the ground floor of the same block was reached by E entrance, closer to the King's Road. Usually Kit and I slept in the front bedroom and Margaret in the back. But the flat was empty tonight, of course, since she was staying on VAD watch. On that same ground floor lived Superintendent Caple and his wife at number 81, and the Haddock family at 82. The Davis family, Mr and Mrs Davis and their three daughters, of whom my touch and kiss companion, Kathy, was the middle girl, were at 83. My aunt's flat at 84 completed the ground floor of Block 3, entrance E.

Upstairs, among others in the remaining three floors on that staircase, were the Revell family at 88, father, mother and son Arthur, the junior monitor at Sloane School. The Ibbs family were at 89. Like me, Arthur Revell had got down to his homework some time before the sirens sounded at 10.07.

In our flat in block 1 the shortbread was baked. My mother was in the scullery taking it out of the gas oven, my father on the Put-U-Up with Kit who was closest to the range which we never used for cooking but whose coal fire was the single form of heating in the flat. They were talking about Kit's drawing. Mrs Corfield was sitting silently. Mr Corfield had his RAF greatcoat on, a grey-blue haversack on his shoulder, cigarette in his month, ready to set off for his camp at West Drayton. The anti-aircraft guns in Battersea Park were exploding with their great hollow resonance across the Thames. It was enough to shake the glass in the windows and difficult not to flinch at, although we all knew the guns might be firing at bombers several miles away. At every fresh explosion of gunfire Mrs Corfield cast a nervous glance at the ceiling.

The raid had been on for about twenty minutes. The Battersea guns had been loud but if there were bombs they were far distant. For some time I remember the adults discussed a mysterious short and powerful crack, quite close by, which we much later discovered was a faulty AA shell exploding just at the end of World's End Passage. That apart, it seemed as if the main raid had passed us by.

But if any of us had been outside in the yard that night at just after

10.30 we would have had an entirely different view of how the raid might develop. Inside the flat behind the thick black-out curtains we were unaware that white and green flares were encircling the whole World's End area. These were the sign of a targeted attack. They were, in fact, a clear indication that the *Kesselhaus und Maschinenhalle*, the boiler room and turbine hall at Lots Road, had finally been selected for destruction.

In number 3 I got up from the desk opposite the window to ask my father what something in the book meant. To show it to him I knelt down on the sisal mat in front of the range. My mother appeared in the doorway from the scullery with a tray of hot shortbread – and stopped.

Everybody in the flat, and I'm sure the occupants of every other flat in Guinness Trust, was listening to the uneven rasp of bomber engines in the brief gaps between exploding AA shells. As we remembered it afterwards, we all knew that these particular bombers were for us. Of course, this is the partial hindsight, partial reconstruction that memory so often comprises. But those moments undeniably had a unique quality. All over Guinness Trust Buildings, throughout its four blocks and 192 flats, people stiffened as the first 2,000lb high-explosive bomb screamed down and exploded in Upcerne Road, between us and Lots Road power station. Seven of my mother's girlhood neighbours were killed outright.

Whether we crouched or threw ourselves to the floor I can't be sure. The impact of the second bomb was so huge, so terrifying, *so much closer*, I remember thinking, eyes closed with my father and brother in front of the Put-U-Up, that one more bomb in the stick would bring the whole block crashing down on us.

We waited. A second or two only, I'm sure. But I can feel that wait today. *One more bomb in the stick will bring the whole block crashing down on us*, was running through my head in that second or two of suspense.

It exploded. The wall behind my mother split a two-foot gap but held. The heavy window frame leapt into the room but was stopped by the back of the Put-U-Up. Plaster was ripped from the ceiling. I fought for air, trying to scoop the dust and soot from my mouth. But dust was not the problem. The first problem in blast, as long as you're still alive that is, is trying to breathe when the shock waves have sucked every millilitre of air from your lungs. Then you're as close to panic as you've ever been since the first airless moment of birth, though now you're still conscious enough to know that one more explosion will detach breath from lungs for ever. *And* bring hundreds of tons of brick and rubble down on your head.

Perhaps it was no more than seconds before we raised our heads. Huge flaring flames were leaping like mad jesters outside the hole where the window had been. The next explosion burst as a more familiar hollow crack and rumble, the sort of bombs we'd heard before, falling a hundred yards or more away.

Dust and soot eddied through the room, swirling around the miraculously undamaged gas mantle. Mr Corfield jumped to his feet and put out the gas, an unthinking reflex when there was a huge fire raging outside. Time now to think about each other. My father was asking Kit and me if we were hurt. My mother crawled from under the Louis XV chair. Two American sailors appeared at the gaping ground-floor window and shouted in, 'Is everybody all right here?'

We looked at each other in shock and astonishment. My mother called back, 'We're all right.' She was turning to the rest of the room as she spoke. Of six people in a room full of thousands of shards of flying glass only Mrs Corfield had been hit in the hand and not badly hurt. The desk I had been working at was deeply pitted with glass but, incomprehensibly, the glass in the display cabinets to either side was unbroken. We had no idea how close the block above our heads was to collapse. We had to move. My mother produced a sheet and wrapped Mrs Corfield's hand. My father looked out of the window and said we'd better try and get out by the front door.

In the entrance hall to our block there was already a clutch of shocked people. Mrs Hartnell from number 4 was bleeding and I gave her my Scout scarf to bind up her arm. Outside in the yard the ground was a fiery orange colour, glittering and undulating. I thought the yard itself was on fire.

My father shouldered his way to the entrance and then back to where we were standing. He was white-faced. 'The King's Road's all down,' he said. 'We're going to try to get to Whitelands.'

He led the way. We stepped out of the entrance and into the yard. I could feel the heat of an enormous flame on my face even before I turned my head. In the middle of the King's Road a gas flame rose high above the Buildings, seventy, eighty feet high, from a boiling, water-filled bomb crater. Beyond it we recognised the line of the King's Road, where perhaps twenty houses were piled rubble or burning ruins. 'That's Ginger Green's house,' Kit said next to me, nodding towards the burning corner of Edith Grove.

The ground about us, inches deep in shattered glass, was rippling with reflections at every gutter of the column of flame. I saw a man run towards it, then, as the flame keeled over until it was nearly parallel to the road, he turned, bent double and raced for his life. From the block opposite, equally stunned people were emerging. My father was leading us across the glittering sea of broken glass. Reach the corner of Block 2, we thought, and we would be safe. 'We'll go down to the river,' he said. 'Then along the embankment to Whitelands.'

We moved forward in a tight group. At the corner of the block we all stopped, staring aghast. Smoke and dust whirled around our heads. Orange light from the gas main gilded the roof of what felt like a huge sparkling cave in the dust-laden air. Within the 'cave' the corner of Block 3, twenty or thirty flats, including Auntie May's number 84, was one enormous pile of rubble, concrete, sections of brick wall, doors, sinks, beds, flapping bits of clothing . . . Behind it, the sixty-foot front wall of Block 4 had been ripped off. In the light from the gas main we stared at exposed rooms that were like an open-fronted doll's house. Except there were still people moving inside it.

Somehow we had to get past the two stricken blocks. Somehow we had to climb the rubble. We began to stumble forward. It would be hard ever to forget those people in the doll's house rooms. Some crawled towards a door, some pressed themselves against the remaining wall, the precipice a matter of feet from them, the floor sloping under them, the drop three or four storeys into the burning rubble below. On the ground more people, mostly women and children, stumbled in circles in torn, bloodstained nightclothes with wardens already trying to herd them together. And all brilliantly illuminated by the biggest gas flame we had ever seen in our gaslit world.

Rescue workers – God knows how they'd got there at that speed, or perhaps much more time had elapsed than I'd realised – were already climbing over the mountain of rubble, calling to voices they heard coming from below them.

Opposite our block, where the fronts of all the houses in the King's Road had been torn off and some totally demolished and left in flames, half-clothed people were scrambling from the ruins. A Heavy Rescue truck was lurching through the rubble covering the road surface. The flaring gas main was at their backs barely twenty yards away as men jumped out and began searching for survivors. Tony Smith, chimney sweep and former World War I Royal Marine, was now a member of Chelsea's Heavy Rescue. For his courage that night, again and again entering the teetering, burning ruins to bring out survivors, he was to be awarded the George Cross, the civilian VC.

We barely had time to glance across at the chaos on the other side of the road. Couldn't in any case have seen much beyond the gas blaze between us and the demolished houses. To judge from the guns and flares we could hear the raid was still at its height. As we stood there in the yard, unable to go forward or back, we seemed to be at the centre of a swirling tornado of dust lit from inside by the flaring gas main. It seemed certain to me that somewhere above us there were German planes circling, ready to drop more bombs.

Then two men in black police helmets ran towards us with outstretched arms. We were to take the other way round the block, get into Tadema Road via the back gate of Guinness Trust and make our way wherever we were going from there. There were other small family groups around us, people in rags helping others forward, the young helping the very old, the old helping the very young. We turned away and crunched over the yard to turn the corner of the block.

Away from the flaring gas main, it was suddenly just broken glass underfoot, no orange iridescence, just an astounding quantity of broken glass blasted from a thousand eyeless windows.

Jo Oakman, a Chelsea Civil Defence worker, kept a diary throughout the war and a record of the bombs that fell on Chelsea on February 23 1944. She was sent to Guinness Trust in the immediate aftermath of the raid.

22.07 Sirens.
Most awful barrage and a spectacular sight of flares and gun flashes.
22.34 Four bombs fell all together on the World's End.
23.12 All Clear.
    Got sent to Guinness Trust which had a heavy bomb on the third wing (block) . . . and gas main in King's Road was alight in crater full of water. The two other bombs were Upcerne Road and Lamont Road.
    It was a truly awful night. The Guinness was one awful heap of rubble and the other blocks were terribly blasted. It was reckoned 200 people were underneath, trapped, and to crown it the heap was smouldering all night. The gas main was late got out. Work

proceeded on Guinness all night (and all day and all the next night).
There were queues at the First Aid Posts of injured – Rest Centres
were full of homeless. We were all up all night doing whatever came
along – at any time. The big shelter had been used and nobody was
killed in it.

She later reports a rumour that 200 people were drowned in the
shelter between Block 3 and Block 4 and repeats: nobody was killed
in the shelter. The denial, she says, was published in the *Daily Herald*
that day. I wonder if we have run into some early spin here? The
photographs of the morning following the bombing clearly show that
the mouth of the shelter was blown open. I don't see any reason to
believe that it was flooded as I saw no water or pumps operating
when we went back the next morning. Yet if there were people in that
shelter, despite its zigzag First World War trench construction, some
of them must have died there. But the government was, of course,
anxious that the populace should continue to think of the shelters as
safe havens from air attack. This might account for the discrepancies
that emerge in reports of that night, both on the effectiveness of the
shelters and even on the number who died.

I have tried to provide a full official list of the dead at the end of this
book but even now some facts are difficult to ascertain. Although the
bombing of the World's End was one incident, a single stick of
bombs undoubtedly aimed at Lots Road power station, casualty
reporting is piecemeal. In the mortuary records the people unearthed
on the corner of the King's Road, where Ginger Green was killed,
were recorded as dying a week later when, presumably, their bodies
were recovered. Ginger Green isn't among them.
    The mortuary records for that week show that in the World's End
73 people died unnatural deaths, mainly from blast and burning.
That includes the eleven bodies recovered from the King's Road and
the seven people killed in Upcerne Road – my mother's old tenement

and the one next door were demolished when the first bomb fell. The bomb that fell in Lamont Road may have been small or perhaps it fell on empty property – it was one of the old brothel streets of Cremorne days – either way there is no record of any deaths from it. But the final total of 73 is clearly an underestimate.

Most people were killed in the upper floors of E entrance Guinness Trust (Jo Oakman's third wing). At number 89 three members of the Ibbs family died, including the sixteen-year-old and fourteen-year-old sons. At number 86 three members of the Horton family died. In flat 88, Arthur Revell, together with his wife and their son, also Arthur, junior monitor at Sloane School, died. He was rumoured to have been trapped by tons of masonry, dying as doctors amputated a leg to free him.

My cousin Margaret's extra VAD watch had meant that Kit and I weren't sleeping in number 84 that night. The flat was empty and under countless tons of brick and concrete by the morning. A plait of Auntie May's auburn hair, cut off as a teenager, streamed from a bed-rail sticking out of the rubble. I rescued it and took it down to her in Windsor. At number 81, Samuel Robert Caple, in his orange tweed trousers and waistcoat, and wearing a body-belt no doubt holding scrupulously accounted for Guinness Trust rents, was crushed and burned to death, as was his wife, Mrs Mabel Anne Caple. At number 82 the Haddock family died. And at number 83 three members of the family of Kathy Davis, her father Owen aged 45. Her sisters Joyce Evelyn aged 17 and Iris aged 10, were killed by blast or burning. I can find no record of what happened to Kathy herself so I assume, with caution, that she somehow survived.

The small group that made its way along the embankment that night was probably not alone. But we felt it. My father wore a steel helmet, my mother shivered as the February river mists penetrated her cardigan, I have no memeory of being cold in my shorts and Air Scout shirt. We were all covered with brick dust. Kit and I walked together watching the flares, green and white, reflected on the river at high tide and the flashes of light from the guns across the river in Battersea Park. Mrs Corfield hurried along beside my mother, the unravelling sheet round her injured hand trailing behind her on the pavement. Mr Corfield had gone to find out about his sister and her family in one of the blocks brought down by the bombs.

At some point on our journey as the flares faded and the gun flashes ceased, perhaps outside the Royal Hospital or as we passed Charles II's Royal Avenue, the All Clear sounded. There was to that sound a sweet relief I'd never felt before. Minutes later we reached Whitelands where, in the servants' corridor where my father had a room, there was hot water for baths, and tea and sandwiches which my mother arranged to be brought up to us by one of the porters.

I remember Kit emerging from his bath. It was impossible not to laugh. He had been nearest the fire. Despite all my mother's efforts, she had not been able to wash off the soot that the blast, roaring down the chimney, had embedded in the skin of his face. It was a week before he began to look less like a circus clown.

I slept in a small service room alone that night, overheated by the great Whitelands boilers below, but with a sandwich and a large mug of tea on the floor beside me. And a copy of *Lilliput*, the magazine with articles by Cyril Connolly and stories by Bill Naughton. And exciting black and white pictures of naked ladies.

NINETEEN

Morning

We returned to Guinness Trust next morning to see what we could salvage from our flat. I'd been in dozens, even hundreds, of collapsing flats and houses before but it was nothing like seeing this, the home we had lived in. There was desolation and, I admit, a certain excitement to it. Our whole world turned upside down.

Within minutes we were all covered with dust again as we tried to fill the sacks and boxes we had brought from Whitelands. My mother was the worst affected. I could see she was close to tears. At one point my father, who had brought a half-bottle of whisky with him, took her aside and pulled it from his pocket. They stood together in the wreckage, she shaking her head, he urging her to drink though she had never touched spirits in her life. In the end she took the bottle, threw her head back and tipped it to her mouth. Whisky bubbled from her lips, making runnels in the dust on her cheeks. She glanced at herself in the cracked scullery mirror, hesitated a second then burst out laughing. After that the morning felt better.

Strange things, we discovered, had been done by blast. Each of the three window frames had been neatly excised and hurled across the room. In the front room the back of the Put-U-Up was shredded by glass and bent by the window frame. In the bedroom the chest of drawers looked as if it had been burgled. The drawers were all pulled open. Bed linen and shirts were hurled across the room, the drawers left hanging barely in place as in a film of a robbery. In the wrecked scullery a piece of raw liver had been sucked from the kitchen cupboard and slapped against one wall. Opposite, the shattered wall between scullery and front room had collapsed overnight. Glass and plaster dust covered every surface. I stood in the front room wondering how so much glass could have left six people virtually unscathed. But then it hadn't missed others, in other flats. As we approached the Buildings that morning we had been told of people badly cut, some blinded.

I remember some of the things we packed, but we left many others. We knew we were heading for a new life. We didn't know where but I think neither of my parents had any idea of re-establishing the old one. My father packed the wireless and his tools. My mother took knives and forks, a few unbroken plates, some sheets from the scullery cupboard, but left everything that had been in the bedroom. There, the bed had been piled with plaster and the heavy wooden window frame had torn up sheets and blankets as it flew across the room and hit the back wall. I remember finding the copy of Margaret Irwin's book undamaged, and my exercise book with the beginning of my essay on Mary Queen of Scots looking as if it had been ripped up by a demented teacher. 'You won't need that,' my father said.

What I don't remember is what I did with my box of treasures. These were pieces of shrapnel, incendiary bomb fins with German factory markings stamped in the green-painted aluminium and, my best items, two bronze medallions, about three and a half inches in diameter, struck by Napoleon in 1800 to commemorate the invasion of England (which, of course, never took place). There were a hundred minted and they were, according to the inscription, to be awarded to the first one hundred men of the Imperial Guard to charge on to English soil. I had seen them as a talisman, much cited to Kit in the early days after the fall of France when it appeared certain that Hitler would attempt his own invasion, as evidence of the inevitable failure of foreign tyrants.

After a couple of hours of clearing up we were all looking exhausted. None of us had had more than half a night's sleep. My father gave me a ten-shilling note and told me to go up to Perry's fish shop for cod and chips. I dawdled outside a bit. There were scenes of desolation all around. The gas main fire had been put out, leaving a huge water-filled crater in the middle of the King's Road. The bomb had been so heavy that it had brought down all the fronts of the houses opposite Guinness. At our end, where number 3 looked out on Edith Grove, the whole corner group of houses had been destroyed.

Round the Hundreds was the saddest sight. You can look at pictures of destruction and be shocked. It's quite different to look at the destruction of buildings you have known every single day of your life. Different to understand that the men moving over the huge mound of rubble were searching for people you knew, with names you could name. Different when you realised with a shiver that you and your brother and your cousin Margaret would have been underneath that if some Naval authority had not required her for an extra watch last night.

I stood watching for a few moments, mesmerised. And over the rubble mound, picking his way carefully, came a familiar figure: my friend Ted Simon. Living out at Notting Hill he had known nothing of the plight of the World's End and had turned up for school that morning to find all the windows blown out and a blackboard at the gate announcing the school was closed until further notice. Now, I squinted through the dust thrown up by the cranes and the drift of smoke to see what he was holding out in front of him. Arm outstretched, he was carrying, with exaggerated care, a badly bent cage with a canary still fluttering inside it.

TWENTY
Epilogue

Of course we returned to Auntie May in Windsor, and then on to Joe
and Jinny's where we lived six months in the familiar squalor. My
father said we would never return to the World's End. I couldn't
imagine where else we would go. After all, I'd seen so little of the rest
of London. Places like Potter's Bar and Friern Barnet, Hampstead
and Islington, sent a shiver down my back. Still do. So we weren't
going back to the World's End but there'd be somewhere else, just
like the World's End, with the same sort of friends and places to play.
I think I still imagined the whole of London was on the river.

As far as my father was concerned I think the bombing had
coincided with the first of his as yet unspoken ambitions: to leave the
World's End for good. Through his work he had seen a different,
more affluent world and although he never thought in terms of
achieving a Whitelands standard of living, he was confident that he
could improve greatly on what we had had. Plans to move had
already been discussed with my mother even before we were
bombed; my father had been making more money but we were still
four people living in a one-bedroomed flat. Indeed, a crucially
important step was already underway by the early spring of 1944.
With the good wishes of Alf Gordon, Fatty the Yid and Darkie Evans

my father was already setting up on his own account, illegally of course, as a street bookmaker. This would mean employing runners who would collect the bets and pass them on to him. There was a fair degree of risk involved as my father built up his network of runners and clients. A fine for any runner apprehended was standard; prison a real possibility for the bookmaker. And any adverse publicity would certainly mean his losing his job at Whitelands. At first, when we still had no fixed abode, he must have taken down the bets at Whitelands House. In my imagination now I see him in his black and silver braided porter's uniform crouched in the basement boiler room where we had spent the nights during the first London blitz. It would have been the only really safe place in the whole building to do what he was doing. Telephones were unknown among any of his friends or family, but there was a phone in the Whitelands boiler room. Down there in the blue-tinged light, the heat, the throat-searing atmosphere of swirling coke dust, he could be sure of being alone as he scribbled furiously while his runners phoned over the bets they had collected for the next day's races. Even today I have no difficulty in conjuring the scene.

Back again at Joe and Jinny's in that spring of 1944 I had a strong sense that my childhood was over. I knew we would not remain long at Windsor but, like all of us, I had no idea where we would be going next. I began to dream of myself, not as a different person, but as someone much older, taking decisions, making plans. This older person (I imagined him as seventeen or eighteen years old) began to develop a definite shape, a personality of his own. He became the sort of young man I thought I should aim at being. A created self. And, of course, girls played an ever more significant part in my dreams.

Two months passed. My mother tactfully managed to take over the cooking again so that we no longer suffered Jinny's efforts. The five of us were by now old friends, family even. My mother became the spokeswoman for the cottages in any dealings with the local council, and even with the Emmets who owned the farm. She succeeded in her negotiations not only because she was quietly persistent and, as I began to realise, infinitely subtle in her choice of fronts to move forward on, but also because she was attractive and imposingly tall for the times.

I remember watching her in the queue at the British Restaurant (sixpence main dish, threepence pudding) at Maidenhead and seeing that she stood a head above the other women in the line. When some minor dispute broke out and the manager was called, it seemed only natural for him to address himself to my mother for her view of what had happened.

Americans were everywhere, many of them black signal corps specialists. At one time every telegraph pole along the Windsor Road seemed to have a black American working at its cross-bar of white china conductors, grinning and waving to the girls who passed by. Every road seemed filled with columns of American infantry. Then, early in June, there was a day and a night of endless convoys on the narrow road to Windsor. Thousands of vehicles emblazoned with big white stars, supply trucks, half tracks and jeeps, took over. Traffic in the opposite direction was stopped by white-helmeted US Military Police. Someone reported to us that the big camp at Hollyport had emptied. I went to see for myself. The American troops had gone, leaving a broad field marked by circles of pressed yellowed grass where bell tents had stood, leaving the dusty baseball diamond and a few fading chewing gum and condom packs in the ditches. Presumably that morning the Reverend Daniels had his Sparborough back to himself as well.

There was a day or two of unnatural silence. Few or no American trucks on the road. No friendly faces at the top of telegraph poles. Then, very early on a June morning, the sky was filled with the sound of our bombers, a very different throb of engines from the Germans'.

The sweepstake we were running on the invasion date was won by Kit later that morning as British, Canadian and American troops fought their way ashore on the Normandy beaches. Walter Oakley Cottages held its breath.

A few days later my mother had news for us. A housing manager from London Underground had agreed to rent us one of their houses. Its back garden was curtailed by the railway line directly opposite the front gates of Wormwood Scrubs Prison. *But three bedrooms and a bathroom and garden!* Twice the size of our flat at Guinness Trust.

We were going back to London. I suppose, given our previous miscalculations about the Luftwaffe's intentions, the decision was about par for the course. The V1 flying bomb onslaught on the capital had just begun.

At the end of this book I have listed all those I can find on record who died in the World's End bombing of February 23 1944. I deeply regret any names omitted or wrongly included but the list is compiled from on-the-spot wartime accounts which had to deal with the records of several mortuaries and treated the night's bombing as four separate incidents. I've no doubt some individual pages in the records are now missing. In addition, deaths after a certain number of days (though they were directly the result of the bombing) seem not to have been included.

In the mortuary records and Record of Civilian War Dead, a total of 55 deaths is recorded at Guinness Trust Buildings that night although the plaque at the rebuilt third block (now named Caple House after the Superintendent who died that night) commemorates the deaths of 59 people. This discrepancy, as we have seen, could be the result of the records not including four people who died as a result of the bombing but at a later date.

A similar confusion seems to exist in the record of the King's Road victims of that night. Eleven deaths are recorded but there is no mention of Ginger Green or his mother. To the best of my knowledge the figures given for the Upcerne Road bomb are accurate at seven dead.

The night's fourth bomb has given rise to more uncertainty. I can find no official record of exactly where it fell. Some say it exploded harmlessly a few yards from Gus the barber's shop in Langton Street.

So although there is a certain degree of confusion in the official figures, I think the most likely figure is a minimum of 73 deaths in the World's End bombing that night with perhaps a maximum of 77. To this number must be added over 100 gravely injured.

Some of the survivors we met the morning after the bombing. Some moved so far away to relatives or to requisitioned houses that we never saw them again. Kit's friend Ronnie Howes survived by walking into the front room a few seconds before the bedroom he had just left slid down three floors below him. He was knocked unconscious by the blast and awoke in an ambulance on the way to Brompton Hospital, with a face 'black as Newgate's knocker' as he described it to me last year. He, like Kit, had caught the blast down the chimney.

Ronnie's grandmother, less able to survive the impact of the blast on her lungs, was taken to hospital but died two days later. Like Ginger Green and his mother on King's Road corner she is one of those not included in the mortuary reports. Jumbo Chandler, who had announced 'the end of the war' to me in 1943, lost an eye; his mother was blinded in both. Though her father Owen Davis is recorded as having been killed along with two girls, presumably her younger and older sister, the fate of Kathy Davis remains a mystery.

Of course, there were dozens who died that night whom we knew by sight or name but had barely talked to. They had peopled our landscape throughout our lives: women struggling with buckets of water from the hot water tap or stopping to talk in the yard; men coming home with tool-bags in one hand and perhaps a cut of purloined carpet or lino for the front room tucked under the other arm. Most of the children we knew from school, Ashburnham, St Mark's or Sloane.

The World's End still exists in name as a pub and an overwhelming brick high-rise 1960s housing estate where anonymity rules. People were moved in from other parts of London, mostly from north of Notting Hill. Not surprisingly, they had never known the World's End as the location of Moseley's meetings and Lord Haw Haw's speeches, never heard of La-di-dah, or Gus the barber. And, too often, were never to know the people in the flat below. The surviving houses of the old World's End are now quoted by local estate agents in the hundreds of thousands, sometimes millions, of pounds. But even their occupants are outdistanced by those the newspapers are beginning to call the World's End Billionaires – among them Roman Abramovich, who bought Stamford Bridge, and Boris Berezovsky was now lives in Stanley House, in the (highly developed) grounds of what was once St Mark's College and Elementary School. Equally unsurprisingly, the billionaires have never head of La-di-dah or Gus the barber either.

Common sense tells me that there's a great deal *not* to regret in the passing of the old World's End, but there's much to mourn, too. I suppose that everyone who lived there in the 1930s and early-40s would weight the equation differently. But everyone I have talked to in preparing this book seems to feel the same about that curious enclave in the life and history of Chelsea, seems to agree that it was a good place to grow up. I must beware of the saccharine sentiment of 'we was all one', we weren't, but the World's End was indeed a privileged place for children to grow up in.

And, of course, those who had the good fortune to survive the so-called tenements of Guinness Trust Buildings (now renamed Guinness Court) feel they were particularly lucky.

*

My grandmother, the good one, Eliza, suffered her final heart attack three months before the bombing that would undoubtedly have killed her. The bad one hung on another ten years or more, her capacity for trouble-making happily diminishing with her strength and mobility. Ma Bash, Alf Gordon, Darkie Evans and Fatty the Yid I never saw to speak to after the war ended, though I did see Fatty, his enormous girth still carried before him, in the 1950s turning into the Weatherby on the corner of Slaidburn Street. But by then his World's End was crumbing, too.

Joe and Jinny, still at Walter Oakley cottages, died early as the 1950s ended. Forget the healthy food, the fresh unpolluted air, the chance to work out in the open. More recognisable aspects of life to Joe and his wife were ditch-digging in winter. Or their heads and shoulders soaked through under a sacking cowl as they bagged potatoes or stripped sprouts in the driving rain. The farm labourer's life was not easy on the body. Auntie May survived into her nineties, as benign as ever, and died five or six years before my mother who spent much of her seventies looking after her.

My father died in 1966 of an immediately fatal heart attack while in his office. Up to a year before he had still stoked the boilers in an emergency although by that time he was manager of Whitelands House and two other blocks in Chelsea, Astell House and Lowndes Court. By then he and my mother were living in a flat in Whitelands, eons away from the sulphur candles of yesterday. His days as a, by then, legal bookmaker had ended by his own decision when a cheap Sunday newspaper printed an entirely baseless story about him taking kick-backs from would-be tenants, illicit profiteering by which he supposedly sent his sons to Cambridge and generally lived the high life – which, by choice, he certainly didn't. When he died Kit took over his accounts book for my mother and discovered money owed from the services he provided for the tenants of Whitelands. The majority owed him money for something, arranging laundry, newspaper delivery, the stocking of fridges for those returning from weekends or trips abroad – even, to our baffled amusement, for the supply of logs although there were no open fires in Whitelands House. All these debts, small and not so small, were scupulously, and when necessary forcefully, collected by Kit. They amounted to several hundred pounds, perhaps two or three thousand in today's money.

Our mother lived on with one or other member of the family, permanently good-humoured and consulted on all sorts of personal questions by us all, until she died a few months short of the year 2000. The way she had survived my father's early death was, I thought, remarkable. But she had a tenacious hold on life and the best it had to offer. She lived in the present while revelling in the past. So she kept his memory alive, not by reminding us all of his birthday each June 9 but by the stories she told of their early life together. Today, because of her, he is no stranger to the great-grandchildren who never saw him.

My brother Kit, my lifetime friend, now lives in Henley, the seat of the large American corporation of whose British, German and French companies he was the highly successful chairman. For myself, I write. And old writers are like old soldiers, aren't they? Or so, despite heart attacks of their own, they like to think.

IN MEMORIAM

Samuel Caple	aged 64	Superintendent	81 Guinness Buildings.
Mabel Anne Caple	62		81 Guinness Buildings
Sarah Haddock	51		82 Guinness Buildings
Owen Davis	45	greengrocer	83 Guinness Buildings
Joyce Davis	17		83 Guinness Buildings
Iris Davis	10		83 Guinness Buildings
Thomas Crumplin	49	driver	85 Guinness Buildings
Julia Crumplin	50		85 Guinness Buildings
Winifred Pearce	22		85 Guinness Buildings
Albert Horton	47	postman	86 Guinness Buildings
Florence Horton	48		86 Guinness Buildings
Norman Horton	10		86 Guinness Buildings
Marjorie Horton	21	clerk	86 Guinness Buildings
Walter Rogers	54	motor fitter	87 Guinness Buildings
Agnes Rogers	54		87 Guinness Buildings
Arthur Revell	43	insurance agent	88 Guinness Buildings
Margaret Revell	41		88 Guinness Buildings
Arthur Revell	13		88 Guinness Buildings
Agnes Ibbs	44		89 Guinness Buildings
Arthur Ibbs	16	apprentice	89 Guinness Buildings
John Ibbs	14		89 Guinness Buildings
Jack Williams	32	RAF	91 Guinness Buildings
Florence Simms	38		93 Guinness Buildings
Henry Simms	16	machine hand	93 Guinness Buildings
John Simms	10		93 Guinness Buildings

Thomas Constant	42	porter	94 Guinness Buildings
Florence Constant	39		94 Guinness Buildings
Walter Stokes	46	mail porter	95 Guinness Buildings
Nellie Harrop	59		98 Guinness Buildings
Isabella Dunn	25	factory inspector	99 Guinness Buildings
William Smith	47	milkman	100 Guinness Buildings
Florence Smith	47		100 Guinness Buildings
Edward Smith	18	despatch clerk	100 Guinness Buildings
Henry Smith	15	schoolboy	100 Guinness Buildings
Olive Smith	13	schoolgirl	100 Guinness Buildings
Frederick Bond	8	schoolboy	136 Guinness Buildings
Annie Barrett	50		141 Guinness Buildings
Richard Newman	55		142 Guinness Buildings
Alice Newman	54		142 Guinness Buildings
Irene Powell	13	schoolgirl	143 Guinness Buildings
Florence McCullough	28		146 Guinness Buildings
Edward Bromley	49	fireman	153 Guinness Buildings
Eileen Bromley	48		153 Guinness Buildings
Elsie Bromley	17		153 Guinness Buildings
Norah Bromley	40		153 Guinness Buildings
Sidney Franklin	28	Home Guard	155 Guinness Buildings
William Hollis	41	labourer	156 Guinness Buildings
John Dennis	44		157 Guinness Buildings
Louisa Dennis	44		157 Guinness Buildings
Ronald Dennis	14		157 Guinness Buildings
Albert Dennis	11		157 Guinness Buildings
Rose Dennis	10		157 Guinness Buildings
Walter Bowles	45	timekeeper	160 Guinness Buildings
Rose Bowles	45		160 Guinness Buildings
Rosina Bowles	21	clerk	160 Guinness Buildings
William Fay	45	munitions worker	514 King's Road
Christina Fay	40		514 King's Road
Ada Platts	47	clerk	514 King's Road
George Smith	54	clerk	516 King's Road
Montague Meyers	39	radio engineer	516 King's Road
Emily Meyers	36		516 King's Road
Henrietta Kitson	60		516 King's Road
Edith Mitchell	43	–	518 King's Road
Edward Mitchell	12		518 King's Road
John Smith	57	furniture porter	518 King's Road
Catherine Smith	54		518 King's Road

Ada Dean	51		15 Upcerne Road
Harry Proudley	57	decorator	15 Upcerne Road
Edith Proudley	–		15 Upcerne Road
Harriet Cordwell	65		15 Upcerne Road
Winifred Cordwell	37	clerk	15 Upcerne Road
George Brodie	78	brass finisher	15 Upcerne Road
Edward Ives	52	road sweeper	15 Upcerne Road